Recognition and Redistribution

This volume takes a fresh approach to issues, challenges, and problems in the global politics of development. The authors challenge conventional perspectives of, and approaches to, development by working with non-state centric and non-state centred perspectives. The chapters in this volume offer critical reinterpretations of historical experiences and analyses of contemporary development strategies, institutional and political constellations around those, and the instances of resistance and struggle they engender.

In moving beyond more economistic approaches to development, this book contributes to uncovering the complexities of the social and political relations of development, *drawing inter alia* on engagements with political theory, anthropological and sociological perspectives, social theory, discourse analysis and historical reconstructions in order to work towards a more integrated account. Integral to all the chapters is the authors' commitment to 'thinking together' relations of recognition and redistribution in the global politics of development. Under investigation are global social relations of power and dispossession, and their impact on state formation, regional flows and cultural spheres. The respective contributions proceed from comprehensively relational premises, thus moving the focus of inquiry away from questions of the impact of globalisation on 'international' politics, and towards an embedded account of the latter within social and political relations, which reach through the coordinates of methodological territorialism.

In framing the project as a whole through the concepts of recognition and redistribution, this book presents a fresh effort to 'rethink development' attuned to the conflictual nature of its relations, and their implications for people linked into the development project. It is timely in an era of global politics and globalisation wherein both, issues of identity and struggles over distribution in the development context challenge us to rethink disciplinary boundaries and their practical implications.

This book was published as a special issue of *Globalizations*.

Heloise Weber is Lecturer in International Relations and Development, School of Political Science and International Relations, University of Queensland.

Mark T. Berger is Professor in the Department of Defense Analysis at the Naval Postgraduate School (Monterey, California).

Recognition and Redistribution

Beyond International Development

Edited by Heloise Weber and Mark T. Berger

Routledge
Taylor & Francis Group

LONDON AND NEW YORK

First published 2009 by Routledge
2 Park Square, Milton Park, Abingdon, Oxon, OX14 4RN

Simultaneously published in the USA and Canada
by Routledge
711 Third Avenue, New York, NY 10017

Routledge is an imprint of the Taylor & Francis Group, an Informa business

© 2009 Edited by Heloise Weber and Mark T. Berger

First issued in paperback 2013

Typeset in Times by Techset Composition Ltd., Salisbury, UK

British Library Cataloguing in Publication Data
A Catalogue record for this book is available from the British Library

ISBN13: 978-0-415-44817-8 (hbk)
ISBN13: 978-0-415-85025-4 (pbk)

Contents

Contributors

Jennifer Bair is Assistant Professor of Sociology and Director of Undergraduate Studies in Ethics, Politics, and Economics at Yale University. Her research interests lie at the intersection of economic sociology, political economy, and development studies, with a regional focus on Latin America. She is the editor of *Frontiers of Commodity Chain Research* (Stanford University Press, 2008) and co-editor of *Free Trade and Uneven Development: The North American Apparel Industry after NAFTA* (2002, Temple University Press). She is currently completing the manuscript *Sewing Up Development? From Boom to Bust in Post-NAFTA Mexico and Beyond*, which draws on several years of fieldwork analyzing how inter-firm networks between US and Latin American exporters have been reshaped by regional trade regimes such as NAFTA and CAFTA, and with what consequences for firms and workers.

Mark T. Berger is Visiting Professor in the Department of Defense Analysis at the Naval Postgraduate School (Monterey, California). He is the author of *The Battle for Asia: From Decolonization to Globalization* (2004), editor of *From Nation-Building to State-Building* (2007), and co-editor (with Douglas A. Borer) of *The Long War: Insurgency, Counterinsurgency and Collapsing States* (2008). He is also co-author (with Heloise Weber) of *Rethinking the Third World: International Development and World Politics* (forthcoming) and the author of *The American Ascendancy and the Fate of Nations: Empires, Nation-States and Changing Global Orders* (forthcoming).

Morten Bøås is a senior researcher at the Fafo Institute for Applied International Studies (Oslo). He has written extensively about international development and African politics. His work has been published in journals such as *Global Governance, Current History, European Journal of Development Research*, and *Journal of Contemporary African Studies*. His most recent book is *African Guerrillas: Raging Against the Machine* (with Kevin C. Dunn, 2007).

Dia Da Costa has a PhD in development sociology from Cornell University (2003). Using the primary analytic lens of political theatre, her research involves ethnographic analyses of world-historical change. She studies theatre groups, Jana Sanskriti in rural West Bengal and Janam in urban Delhi, to conceptualize political action and social justice in a postcolonial democracy. Her recent and forthcoming publications appear in *Journal of Contemporary Ethnography, Journal of South Asian Popular Culture, Signs, Journal of African and Asian Studies, Contributions to Indian Sociology*, and in an edited volume *Theatre of the Streets*. Currently, she teaches courses on culture and development at Queen's University, Canada.

Shelley Feldman is Professor of Development Sociology and Director of Feminist, Gender, and Sexualities Studies at Cornell University. Building on over two decades of research in

Bangladesh, she explores the political economy of economic and social restructuring, changing gender relations, NGOs and civil society, and rural subsistence and social provisioning. Her research has been featured in *REVIEW, SIGNS, Interventions, Economy and Society*, and numerous other journals and collections. She co-edited *Unequal Burden: Economic Crises, Persistent Poverty and Women's Work* and *Informal Work and Social Change*. Her current projects include an institutional history of the post-1947 period in East Pakistan, and a study of the Bangladesh Liberation War Museum as a window on Bangladeshi independence.

Sandra Halperin is Professor of International Relations and Co-Director of the Centre for Global and Transnational Politics at Royal Holloway College, University of London. Her main research interests include global development, the historical sociology of global relations, the causes and conditions of war and peace, and Middle East politics. Her publications include *In the Mirror of the Third World: Capitalist Development in Modern Europe* (1997). *Global Civil Society and Its Limits* (co-edited with Gordon Laxer, 2003), *War and Social Change in Modern Europe: The Great Transformation Revisited* (2004), and articles on contemporary Middle East politics, Islam, nationalism, ethnic conflict, state-building, historical sociology, and globalisation.

Kathleen M. Jennings is a researcher at the Fafo Institute for Applied International Studies (Oslo), and coordinates its New Security Programme. She focuses on international interventions in conflict and post-conflict environments, human security, and security privatisation. Recent and forthcoming publications include articles in *International Peacekeeping*, *Global Governance*, and the *European Journal for Development Research* (with Morten Bøås). She was previously a research associate at the Council on Foreign Relations in Washington, DC.

Philip McMichael is Professor of Development Sociology, Cornell University. He has authored *Settlers and the Agrarian Question* (1984) and *Development and Social Change* (2008), and has edited *The Global Restructuring of Agro-Food Systems* (1994), *Food and Agrarian Orders in the World Economy* (1995), and *New Directions in the Sociology of the Global Development* (2005; with F. H. Buttel). He has chaired the Political Economy of the World-System Section of the American Sociological Association (1995), and was President of the Research Committee on Food and Agriculture of the International Sociological Association (1998–2002). Recently a visiting scholar at Oxford University and the University of Queensland, he researches global food politics.

Dieter Plehwe, Dr. Phil., is a permanent researcher at the Berlin Social Science Research Centre's Department of Internationalization and Organization. His work focuses on global networks of intellectuals and think-tanks, and on regional integration in Western Europe and North America. He recently participated in the NYU International Centre for Advanced Studies Program 'The Authority of Knowledge in a Global Age', and edited the 2006 Routledge volume *Neoliberal Hegemony: A Global Critique* with Bernhard Walpen and Gisela Neunhöffer.

Cristina Rojas is Professor in the School of International Affairs, Carleton University (Ottawa, Canada), and a visiting scholar at the Institute of Latin American Studies, University of North Carolina, at CERLAC at York University, and at the David Rockefeller Center for Latin American Studies at Harvard University. Her most recent books are *Elusive Peace: International, National and Local Dimensions of Conflict in Colombia* (2005; edited with

Judy Meltzer) and *Civilization and Violence: Regimes of Representation in Nineteenth Century Colombia* (2002). Her articles have been published in *Canadian Journal of Development Studies*, *Revista Venezolana de Economía y Ciencias Sociales*, *Review of International Political Economy*, and *Alternatives.*

Susanne Soederberg is Canada Research Chair in Global Political Economy and Associate Professor in the Department of Global Development Studies at Queen's University, Kingston, Canada. She is author of *The Politics of the New International Financial Architecture: Reimposing Neoliberal Dominance in the Global South* and *Global Governance in Question: Empire, Class, and the New Common Sense in North-South Relations.* She is currently completing a book manuscript on corporate power and shareholder activism in the era of financialization.

Marcus Taylor is an Assistant Professor in the Department of Global Development Studies at Queen's University, Kingston, Canada. He is author of *From Pinochet to the Third Way: Neoliberalism and Social Transformation in Chile* (Pluto, 2006), editor of *Global Economy Contested: Power and Conflict Across the International Division of Labour* (Routledge, 2008), and is currently undertaking a comparative study of labour market transformation in Mexico and China.

Heloise Weber is Lecturer in International Relations and Development Studies at the School of Political Science and International Studies, University of Queensland. Her research interests are in the global politics of development and inequality, critical development theory, international relations theory, and the politics of international institutions in development. Her research has been published in (among others) *Review of International Political Economy*, *Review of International Studies*, and *Third World Quarterly.* She is also co-author (with Mark T. Berger) of *Rethinking the Third World: International Development and World Politics* (forthcoming). She is currently working on a monograph *Organizing Poverty: The Global Politics of Microfinance.*

Martin Weber lectures in international relations and peace and conflict studies as the University of Queensland, Australia. His research interests are in international social and political theory, and in political economy/international political economy, and his work has been published in the form of journal articles (*Review of International Studies*, *Alternatives*, *Review of International Political Economy*, *Global Environmental Politics*, and *Global Governance*) and contributions to edited volumes. Currently he is working on a monograph, *Critical Theory and Global Political Ecology.*

Introduction: Beyond International Development

MARK T. BERGER & HELOISE WEBER

Development and inequality have been central issues in the wider history of the transformation of the world order since 1945. The formation of the United Nations and ancillary bodies (such as the World Bank and the IMF) and the universalization of the nation-state system against a backdrop of decolonization and the Cold War focused increasing attention on inequality and development. Different disciplines within the social sciences increasingly addressed these issues, albeit in different ways. In fact, the 'discovery of development' after 1945 led to the emergence of entire new fields of study. For instance, area studies (AS) and development studies (DS) were both consolidated in the 1950s. They explicitly targeted 'non-Western' geographical spaces and tended to focus on the domestic (or 'internal') dimensions of societies in Asia, Africa, the Middle East, and Latin America. International studies (IS) and international relations (IR), meanwhile, tended to focus on political factors and processes deemed unique to the domain of the 'international'. The former only fully came of age as a field of study with the end of the Cold War, while the latter was consolidated as sub-discipline of political science in the aftermath of the First World War. In all of these cases, analysis was premised on the notion of the political as demarcated by the territorial boundaries of modern nation-states.

At the same time, there is a long history of mutual neglect of, or ignorance about, the work of the other, on the part of diplomats and development practitioners. This is closely connected to the mutual neglect between IR, and even IS, on the one hand, and DS on the other hand. This has occurred despite conventions in IR, IS, and DS that take as their point of departure certain shared norms and assumptions about the ordering of world politics. These shared assumptions include a generally technocratic commitment to the theory and practice of development that takes the 'international' as its point of departure. The consequence of this has been the privileging of certain forms of knowledge, such as evolutionary theories of modernization and state-centric conceptions of development, as well as an underlying commitment to a highly formalized comparative method that takes the nation-state for granted as an unproblematic and even natural unit of a wider system of nation-states. Comparing what are perceived to be independent and like units, in relation to predefined standards (such as indicators of growth), provides a flawed analysis of the spatio-temporal dimensions of global politics. Such an approach is unable even to begin to capture the social relations and cultural imaginations that inform the struggles over development. Neither can it register the way in which historical legacies combine with contemporary context-specific conjunctures to reshape and reconfigure the dynamics of struggle in the organization of the global politics of development.

The objective of this volume is to address the causes and consequences of this neglect of the social in general and the continued lack of genuine inter-disciplinary approaches to development more specifically. We seek to demonstrate how and why conventional methodologies and epistemologies work to routinize and naturalize a particular common-sense set of ideas about development. This framing obscures the *social relations* that transcend the territorial boundaries of the modern nation-state. For example, we address how social power operates in world politics even as the *social* has been marginalized by dominant discourses on international relations and development, which continue to take the 'international' as their point of departure. The widespread use and acceptance of the comparative method to evaluate national development experiences in an 'international' framework render global (or, if one prefers, transnational) social relations and political power virtually invisible. The dominant approach to development continues to be articulated in relation to international development generally, and the 'Third World' more specifically, even if the latter concept has been substituted by 'least developed' states or 'low income' states. This formal comparative method in development (and the social sciences more generally) is non-relational and ahistorical, and by implication also constructs a conceptual understanding of 'development' in terms of differential processes *extraneous* to world historical development.

To be sure, debates outside these narrow confines have already problematized to some degree the ahistorical character of the formal comparative method, but they have not necessarily transcended its basic assumptions. For example, while world-system theory (see McMichael, 1990) offered a historically grounded analysis of world development, it conceived of world historical processes in a way which was deterministic and at the same time naturalized the nation-state system. Despite its many insights, it does not engage specific social contexts and political and social relations, which always transcended its rigid 'spatial' differentiation of core, semi-periphery, and periphery. Also, while many of the arguments presented by the contributions that follow will resonate with globalization theorists, our project as a whole is not confined to the meta-theoretical arguments which underpin this debate, as important as these are. Rather, we also look at the more particular *substantive* relations of social power, offering a historically embedded study of the organization of development and inequality in global politics.

We recognize the complex context in which struggles for development have occurred in the past and continue to occur. In the immediate post-1945 period, the 'self-determination of peoples' was going to be realized through the nation-state in the context of the universalization of the nation-state system. It was at this time that the nation-state became the vehicle for and embodiment of modernity. It was also at this time that the issue of 'development' came increasingly to be framed as a need for the nation-states of the 'Third World' to emulate and catch up with the First World. Alternatively, in some cases they sought to emulate and catch up with the Second World, if they were seeking to follow the state-socialist model of national development held out by the Soviet Union during the Cold War. From the onset of the Cold War to the present, the dominant ideas about the pursuit of modernity have been framed via the concept of international development.

Adopting a variety of approaches, the contributors to this volume evaluate the problems related to the continued presence of the power of an imaginary framed in terms of international development. By reflectively transcending existing disciplinary boundaries they offer alternative accounts

of the politics of development. With non-state-centric approaches, and reinterpretations of historical experiences of development practices (in some cases in relation to wider questions of political
theory), this volume as a whole offers an exploration of the complicated legacy of development
theory and the contemporary practices it has engendered. In moving beyond both economic-
centred and technocratic approaches to development, and more importantly beyond the imagination of international development itself, most of the contributors seek to uncover the complexity
of development in ways that account for and emphasize the importance of social relations of power
and identity. We pose a direct challenge to the intellectual credibility of a range of established
conceptions of international development.

At the same time, our approach entails an implicit foregrounding of the concept of recognition
(Fraser and Honneth, 2003). We demonstrate that the concept of recognition—whether
expressed in a negative form or tied to positive development interventions—is a useful way
of rethinking social and political ordering. It has particular implications for understanding
notions and perceptions of justice and injustice in the context of a wide range of claims for redistribution by both the affluent and the disenfranchised. Framing this volume as a whole via the
concepts of recognition and redistribution marks a genuine effort to move beyond the dominant
discourse of international development. We feel that in an era of globalization in which issues of
identity and struggles over development constantly challenge the anachronistic approaches to
international relations and international development, the need to move beyond the imaginary
of international development is long overdue.

More broadly, this volume makes a contribution to calls to rethink the dominant framework of
analysis which has defined orthodox approaches to IR and DS (Berger, 2001; Kratochwil, 2003;
McMichael, 1990; Murphy, 2001, p. 354; Saurin, 1995; Smith, 2003). There has been no comprehensive effort to theorize and analyse the politics of international development from an analytical
perspective that combines historical dynamics and conjunctures (such as the social struggles which
underpinned decolonization, the Cold War, and the universalization of the nation-state system) and
what can be called synchronic dynamics. As a consequence, approaches to development have
either been incomplete or flawed, resulting in inappropriate and misplaced policy.

A number of the contributors critically examine key conceptions and institutional dynamics
that have been central to development processes. Mark T. Berger offers a historically grounded
analysis of the role and implications of the universalization of the nation-state, which was at a
particular historical moment conceived of as the key 'agent' and 'actor' of development. His
study carefully considers the historical specificity of state formation, the violence this has
entailed—both physical and structural—and the limits and problems of 'naturalizing' the
modern nation-state. This is done in relation to the more specific geo-politics of nation-building
and its relationship to IS, AS, and DS. In particular, Berger points to the need to move beyond
AS and DS and at a minimum dramatically recast IS in order to produce viable alternatives to the
dominant liberal and neo-liberal conceptions which frame global politics in terms of an imaginary of IR and IS. In her contribution, Shelley Feldman highlights the complex ways in which
state violence is constituted, through an analysis of the politics of representation. She demonstrates the way in which discourses of 'othering' in terms of 'insiders' and 'outsiders' are
deployed to advance and manage the contradictions of capitalist global social relations.
Martin Weber continues with the theme of recognition and redistribution that underlies the contradictions of modernity. He specifically examines the historical legacy of the construction of
identity in terms of an individualized notion of a proprietary self in the image of *Homo oeconomicus* in the context of the justification of private property. These three papers broadly address
the historical legacy and contradictions of the project of modernity.

The other contributions go on to substantiate further the argument about the changing social and political contexts of development, through insightful examples that problematize the territorial assumptions that underpin IR and DS. In particular, they highlight the limits of spatio-political analysis and state-centrism inherent in the theory and practice of development. For example, Morten Bøås and Kathleen M. Jennings examine the politics of the contemporary discourse of 'state failure' and 'failed states'. They draw on the examples of Afghanistan, Liberia, and Somalia. They demonstrate the way in which the discourse of 'failed states' reworks a particular disciplinary logic in ways that obscure the failure of the vast majority of states (that are not viewed as 'failed') to provide for the social and economic well-being of their citizens. Jennifer Bair, in keeping with our historically embedded approach, examines the struggles by the erstwhile Third World to realize a new international economic order (NIEO) prior to the rise of neo-liberalism. Her study carefully scrutinizes the role that identity played in attempts at the United Nations to construct a broad Third Worldist coalition to challenge the dominant international power structure of the 1970s. At the same time, her analysis demonstrates the limits of the idea and practice of national development to provide human security, broadly conceived, within a political reordering of global capitalism.

Susanne Soederberg picks up these emerging trends and discusses the transformation of a redistributive-oriented—however limited—approach to development and the formation of a market-based, corporate rights approach. Her political analysis of the UN-led project of the Global Compact is illustrative of the global reach of new actors and agents in attempts to organize and manage the neoliberal variant of global capitalism. Continuing with the theme of illustrating contemporary struggles over development, Dieter Plehwe examines the politics of knowledge production for neoliberal development. His analysis of the World Bank's efforts to institutionalize and consolidate 'knowledge' for development through the global development network draws out the extent to which 'managing knowledge' has been part of struggles in the politics of development. Meanwhile, Marcus Taylor restates the need for critical development studies to avail itself of a deeper sociological understanding of the uneven relations of production at the global level. Development theory, he argues, has yet to engage fully with the lessons that can still be drawn from Marx's social theory of the relations of production. Taylor diagnoses a lack of attention in contemporary development analysis to the uneven production of labour/labouring bodies, and demonstrates the need to move beyond recent institutionalist and technocratic notions of development in order to arrive at an adequate critical conceptualization of uneven development. These five papers engage the contemporary context of struggles over development, and they do so by situating their analysis within a wider historical and global context.

The remaining contributions re-examine conventional and historical narratives about development, drawing out the way in which social relations have historically transcended territorial borders even as the nation-state is assumed to be a coherent and even relatively autonomous social entity. They also consider this dynamic in ways that conceptualize macro-political contexts in relation to micro-social and political relations, and offer new ways to think about development in the twenty-first century. Sandra Halperin offers a reinterpretation of the history of class formation in a way that demonstrates the formation of 'horizontal' global social relations, primarily around class and class interests. Heloise Weber continues the focus on demonstrating the relevance of foregrounding global social relations by examining the politics of methodological choices. In particular, she engages directly with the politics of the formal comparative method and the disciplinary practices it produces. Cristina Rojas explores conceptual and practical efforts to retrieve the 'sociology of the absences'. She does this via an examination of the politics of knowledge production and power in struggles over development. Finally, Dia Da Costa and Philip McMichael continue with this theme and examine the way in which struggles over knowledge and the theory and practice of development play out through the politics of representation, in what they refer to as the 'poverty of the global order'.

Overall, this volume provides a range of critiques of the dominant theoretical and practical approaches to international development. At the same time it maps out alternative insights for progressive politics and emphasizes the necessity of moving beyond international development in order to understand the causes of poverty and inequality, and the social and political consequences of a mainstream development discourse. As this volume emphasizes, progress, as such, will always be contingent upon social and political contexts. Furthermore, it will continue to be limited by pre-conceived ideas. It should, however, be clear by now that a liberal social ontology that posits progress in terms of rational, self-interested individuals will no longer suffice if we are to engage seriously with complex issues of identity, social power, and proprietary notions of 'freedom'. Ultimately, the challenge is to think beyond the notion of rational self-interest and a technocratic conception of international development, which are at best abstractions from concrete social relations of struggle for diverse and alternative worldviews. Rendering such struggles visible—which by no means constitutes a resolution to the crisis of development— does, at least acknowledge their existence. Our hope is that in so doing, we will also enable an appreciation of struggles for recognition and redistribution in the wider context of the increasingly crucial need to move theory and analysis beyond its current *representation* in terms of international development.

Note

1   We would like to thank Barry Gills sincerely for his support of this project. Our thanks also go to Elizabeth Pallister for her previous editorial support, and Calum Miller who has since taken over. Both have been a real pleasure to work with.

References

Berger, M. T. (2001) The rise and demise of national development and the origin of Post-Cold War capitalism, *Millennium, Journal of International Studies*, 30(2), pp. 211–234.

Fraser, N. & Honneth, A. (2003) *Redistribution or Recognition: A Political–Philosophical Exchange* (London: Verso).

Kratochwil, F. (2003) The monologue of science, *International Studies Review*, 5(1), pp. 124–128.

McMichael, P. (1990) Incorporating comparison within a world-historical perspective: an alternative comparative method, *American Sociological Review*, 55(3), pp. 385–397.

Murphy, C. N (2001) Political consequences of the new inequality, *International Studies Quarterly*, 45(3), pp. 347–356.

Saurin, J. (1995) The end of international relations? The state and international theory in the age of globalization, in J. Mcmillan & A. Linklater (eds) *Boundaries in Question* (London: Pinter).

Smith, S. (2003) Dialogue and the reinforcement of orthodoxy in international relations, *International Studies Review*, 5(1), pp. 141–143.

Keeping the World Safe for Primary Colors: Area Studies, Development Studies, International Studies, and the Vicissitudes of Nation-Building

MARK T. BERGER

Introduction: Keeping the World Safe for Primary Colors

Nation-building is back. Since the end of the Cold War and particularly since 9/11, it has returned to the center of academic and policy debates in the context of various attempts to revitalize or establish regional or international security organizations and development frameworks. This essay links the formulation of contemporary nation-building strategies to a critical examination of the history of earlier nation-building efforts. It does this by setting the idea and practice of nation-building against the backdrop of the international history of the twentieth century. In particular, there is a need to talk about security and development in relation to: decolonization, the Cold War, the universalization of the modern nation-state system, the vicissitudes of the global political economy, the transformation of international relations since 9/11, and the contemporary crisis of the nation-state system. More particularly, this paper focuses on the history of the idea and practice of nation-building in an effort to explicate the roles of development studies (DS) and area studies (AS) in the constitution and transformation of the field of international studies (IS). The aim here is to clarify in broad terms how all these fields of study have been, and continue to be, embedded in international security and economic/development policy processes and questions of international relations and global governance.[1]

The central argument here is that at this world-historical juncture the nation-state system and the pursuit of modernity via the nation-state generally, or nation-building more specifically is the key obstacle to the achievement of a genuinely emancipatory modernity in a global era of emergent oligopolistic capitalism. This approach challenges the way in which the nation-state and the nation-state system remain central to, and continue to be routinized and naturalized by, the dominant discourses within IS (Berger and Weber, 2005, pp. 95–102; Berger and Weber, 2006, pp. 201–208). With the end of the Cold War, furthermore, the boundaries between DS and AS, and their relationship to international relations (IR) and other disciplines, have become increasingly blurred (Palat, 2000). In fact, it can be argued that the future of these fields of study, whether as critique of or complement to the IS.

This paper begins by looking at the history of DS (particularly development economics). It then turns to AS (especially modernization theory). The rise of these fields is outlined with an emphasis on the international politico-economic and security context that framed their institutionalization, professionalization, and transformation after 1945. I conclude that the future of DS and AS lies in their implicit or explicit convergence on IS. Furthermore, as a set of critical practices and structures, IS generally, and the theory and practice of nation-building more specifically, needs to be reconceptualized in ways that carry it well beyond its contemporary international framework.

Development Studies, Nation-Building, and Economic Development

Development Studies and Development Economics

The emergence of DS programs after the Second World War was grounded in wider processes of decolonization, the universalization of the nation-state system, and the onset of the Cold War. More specifically the rise of DS was closely connected to the emergence of development economics in this period. From its inception the discipline of economics was preoccupied with understanding economic growth in North America and Western Europe. However, against the backdrop of the Cold War, the emergent discipline of development economics (and what eventually became known as development studies more broadly) explicitly sought to understand the causes of poverty and underdevelopment in what became known as the Third World.

A key role in the establishment of development economics is often assigned to economists working in Britain during the Second World War, in particular Paul N. Rosenstein-Rodan. During the Second World War Rosenstein-Rodan encouraged research on economic development at the Royal Institute of International Affairs, Nuffield College, where he was secretary of the committee on post-war reconstruction. In the 1950s he emerged as a key figure at the Center for International Studies (CENIS) at the Massachusetts Institute of Technology (MIT). Following its establishment in 1951 CENIS emerged as an important nexus for development economics and modernization theory. MIT itself had already emerged as the biggest defense contractor of any university in the United States by the end of the Second World War, a position it occupied, followed closely by Stanford University, throughout the Cold War and into the post-Cold War era (Leslie, 1993, pp. 11–12).

For Rosenstein-Rodan and his colleagues, government-planned industrialization was the key to national economic development. The importance of industrialization was exemplified in the writings of W. Arthur Lewis. Apart from writing a number of influential works on development economics in the 1950s, Lewis also made a major contribution to the 1951 United Nations report *Measures for the Economic Development of Underdeveloped Countries*. Lewis embodied the growing concern of many North American and Western European policy-makers, and development economists, that the Soviet model of nation-building was gaining support in Asia, Africa, the Middle East, and Latin America (for example, see Lewis, 1955, p. 431). Lewis's work also represented a major point of departure for W. W. Rostow's efforts to articulate a developmental alternative to Marxism. In the 1950s Rostow was closely associated with CENIS, then in the 1960s he served in various positions under both John F. Kennnedy and Lyndon B. Johnson.

Rostow's book, *The Stages of Economic Growth: A Non-Communist Manifesto*, symbolized the high modernist and anti-Communist approach to nation-building emanating from Washington in the early 1960s. First published in 1960, the book called on 'we of the democratic north' to 'face and deal with the challenge implicit in the stages-of-growth … at the full stretch of our moral commitment, our energy, and our resources' (Rostow, 1960, pp. 162–167).

During the 1960s, however, development economics increasingly lost its luster (Krugman, 1999, pp. 6–7; Seers, 1979). A central factor in this decline, as manifested in the highly politicized conclusions of Rostow's work, was that the political and social complexities that development economists faced were not given sufficient consideration at the outset. For example, the work of Gunnar Myrdal exemplified the view that underdeveloped nations could not escape from poverty unless they embarked on major state-guided national development efforts, supported by substantial foreign aid (Myrdal, 1957). However, writing many years later, Myrdal conceded that what had been needed in underdeveloped nations 'in order to raise the miserable living levels of the poor masses' was 'radical institutional reforms' and the governments of the new nations had not been able to bring these about (Myrdal, 1968, pp. 47, 66–67).

More broadly, one of the most significant weaknesses of development economics, and of a wide range of theories of modernization in the high period of national development, was the taking of the nation-state as the unquestioned object of their technocratic and paternalistic efforts. The emergence of modernization theory in the 1950s and early 1960s is generally seen, in part, as a response to the failure of development economists to address the wider political questions associated with nation-building. The radicalization of DS by the 1960s, and its broadening to incorporate an increasing array of social science disciplines, also reflected a reaction to the failure of DS and its consolidation around development economics as the key to the delivery of modernity.

Development Studies and Neo-Classical Economics

The influence of development economics as a dominant set of ideas about economic development and nation-building, and the overall character of DS, shifted in the 1970s and 1980s with the growing ascendancy of neo-classical economics against the backdrop of the rise of neo-liberalism and the US-led globalization project. This reorientation was readily apparent at the World Bank. By the 1980s, US influence over the Bank and beyond was increasingly grounded in the Bank's dependence on world financial markets, the position of the US as a global financial center, and the closely aligned interests of key financial actors with those of US foreign policy.

The high period of neo-classical fundamentalism at the World Bank peaked by the second half of the 1980s as ideologues gave way to technocrats in Washington during the second Reagan administration. This shift was marked by the change of presidents at the Bank from Clausen to Barber Conable (1986–1991). With Conable at the helm, the organization's public image was seen to be more consensual than under Clausen, while poverty alleviation and the mitigation of the social costs of structural adjustment were given greater prominence.

The World Bank's understanding of development into the 1990s, despite the relative retreat from neo-classical fundamentalism, continued to be, or increasingly became, influenced by the rise of rational choice theory. The dramatic ascendance of rational choice theory (or the new institutionalism and the new political economy) in this period resulted in a highly mechanistic approach to the dynamics of political and economic change. Like the approach to economic behavior taken by neo-classical economics, rational choice theory built its explanations for political behavior on assumptions about the rational calculations that informed the policies and actions of the individuals and groups concerned. By the 1990s, the terminology of rational choice theory, if not the more rigorous versions of its conceptual framework, was being widely deployed, facilitating the revision and the strengthening of the neo-liberal ascendancy (Leys, 1996, pp. 36–37, 80–82).

By the end of the 1990s, however, the World Bank had ostensibly made a shift from 'structural adjustment' to a focus on a 'comprehensive development framework' that again foregrounded poverty alleviation (Pender, 2001, pp. 397–411). This shift has been reinforced, although not necessarily manifested to a great degree in practice, by a renewed emphasis in the wake of September 11, 2001, on the importance of foreign aid and poverty alleviation to engender economic and political stability and undercut the appeal of fundamentalist Islam.

However, as contemporary neo-liberal nation-building in Iraq, which will be discussed below, demonstrates, this does not represent a retreat from any of the core elements of the US-led globalization project within which the World Bank plays a central role (Cammack, 2002, pp. 125–132). In fact, since 9/11 the primary emphasis of key international actors, such as the US government and its various agencies, has been to reinforce the neo-liberalism at the center of the globalization project. One result of this trend has been to marginalize further the social development agenda of branches of the World Bank and the United Nations. As more than one commentator has noted, since 9/11 the administration of George W. Bush has increasingly defined security in a way that views brute force as the only solution to 'any and all opposition, regardless of its origins or goals' (Murillo, 2004, p. 15, also see pp. 27–28). This has been reinforced by the steadily increasing expenditure on defense by the US government. The Secretary of Defense, Donald Rumsfeld, appeared to make a concession in the early months of 2006 that the US needed to focus on 'hearts and minds' as well as 'shock and awe'. However, neither his public utterances nor the *Quadrennial Defense Review* (which came out in February 2006) reflected movement on the part of the White House, or the Pentagon, towards a broader conception of security. Despite Rumsfeld's subsequent resignation at the end of 2006, there is still no apparent recognition that what the Bush administration and the Pentagon are now calling the 'Long War' is also a new war. In practice there has been little or no serious reconceptualization of counterinsurgency and nation-building or rethinking of the war on terror itself (Berger and Borer, 2007).

Area Studies, Nation-Building, and Modernization

Area Studies and Modernization Theory

Modernization theory and nation-building were central to the rise of AS after 1945. During the Second World War and the early Cold War a large number of academics took up full-time or part-time posts with various government agencies. This was linked to a wave of institutional growth and expansion in AS and IS that began during the Second World War. The Office of Strategic Services (OSS), the forerunner of the Central Intelligence Agency (CIA), was one of the best known postings for political scientists and historians. In fact, McGeorge Bundy, one-time president of the Ford Foundation, which provided considerable support for AS in the 1950s and 1960s, characterized the Office of Strategic Services as the 'first great center of area studies in the United States' (Bundy, 1964, pp. 2–3). For example, a number of younger academics were attracted to Asian Studies after having served with the OSS or the armed forces in the Pacific during WWII. This group embarked on their higher degrees after 1945, at a time when large amounts of money from government and private foundations became available as part of the wider geo-politics of the Cold War. The disciplinary range of AS grew dramatically as a new generation of academics entered new or revised fields of study that emerged with the expansion and diversification of the social sciences after 1945.[2]

In the 1950s, Southeast Asia emerged as a major arena of the Cold War. Policy-makers in Washington were increasingly concerned about the stability of the emerging new nations in the region in the context of the consolidation of the People's Republic of China and the rise of 'guerrilla communism' in a number of former colonies. The rising interest in Southeast Asia, in the context of the growing concern with developing areas generally, is apparent in the work of Lucian W. Pye, a founding member of the Committee on Comparative Politics, who emerged as a particularly influential advocate of modernization theory. Pye succeeded Almond as head of the Committee in 1963, and remained in that post until its dissolution in 1972. Pye's work combined an explicitly psychological approach to politics and nation-building. His first book, published in 1956, was *Guerrilla Communism in Malaya: Its Social and Political Meaning*. It built on Almond's 1954 study, which had concluded that the communist parties of Western Europe drew their recruits from members of the population who were 'alienated', 'deviational', or 'psychologically maladjusted'. These new recruits were attracted to the structure provided by the communist parties primarily as a means to resolve personal identity crises (Almond, 1954, pp. 234, 370, 380). Pye argued that the fundamental basis of the appeal of communism in Malaya and other underdeveloped nation-states was the insecurity and psychological stress experienced by people who had lost their 'traditional way of life' as part of their effort to achieve a 'modern' existence (Pye, 1956, pp. 3, 7, 201–202).

In 1962 Pye published a major study (supported by CENIS at MIT) that focused on the 'problems of building a modern nation-state'. This book, *Politics, Personality and Nation-Building: Burma's Search for Identity*, used Burma as a case study, but drew examples from a wide range of emergent nation-states in Asia and Africa. Making clear the concern with order that was central to modernization theory from the outset, he lamented the apparent lack of 'doctrines on nation building'. The formulation of such a doctrine, he argued, had been inhibited primarily by an 'unreasoned expectation' that democracy was 'inevitable' and by the 'belief that political development is a natural and even automatic phenomenon which cannot be rationally planned or directed'. Pye emphasized that there was a 'need to create more effective, more adaptive, more complex, and more rationalized organizations' to facilitate nation-building. However, the 'heart' of the nation-building 'problem', for Pye, still centered on the 'interrelationships among personality, culture, and the polity' (Pye, 1962, pp. xv–xvi. 6–8, 13, 15–31, 38–39, 42).

By the 1960s the work on nation-building by Pye, as well as other modernization theorists, intersected with an increased emphasis in US foreign policy circles (symbolized by the election to the US presidency of John F. Kennedy) on the need for a more ambitious nation-building strategy. This involved taking the initiative in the Third World to counter the communist threat: the key means by which this was to be done was via the infusion of increased levels of military and economic aid, advice, and support. The country at the center of US nation-building efforts by the early 1960s was South Vietnam.

By the late 1950s CENIS luminaries such as Walt Whitman Rostow advocated and symbolized this shift. For example, in January 1960, the US Senate Committee on Foreign Relations (of which Kennedy was a member and to whom Rostow provided advice and counsel) received (at the Committee's request) a report from CENIS. The report's title made clear the importance that CENIS attached to the emerging Third World: it was entitled *Economic, Social, and*

Political Change in the Underdeveloped Countries and Its Implications for United States Policy.
The authors expounded CENIS's view on the importance of the developing nations for US foreign policy. The report's main recommendations were as follows. US foreign economic aid should be disbursed on a 'long-term' and 'unlinked' basis following clear economic criteria. Technical assistance, particularly in agriculture, needed to continue and land reform needed to be promoted. The US needed to coordinate the distribution of aid with other aid-donor governments in the developed world, and a corps of development professionals should be established. Aid for particular capital-intensive projects, it was argued, should be increased and spread over a number of projects to facilitate a 'big push' in the developing nations.[3]

Area Studies and Military Modernization Theory

In South Vietnam the US-backed nation-building initiative entered a new phase during the Kennedy administration. The Strategic Hamlet Program became the 'centerpiece' of Washington's policy towards South Vietnam in 1962 and 1963. The Kennedy administration facilitated the removal of peasants from widely dispersed villages, placing them in concentrated settlements under the control of the government in Saigon. Washington's commitment to this program was apparent in the fact that the State Department scheduled almost US$90 million to be spent on it in the fiscal year 1963. With this strategy the US Military Assistance Command (MACV) and USAID sought to prevent, or at least seriously weaken, the National Liberation Front's (NLF's) ability to obtain intelligence, food, and other supplies, as well as recruits from the southern population. They also sought to inculcate new ideas about national citizenship that were centered on loyalty to the government of South Vietnam. In 1962 it initially appeared as if the strategic hamlets were undermining the influence of the NLF; however, the guerrillas acted rapidly and effectively to counter this trend. The NLF (which had been formed in December 1960 as a popular front organization to spearhead the guerrilla war in South Vietnam) promised the peasants (many of whom were, not surprisingly, hostile to resettlement, the forced labor demands, and other coercive aspects of the US-backed program) that following the revolution they would be allowed to return to their old villages. The NLF also intensified military attacks on and recruitment in the strategic hamlets.

In a wider sense, however, the Strategic Hamlet Program failed because US officials and advisors were unable or unwilling to examine the ideas it rested on. The assumption that rural practices and values could be eradicated, or at least revised, to fit anti-Communist modernizing and nation-building goals remained entrenched as the war deepened. After President Ngo Dinh Diem, who ruled from 1955 to 1963, was overthrown and killed, the term 'strategic hamlet' was excised from counterinsurgency discourse. However, subsequent efforts to resettle and control the rural population did little to change the basic modernization framework that underpinned the failed Strategic Hamlet Program of 1962–1963 (Latham, 2000, pp. 153–154, 180–182, 197–198, 203–204; see also Hunt, 1995).

A number of observers have argued that the war in Vietnam provided the backdrop for the consolidation of what is sometimes called military modernization theory (Bienen, 1971, p. 7; Gutteridge, 1962, 1965; Janowitz, 1964; Johnson, 1962; Kolko, 1988, pp. 132–134). Samuel Huntington is generally seen as one of the most prominent exponents of the shift from classical modernization theory to military modernization theory (Huntington, 1968). In an implicit critique of development economics and Cold War policy-makers, he argued that the instability in the Third World was primarily the result of 'rapid social change and the rapid mobilization of new groups into politics coupled with the slow development of political institutions'.

In his view, US foreign policy since 1945 had missed this point, because Washington had focused on the 'economic gap' and ignored the 'political gap'. He emphasized that the political gap had been ignored because of the assumption in North America that political stability flowed from 'social reform' stimulated by economic development. However, in his view it was actually the process of modernization that resulted in political instability. For Huntington, organization was the 'road to political power' as well as the 'foundation of political stability'. While the 'vacuum of power and authority' which was seen to exist in 'so many modernizing countries may be filled temporarily by charismatic leadership or by military force', he argued that it could only be 'filled permanently' by 'political organization' (Huntington, 1968, pp. vii, 4–5, 40–41, 43–45, 460–461).

The prescriptions of Huntington, and other modernization theorists who viewed order as the primary objective, held out the possibility that successful nation-building in South Vietnam and elsewhere remained within Washington's power. However, with the Tet Offensive in early 1968 any idea that US power could turn South Vietnam into a viable capitalist nation-state and achieve military victory against the North disappeared. For the architects of the US war in Vietnam, the Tet Offensive represented what Gabriel Kolko has described as a 'long-postponed confrontation with reality' (Kolko, 1994 [1985], pp. 303–337, 341–355.). Against the backdrop of the failing US effort to turn South Vietnam into a Southeast Asian version of South Korea or Taiwan (which, in Cold War terms, were superficially similar but had very different histories), Huntington's book represented an important reorientation and revision of modernization theory. It also represented an inability, or an unwillingness, to probe the deeper assumptions on which the US-led modernization project rested. *Political Order in Changing Societies* (Huntington, 1968) highlighted the close connection between political science and the 'policy concerns of the day' (Shafer, 1988, p. 12). The assumptions and concerns of the officials who carried the US into full-scale war in Vietnam were closely connected to the theories of modernization that emerged in the 1950s and 1960s (Gilman, 2003).

Despite revisions, modernization theory continued to be constrained by the way in which change was conceptualized as a process in which nations evolve, or ought to evolve, along a single path, or a limited number of paths, towards capitalist modernity. This outlook was grounded implicitly, and often explicitly, in romanticized visions of the history of North America and Western Europe (especially the US and Great Britain). The naturalization of the nation also meshed with and reinforced the wider organic metaphors that had come to underpin a great deal of work on modernization. Organic and evolutionary conceptions of development glossed over the uneven and destructive aspects of capitalist development.

By the 1970s, the elaboration of military modernization theory and the politics-of-order approach was part of a much wider process of both diversification and relative decline in modernization theory as various new radical and moderate theoretical challengers emerged. This process included the emergence of the theory of bureaucratic authoritarianism. Associated initially with the work of Guillermo A. O'Donnell, the idea of bureaucratic authoritarianism had gained some prominence by the 1970s (O'Donnell, 1973, 1976, 1977, 1978, 1979, 1988). O'Donnell argued that in late-industrializing nation-states, economic development intersected with the end of democracy and greater, rather than less, inequality. Central to O'Donnell's analysis was the argument that a bureaucratic-authoritarian state emerged when the limits of import-substitution industrialization were reached. At this point, the alliance forged between the working class and the bourgeoisie broke down and the national bourgeoisie moved to form an alliance with the military and the technocracy, resulting in bureaucratic-authoritarianism. A central characteristic of a bureaucratic-authoritarian regime, as defined by O'Donnell, was that it was an attempt by the national bourgeoisie, linked to transnational capital, to protect their interests and guide the economy in a direction commensurate with their needs. By the second half of the 1970s the more deterministic elements of the theory of bureaucratic authoritarianism were increasingly challenged and it was used as a relatively open conceptual framework to guide research rather than as a verifiable theory (Collier, 1979; Remmer and Merkx, 1982).

Although its primary impact was in Latin American studies, bureaucratic authoritarianism had a broad influence on the study of modernization and nation-building. It played a role in, or was connected to, the shift towards 'bringing the state back in' that followed on from the diversification of modernization theory generally and from the demise of the Committee on Comparative Politics in 1972 (Geddes, 1991, p. 49; Rudolph and Rudolph, 1967; Tilly, 1975). This shift was formalized with the establishment of the SSRC's Committee on States and Social Structures in 1983. In the 1970s and 1980s, meanwhile, governments in Washington sought to avoid the nation-building of an earlier era (particularly the use of large numbers of US troops).

International Studies, Nation-Building, and Global Security

International Studies and the New 'Liberal Imperialism'

Post-Cold War, and particularly in the post-9/11 era, however, nation-building (or state-building as some observers now prefer to describe it) has taken on renewed significance (Fukuyama, 2004, 2006). This has increasingly gone hand in hand with a call for Washington to engage in a more explicit exercise in a new 'liberal imperialism' (Mallaby, 2002, pp. 2–7).

In a similar vein, the prominent historian Niall Ferguson asked rhetorically whether 'the leaders of the one state with the economic resources to make the world a better place have the guts to do it?' (Ferguson, 2001, p. 141; see also Ferguson, 2003). In a more recent book, Ferguson again suggested that the US take up the imperial burden. However, he also expressed serious doubts about its ability to do so, focusing particularly on what he regarded as a lack of political will and social and cultural commitment to nation-building within a wider US imperial framework. He also called into doubt the ability of the US to meet the financial costs of a global imperium in a world that Ferguson represented as increasingly anarchic (Ferguson, 2004).

From a somewhat different angle, some observers have expressed concerns that in the post-Cold War and post-9/11 order the US places too much emphasis on the role of the military in nation-building. In *The Mission: Waging War and Keeping Peace With America's Military*, Dana Priest observed that in the years prior to 9/11 Washington grew 'increasingly dependent on its military to carry out its foreign affairs'. Over time the military 'filled a vacuum left by an indecisive White House, an atrophied State Department, and a distracted Congress'. Following 9/11, 'the trend accelerated dramatically' and 'without a doubt, U.S.-sponsored political reform abroad is being eclipsed by new military pacts focusing on anti-terrorism and intelligence-sharing'. For Priest, this is a major shortcoming of US foreign policy. She lamented that after 'twelve years of reluctant nation-building' in the post-Cold War era Washington has unfortunately still not 'spawned an effective civilian corps of aid workers, agronomists, teachers, engineers—a real peace corps—to take charge of post-war reconstruction in Afghanistan or anywhere else' (Priest, 2003, pp. 14, 390–392).

Central to the wider call for the US to take up the imperial mantle and/or embrace the nation-building mission is the assumption that the US (and those allies, and/or the European Union and the United Nations if they accept US leadership) needs to universalize economic and political liberalism. This is assumed to be for both the US's own security and for the benefits that will flow to the rest of the world. 'Freedom' is the term most widely used by the Bush administration to describe what the US has to offer the world. Furthermore, on this reading, instability and conflict around the world are regularly assumed to flow from the cultural, ethnic, or religious shortcomings and/or civilizational rigidities of those on the receiving end of the US-led pursuit of global liberal modernity. In popular rendition, conflict and instability in the post-Cold War era are generally represented as flowing from primordial animosities and long-standing and irrational ethnic or religious hatreds.

A particularly influential observer and policy intellectual whose work has helped to reinforce a primordial reading of post-Cold War instability is Samuel Huntington. For Huntington, as for other traditional realists, and in contrast to the neo-conservatives, Washington needs to remain extremely wary of grand imperial and nation-building missions (Brzezinski, 1997; Mearsheimer, 2001). In Huntington's view, Washington should focus on its vital national interests and recognize the serious constraints on trying to create a global order in its own image (Huntington, 1996a, 1999). In a 1993 article in *Foreign Affairs* he argued that international politics was increasingly converging on the often violent reaction of 'non-Western civilizations to Western power and values' (Huntington, 1993, p. 41). These concerns were outlined in greater detail in *The Clash of Civilizations and the Remaking of World Orde*r (1996b), which contributed to the culturally reductionist views which were steadily gaining influence in the post-Cold War era. Huntington has recently followed up his earlier prognostications with a book that warns his fellow citizens that globalization and immigration represent serious threats to America's 'traditional' values (Huntington, 2004).

The debate about the future of international order and the form and extent of the new 'liberal imperialism' to which *The Clash of Civilizations* was connected has also increasingly focused on whether the instability and violence in collapsing or collapsed nation-states is economically based. For example, David Keen has argued that 'there may be more to war than winning' (Keen, 2000, p, 26). Nazih Richani has argued that under certain identifiable conditions, 'war systems' or 'systems of violence' emerge that are self-perpetuating (Richani, 2002, pp. 3–4.).

The view that civil wars and endemic political violence flow primarily from the pursuit of economic gain by the key combatants was given its most reductive articulation in a series of studies supported by the World Bank and conducted under the leadership of Paul Collier and Anke Hoeffler. As the result of a broad statistical analysis of virtually all civil wars since the mid-1960s, they concluded that variables such as regime type, economic mismanagement, political rights, and levels of ethnic homogeneity or heterogeneity were statistically irrelevant to explaining the causes of civil wars: instead, economic factors were the crucial explanatory variable. In their analysis low economic growth rates and low incomes predisposed nation-states to civil war, but there was, it was argued, no strong connection between high levels of social inequality and civil conflict. They also emphasized that polities that were highly dependent on the export of primary commodities and were populated by large numbers of young men, with limited or no education, were also highly susceptible to civil conflict and political instability. Their overall conclusions were that political grievances were not directly connected to the outbreak of civil wars. In their view, nation-states that contained significant cohorts of poorly educated youths and readily accessible natural resources were particularly susceptible to civil conflict and the emergence of rebels driven primarily by powerful economic incentives ('greed') to use violence to acquire wealth (Collier, 2000; Collier and Hoeffler, 2000).

More recently, in the wake of considerable debate about what are highly stylized conclusions that explain political instability and state collapse primarily in terms of actors motivated by 'greed' rather than legitimate political 'grievances', Collier and his collaborators have altered their analysis somewhat. They now emphasize the way in which factors such as access to finances (particularly natural resources) and regional and global diaspora networks, along with a significant number of uneducated youths and opportunities for organized violence, all contribute to civil conflicts that also flow from other motivating factors (Collier, 2003). While this modification of the 'greed and grievance' argument satisfied some of its critics, its reliance on quantitative analysis and its economic determinism continue to be challenged (both directly and indirectly) by observers who seek to situate their analysis of civil conflict, national instability, and post-conflict transitions within an historical and politico-economic context (e.g., see Reno, 1998).

Unlike Collier and other proponents of the 'greed and grievance' duality, who support their position with reference to quantitative research, these writers rely more on the qualitative research of historians and political economists. A particularly self-conscious effort to go beyond greed and grievance has been mapped out by Karen Ballentine and Jake Sherman (2003). At the outset they emphasize that while there is considerable agreement that the dynamics of conflict can only be understood with reference to economic factors, what remains to be clarified is why, when, and how (much) economics matters. Furthermore, the highly normative character of the terms 'greed' and 'grievance' has combined with their terminological imprecision to generate considerable disagreement about their usage. Ballentine and Sherman conclude that the 'greed theory of civil war' (grounded as it is in statistics) generates propositions about the role of economic factors (in relation to 'motive' or 'opportunity') that are 'probabilistic' assessments of the risk of conflict. However, most importantly, Collier's approach is not an actual description of the dynamics of civil conflict in 'specific real-world instances'. As a result, ascertaining the role of economics can only be achieved via comparative examination and descriptive analysis of particular examples of civil conflict. For them, moving beyond greed and grievance in this fashion is 'essential' to any effort to devise policies to prevent civil conflicts, to facilitate nation-building, and to enhance international security and stability more generally (Ballentine and Sherman, 2003, pp. 4–5.).

Despite the improvements advocated by Ballentine and Sherman, however, the most influential academic narratives on nation-building and international security in the post-Cold War era continue to avoid or downplay issues of history, culture, and identity, in favor of a quantitative and technocratic approach. This, in turn, is linked to an even more fundamental problem—the fact that the dominant theories of nation-building and international security continue to routinize the nation-state as their key unit, or sub-unit, of analysis. The growing array of theories and policy proposals seeking to explain and facilitate conflict resolution and nation-building in the post-Cold War era continue to be outlined and/or implemented on the assumption that nation-states are the basic, even the natural, units of a wider international order. This is further underpinned by the assumption that capitalism, or the currently dominant and romanticized neo-liberal conception of capitalism, is an equally natural part of the post-Cold War order. The history of nation-state formation and consolidation following decolonization and the onset of the Cold War, and the significant changes associated with the reorientation of the global political economy since the 1970s, is complex. Nevertheless, the continued glossing over of this history has ensured that the routinization of the nation-state has remained central to the dominant narratives on nation-building and international security at the start of the twenty-first century (e.g., see Rotberg, 2003a, 2003b).

International Studies and Neo-Liberal Nation-(State-)Building

In the wake of 9/11, the Middle East in general, and Iraq in particular, has become even more of a focus of US foreign policy than in the past, and a key proving ground for post-Cold War nation-building. The US overthrow of Saddam Hussain came at a time when not only the nation-state of Iraq was in crisis (arguably it had been in crisis since its creation in 1920), but when the wider UN-centered nation-state system itself had entered a prolonged crisis. This crisis is being played out against the backdrop of the end of the Cold War, the uneven, incomplete, and increasingly unequal transition to globalization, and the emergence of a unipolar world centered on US dominance and grounded in overwhelming US military power.

From the outset the US occupation of Iraq after 20 March 2003 failed to confront the profoundly flawed legacy of British-led nation-building efforts in the 1920s, which were succeeded by years of brutal and narrowly-based authoritarianism in which national institutions were increasingly overlaid by patrimonial lines of control (Berger, 2004b). Even if the US was willing to engage in a far more sustained struggle for hearts and minds in the Tigris and Euphrates valleys today than it ever did in the Mekong Delta and the highlands of South Vietnam 30 years ago, the obstacles it faces today remain insurmountable. The failure to learn the lessons of an earlier era are compounded by the fact that earlier approaches to nation-building (apart from the central emphasis on security and brute military force, which remains intact) have been displaced by neo-liberal nation-building. The emphasis on the latter has ensured that the likelihood of success is even lower than it was in an earlier era (the best analysis on this point is by Dodge, 2005).

Even in the Middle East, Iraq is distinctive in the way in which, since the late 1960s, the Ba'thist regime used a combination of extreme forms of violence and the distribution of oil-based patronage to eliminate or domesticate any significant autonomous political activity. In this context, the US occupiers often latch on to political elements that appear to be autonomous and authentic, or they may even embrace 'primordialization', as did the British colonial rulers of the 1920s. The latter approach involves assuming that Iraqi society is still completely dominated by pre-modern tribal and religious structures. At this juncture there are clear indications that both the US and their British allies have used these ostensibly pre-modern structures. However, they need to be seen not as traditional institutions or practices with roots deep in the region's history, but as social structures destroyed and then reconstructed as pillars of the regime of Saddam Husain (Dodge, 2003, pp. 159–163). The UK's failed effort early in the twentieth century to construct a liberal nation-state out of three former Ottoman provinces continues to be central to any understanding of post-Saddam Iraq in the early twenty-first century. And Washington's inability, or unwillingness, to understand this means that it has already embarked on an early twenty-first-century version of the failed nation-building effort presided over by the British in the 1920s and early 1930s. The US has also embarked on a repetition in Iraq, albeit a revised neo-liberal version, of its own earlier failure in South Vietnam. The chances of success in the Middle East in the early twenty-first century are even more remote than they were in Southeast Asia in the 1960s (Dodge, 2006).

The failing US-led nation-building effort in Iraq is now taking place against the backdrop of an incipient civil war with regional ramifications. It is also occurring in the context of a post-Cold War and post-9/11 global order in which the number of collapsed/collapsing and failed/failing nation-states in both the Islamic world and beyond is increasing. In this context, if IS as a complex series of structures and professional practices is to be of any relevance it needs to move beyond its predominant commitment to the maintenance and rehabilitation of the international system of nation-states. In particular, it needs to move away from technocratic questions about facilitating nation-building. In contrast, what is called for is a serious effort to locate the fate of nations in an analytical framework that builds on the assumption that the limits of the nation-state as a vehicle for modernity have already been reached. The way forward, if you like, is to accept that contemporary efforts at nation-building are fundamentally compromised by their reliance on pseudo-anthropological ideas about primordialism on the one hand and their commitment to the corrosive and contradictory effects of market reform and globalization on the other hand (Berger, 2006).

Conclusion: Area Studies, Development Studies, International Studies, and the Vicissitudes of Nation-Building

As emphasized at the outset, nation-building has been rediscovered. However, the growing preoccupation with nation-building and counterinsurgency in the post-Cold War, post-9/11 era have limited (and in some cases no) prospects for success if those involved in the process fail to locate what they are doing in a critical historical context. As a bare minimum there is, as noted earlier, a need to link the formulation and implementation of contemporary nation-building and counterinsurgency strategies to a critical examination of the history of earlier efforts at nation-building specifically and the history of the twentieth century more generally. Arguably the single most important historical example of a US-led nation-building effort during the Cold War was South Vietnam. This was the *locus classicus* of nation-building in the 1960s and early 1970s, and now Iraq has become the epicentre of the geo-politics of nation-building and counterinsurgency for the foreseeable future.

In many parts of the Third World the processes of nation-building in the past were linked to an ongoing struggle that pitted insurgency against counterinsurgency in the context of the wider Cold War contest between capitalist and state-socialist forms of national development. One of the key characteristics of the post-Cold War era is the growing number of failing/failed or collapsing/collapsed states: an increasing number of nation-states are mired in high levels of civil conflict and/or civil war and displaying a decreased, or complete absence of, political stability and social order. This, in turn, particularly since September 11, 2001, has resulted in a new 'Long War' (the term now apparently being used by the Bush administration to replace the 'War on Terror'), combining both older and newer forms of insurgency and counterinsurgency, and challenging or defending the post-Cold War international order. At the end of the day, nation-building was a Cold War project and its results at the time, regardless of how one measures them, were mixed at best. In the post-Cold War era, the main proponents of US-led nation-building and counterinsurgency (a latter-day effort to keep the world safe for primary colors) appear unwilling or unable to realize that they are pursuing yesterday's project with tragic consequences for all concerned.

In this context, the future of DS and AS is to be found in their convergence on IS. At the same time, the future of IS as a set of critical practices and structures generally, and the study of nation-building more specifically, needs to be dramatically reconceptualized and reorganized in a direction that addresses the growing significance of the 'transnational' and the global. Only in this way will international studies generally, and the critical study of the idea and practice of nation-building more specifically, make a contribution to furthering global emancipation, social prosperity, and political stability (Berger and Weber, 2007).

Notes

1   While I do not discuss international relations (IR) directly, the central role of IR in IS obviously needs to be acknowledged, as does the fact that IR emerged and was consolidated as a field of study prior to DS and AS (Knutsen, 1997).

2   A key site for AS, and the elaboration of the central concepts of modernization theory and nation-building during the early Cold War, was the Social Science Research Council's (SSRC) Committee on Comparative Politics. Established in 1954 and chaired by Gabriel Almond until 1963; the Committee provided a key focus for the production and dissemination of modernization theory (see Berger, 2004a, chapter 3).

3   A revised and expanded version of the report was published in 1961 as *The Emerging Nations: Their Growth and United States Policy*. It included chapters by Rostow and Lucian Pye (Millikan and Blackmer, 1961).

References

Almond, G. A. (1954) *The Appeals of Communism* (Princeton, NJ: Princeton University Press).

Ballentine, K. & Sherman, J. (2003) Introduction, in K. Ballentine & J. Sherman (eds) *The Political Economy of Armed Conflict: Beyond Greed and Grievance* (Boulder, CO: Lynne Rienner).

Berger, M. T. (2004a) *The Battle for Asia: From Decolonization to Globalization* (London: RoutledgeCurzon).

Berger, M. T. (2004b) From Saigon to Baghdad: nation-building and the specter of history, *Intelligence and National Security: An Inter-Disciplinary Journal*, 19(3), pp. 344–356.

Berger, M. T. (2006) From nation-building to state-building: the geo-politics of development, the nation-state system and the changing global order, *Third World Quarterly*, 27(1), pp. 5–25.

Berger, M. T. & Borer, D. A. (2007) The Long War: insurgency, counterinsurgency and collapsing states, *Third World Quarterly*, 28(2), pp. 197–215.

Berger, M. T. & Weber, H. (2005) Beyond U.S. grand strategy? Critical analysis and world politics, *Critical Asian Studies*, 37(1), pp. 95–102.

Berger, M. T. & Weber, H. (2006) Beyond state-building: global governance and the crisis of the nation-state system in the 21st century, *Third World Quarterly*, 27(1), pp. 201–208.

Berger, M. T. & Weber, H. (2007) *Rethinking the Third World: International Development and World Politics* (London: Palgrave Macmillan).

Bienen, H. (1971) The background to contemporary study of militaries and modernization, in H. Bienen (ed.) *The Military and Modernization* (Chicago: Aldine Atherton).

Brzezinski, Z. (1997) *The Grand Chessboard: American Primacy and Its Geostrategic Imperatives* (New York: Basic Books).

Bundy, M. (1964) The battlefields of power and the searchlights of the academy, in E. A. G. Johnson (ed.) *Dimensions of Diplomacy* (Baltimore, MD: Johns Hopkins University Press).

Cammack, P. (2002) Attacking the global poor, *New Left Review*, 2(13), pp. 125–134.

Collier, D. (1979) The bureaucratic-authoritarian model: synthesis and priorities for future research, in D. Collier (ed.) *The New Authoritarianism in Latin America* (New York: Columbia University Press).

Collier, P. (2000) Doing well out of war: an economic perspective, in M. Berdal & D. M. Malone (eds) *Greed and Grievance: Economic Agendas in Civil Wars* (Boulder, CO: Lynne Rienner).

Collier, P. (2003) *Breaking the Conflict Trap: Civil War and Development Policy* (Washington, DC: World Bank and Oxford University Press).

Collier, P. & Hoeffler, A. (2000) *Greed and Grievance in Civil War*, World Bank Working Paper Series, Washington, DC.

Dodge, T. (2003) *Inventing Iraq: The Failure of Nation Building and A History Denied* (New York: Columbia University Press).

Dodge, T. (2005) *Inventing Iraq: The Failure of Nation Building and A History Denied*, 2nd ed. (New York: Columbia University Press).

Dodge, T. (2006) Iraq: the contradictions of state-building in historical perspective, *Third World Quarterly*, 27(1), pp. 187–200.

Ferguson, N. (2001) Clashing civilizations or mad mullahs: the United States between informal and formal empire, in S. Talbott & N. Chanda (eds) *The Age of Terror: America and the World After September 11* (Oxford: Perseus Press).

Ferguson, N. (2003) *Empire: The Rise and Demise of the British World Order and the Lessons for Global Power* (New York: Basic Books).

Ferguson, N. (2004) *Colossus: The Price of America's Empire* (London: Penguin Press).

Fukuyama, F. (2004) *State-Building: Governance and World Order in the 21st Century* (Ithaca, NY: Cornell University Press).

Fukuyama, F. (ed.) (2006) *Nation-Building: Beyond Afghanistan and Iraq* (Baltimore, MD: Johns Hopkins University Press).

Geddes, B. (1991) Paradigms and sand castles in comparative politics of developing areas, in W. Crotty (ed.) *Comparative Politics, Policy, and International Relations*, Political Science: Looking to the Future, Vol. 2 (Evanston, IL: Northwestern University Press).

Gilman, N. (2003) *Imposing Modernity: Modernization Theory and Cold War America* (Baltimore, MD: Johns Hopkins University Press).

Gutteridge, W. (1962) *Armed Forces in the New States* (London: Oxford University Press).

Gutteridge, W. (1965) *Military Institutions and Power in the New States* (New York: Praeger).

Hunt, R. A. (1995) *Pacification: The American Struggle for Vietnam's Hearts and Minds* (Boulder, CO: Westview Press).

Huntington, S. P. (1968) *Political Order in Changing Societies* (New Haven, CT: Yale University Press).

Huntington, S. P. (1993) The clash of civilizations? *Foreign Affairs*, 72(3), pp. 44–57.

Huntington, S. P. (1996a) The West: unique, not universal, *Foreign Affairs*, 75(6), pp. 28–46.

Huntington, S. P. (1996b) *The Clash of Civilizations and the Remaking of World Order* (New York: Simon and Schuster).

Huntington, S. P. (1999) The lonely superpower, *Foreign Affairs*, 78(2), pp. 35–49.

Huntington, S. P. (2004) *Who Are We? The Challenges to America's National Identity* (New York: Simon and Schuster).

Janowitz, M. (1964) *The Military in the Political Development of New Nations: An Essay in Comparative Analysis* (Chicago: University of Chicago Press).

Johnson, J. J. (ed.) (1962) *The Role of the Military in Underdeveloped Countries* (Princeton, NJ: Princeton University Press).

Keen, D. (2000) Incentives and disincentives for violence, in M. Berdal & D. M. Malone (eds) *Greed and Grievance: Economic Agendas in Civil Wars* (Boulder, CO: Lynne Rienner Publishers).

Knutsen, T. L. (1997) *A History of International Relations Theory*, 2nd ed. (Manchester: Manchester University Press).

Kolko, G. (1988) *Confronting the Third World: United States Foreign Policy 1945–1980* (New York: Pantheon).

Kolko, G. (1994) *Anatomy of a War: Vietnam, the United States and Modern Historical Experience*, 2nd ed. (New York: New Press).

Krugman, P. (1999) The fall and rise of development economics, in P. Krugman, *Development, Geography and Economic Theory* (Cambridge, MA: MIT Press).

Latham, M. E. (2000) *Modernization as Ideology: American Social Science and 'Nation-Building' in the Kennedy Era* (Chapel Hill: University of North Carolina Press).

Leslie, S. W. (1993) *The Cold War and American Science: The Military–Industrial–Academic Complex at MIT and Stanford* (New York: Columbia University Press).

Lewis, W. A. (1955) *The Theory of Economic Growth* (London: Allen and Unwin).

Leys, C. (1996) *The Rise and Fall of Development Theory* (Bloomington: Indiana University Press).

Mallaby, S. (2002) The Reluctant Imperialist: Terrorism, Failed States and the Case for American Empire, *Foreign Affairs*, 81(2), pp. 2–7.

Mearsheimer, J. J. (2001) *The Tragedy of Great Power Politics* (New York: W. W. Norton).

Millikan, M. F. & Blackmer, D. L. M. (eds) (1961) *The Emerging Nations: Their Growth and United States Policy* (Boston, MA: Little, Brown and Company).

Murillo, M. A. (2004) *Colombia and the United States: War, Unrest and Destabilization* (New York: Seven Stories Press).

Myrdal, G. (1957) *Economic Theory and Underdeveloped Regions* (New York: Harper).

Myrdal, G. (1968) *Asian Drama: An Inquiry Into the Poverty of Nations* (London: Penguin).

O'Donnell, G. A. (1973) *Modernization and Bureaucratic-Authoritarianism: Studies in South American Politics* (Berkeley: University of California Institute of International Studies).

O'Donnell, G. A. (1976) Modernization and military coups: theory, comparisons and the Argentine case, in A. F. Lowenthal (ed.) *Armies and Politics in Latin America* (New York: Holmes and Meier).

O'Donnell, G. A. (1977) Corporatism and the question of the state, in J. M. Malloy (ed.) *Authoritarianism and Corporatism in Latin America* (Pittsburgh: University of Pittsburgh Press).

O'Donnell, G. A. (1978) Reflections on the patterns of change in the bureaucratic-authoritarian state, *Latin American Research Review*, 13(1), pp. 3–38.

O'Donnell, G. A. (1979) Tensions in the bureaucratic-authoritarian state and the question of democracy, in D. Collier (ed.) *The New Authoritarianism in Latin America* (New York: Columbia University Press).

O'Donnell, G. A. (1988) *Bureaucratic-Authoritarianism: Argentina, 1966–1973, in Comparative Perspective* (Berkeley: University of California Press).

Palat, R. A. (2000) Fragmented visions: excavating the future of area studies in a post-American world, in N. L. Waters (ed.) *Beyond the Area Studies Wars: Towards a New International Studies* (Hanover, NH: University Press of New England).

Pender, J. (2001) From 'structural adjustment' to 'comprehensive development framework': conditionality transformed? *Third World Quarterly: Journal of Emerging Areas*, 22(3), pp. 397–411.

Priest, D. (2003) *The Mission: Waging War and Keeping Peace with America's Military* (New York: W. W. Norton).

Pye, L. (1956) *Guerrilla Communism in Malaya: Its Social and Political Meaning* (Princeton, NJ: Princeton University Press).

Pye, L. W. (1962) *Politics, Personality and Nation-Building: Burma's Search for Identity* (New Haven, CT: Yale University Press).

Remmer, K. L. and Merkx, G. W. (1982) Bureaucratic-authoritarianism revisited, *Latin American Research Review*, 17(2), pp. 3–40.

Reno, W. (1998) *Warlord Politics and African States* (Boulder, CO: Lynne Rienner Publishers).

Richani, N. (2002) *Systems of Violence: The Political Economy of War and Peace in Colombia* (Albany: State University of New York Press).

Rostow, W. W. (1960) *The Stages of Economic Growth: A Non-Communist Manifesto* (New York: Cambridge University Press).

Rotberg, R. I. (ed.) (2003a) *State Failure and State Weakness in a Time of Terror* (Washington, DC: Brookings Institution Press).

Rotberg, R. I. (ed.) (2003b) *When States Fail: Causes and Consequences* (Princeton, NJ: Princeton University Press).

Rudolph, L. I. & Rudolph, S. H. (1967) *The Modernity of Tradition: Political Development in India* (Chicago: University of Chicago Press).

Seers, D. (1979) The birth, life, and death of development economics, *Development and Change*, 10(4), pp. 707–719.

Shafer, D. M. (1988) *Deadly Paradigms: The Failure of US Counterinsurgency Policy* (Princeton, NJ: Princeton University Press).

Shepard, L. (1998) *Life During Wartime* (London: Orion Books).

Tilly, C. (ed.) (1975) *The Formation of National States in Western Europe* (Princeton, NJ: Princeton University Press).

United Nations (1951) *Measures for the Economic Development of Underdeveloped Countries* (New York: United Nations).

Social Regulation in the Time of War: Constituting the Current Crisis

SHELLEY FELDMAN

Introduction

The 'war on terror' is an iconic example of state violence—the transgression by one state violating the rights of another, challenging the understanding of territorial sovereignty that established the doctrine of noninterference in the affairs of other nations. This doctrine remains enshrined, if tenuously, in current international law. Importantly, state violence and its attendant disciplinary practices and strategic deployment are neither limited to cross-national transgressions nor associated only with wartime. Rather, state violence, and not only the threat of violence, constitutes politics everywhere. To recognize state violence as constituting more than contraventions of extra-state transgressions within the development project requires rethinking development in the idiom of violence. This, in turn, depends on interpreting violence not only, although it is important, in terms of the effects of development interventions—marked by increasing inequality as well as poverty, extended ecological devastation from which there is probably no return, and declines in public and personal security as class wars increase and public goods are eroded in what were once referred to as dependent country contexts—but also in terms of how violence is constituted in transgressor states. The war on terror, then, is an aspect of the current neoliberal crisis that is constituted differently across the spatial domains of the global economy.

A focus on violence, specifically state violence, appreciates Weber's (2004) interrogation of territoriality and its attendant political imaginaries for what it tells us about how the development map elides and legitimates particular relations of political authority. It also acknowledges Sparke's (2003) challenge to an imaginary of globalization that is constructed to ignore relations of power and American dominance. Robinson's (1998) reference to the 'Latinamericanization' of the US, while drawing parallels between countries mapped in three worlds, signals the need to challenge categorical formulations. What these authors remind us is that how we interpret global interdependence may underestimate the unevenness of neoliberal practice across dependent and hegemonic national formations. These interpretations create what one might call violence to our imagination, since it constrains thinking creatively about the varied relations and practices that constitute hegemony. By focusing on state violence we recognize the importance of incorporating intra-state violence, centered in the US,[1] as a critical site for unmasking cultural practices within a global politics of development.[2]

In this paper I explore the creative masking of this violence in order to identify selected institutional and political practices that have, until quite recently, generated broad compliance with the policies of the current neoliberal project. Importantly, these may find expression in the particularities of the Bush regime and the extremism of the Republican Party, but our understanding should not be limited to this administration alone since state violence is a characteristic of the contemporary crisis of capital as expressed through new relations of dispossession and enclosure. A concern with popular compliance contributes to the burgeoning literature on citizenship, sovereignty, and rights, as well as centrist and left critiques of the war on terror, by focusing on efforts to build conformity and complicity with the US war initiative.[3]

Using the Danish cartoon scandal and the Dubai Ports World crisis in 2006, I offer two linked arguments. First, I suggest that the rhetorical climate surrounding events in the US cast inequality, particularly gender inequality, and violent opposition as occurring 'elsewhere', while framing inequality as difference and opposition as terrorism 'at home'. This framing is refracted through a view of individualism as personal responsibility and rational action to provide a basis for patriotism, while offering a collective formulation of Islam as a threat and the basis of communal transgressions of individual rights and freedoms.[4] Second, I query critical studies of global hegemony for failing to acknowledge adequately hegemonic projects within the US as constitutive of its position in the world economy. Here I emphasize the contradictory tensions among transgressions of war, legal violations, and invasions of individual liberties in the idiom of liberal democracy (Giroux, 2005; Johnson, 2004).

Theoretically, I am concerned with why development debates consistently ignore the place of the US as a political space and assume, instead, its givenness as a political, economic, and military hegemon. Recentering the practices that support US hegemonic status opens to scrutiny the role of US cultural practices as vehicles for constructing imaginaries and normalizing specific interpretations of events. Institutionally, these practices share a stage with what Althusser (1971) refers to as ideological state apparatuses. The emphasis on cultural practices in debates on global political economy connects intra-state militarization, securitization, and privatization to inter-state violence, recognizing that the 'war overseas always has a homefront and domestic fallout' (Piven, 2004, p. 1). This ties the neoliberalist ambitions of Bush and the Republican Party to a 'domestic strategy, rooted ... in calculations geared to shoring up the Bush regime's domestic power and ... policy agenda' (p. 11), the privatization and corporatization of social services—education, health care, welfare, and social security—in the wake of a disputed election, conflagrations over political appointees, revelations about the corruption associated with military contracts, and low poll ratings.

The incorporation of the US as a specific site of analysis in development debates, however, is intended to move beyond limiting the inclusion of the US to discussions of the war's domestic fallout or to its policy effects. A more robust view of inclusion requires a theoretical stage able to reveal the construction of discourses of development and globalization in ways that connect development practices 'at home' with development initiatives 'abroad'. In this effort, Midnight Notes' (1990) focus on the new enclosures and Harvey's (2003) reworking of primitive or primary accumulation are extremely suggestive. Each takes a view of the world map that remains attentive to the particularities of national histories and colonial encounters while recognizing that the current crisis of accumulation depends on understanding the world economy as a whole. Sparke's (2003, pp. 374–375) appreciation for the ways in which globalization 'represents economic interdependency as constitutive of a smooth and decentred global space [that]. . . elides and enables American dominance' likewise suggests the ways in which it foregrounds spatial imaginaries and the reworking of the commons. Importantly, as Sparke (2003, p. 376) argues, this imagery 'is partially constitutive of global systems of management and governance and, as such, partially enabling of the very asymmetries it obscures'. Thus, for Sparke, McDonalds depends on McDonnell Douglas just as particular governance relations and consumption practices depend on exploitation. As an interpretation of global capitalist relations, rather than a phenomenon solely of US capital, Aboulafia (in Gross, 2006) offers a 'guns to caviar index':

> The last few years have seen a global orgy of wealth creation in the developed world (hedge fund managers, CEOs, overpaid sports stars), in the semi-developed world (Middle East petro-sheikhs, Mexican tycoons), and in the developing world (Indian software moguls, Chinese industrialists). Spending on business jets rose about 47 percent between 2003 and 2005, and 2006 is shaping up to be a record year.[5]

Debates on hegemony have been unable to capture this process adequately. For instance, even though the language of hegemony debated by Harvey (2003, 2005) and Arrighi (2005a, 2005b) recognizes the US as the world's economic and military hegemon, they are less interested in exploring how hegemony is constituted relationally and experientially. In each case, hegemony refers to a status, a hegemon, as an effect of economic, military, and political power, rather than to a set of practices and relations that create political compliance through, among other relations, violence. Wallerstein (2000) suggests that the US decided to go to war to demonstrate its overwhelming military power, to intimidate European nations who no longer depend on the US in ways similar to the period prior to the demise of the Soviet threat. Today, moreover, the threat of nuclear proliferation among countries of the south is not contained by the soft power of persuasion.

Examining the current war on terror through the Danish cartoon scandal and the Dubai Ports World crisis offers a starting point for exploring these themes. Since a crucial aspect of neoliberal practice concerns securing legitimacy and popular support for potentially unpopular interventions, I begin with a discussion of moral regulation. Here, Hall (1988) is extremely suggestive in showing how the power of Thatcherism lay in its ability to constitute subjects for whom its discourses about the world made sense.[6] He builds his argument by creatively interpreting Gramsci's understanding of hegemony as the ability of an alliance of ruling class factions 'not only to coerce a subordinate class to conform to its interests, but [to exert] total *social* authority over those classes and the social formation' (Hall, 1979, p. 232). Abrams (1988) and Corrigan and Sayer (1985) situate cultural production as a constitutive aspect of state practice and, as the latter clarify, the 'idea of the state . . . is a claim to legitimacy, a means by which politically organized subjection is simultaneously accomplished and concealed, and it is constituted in large part, [but not solely] by the activities of institutions of government themselves' (pp. 9–10).

This, of course, does not presume that hegemonic practices are uncontested or secure in the US,[7] but, rather, highlights the need to explain the relative absence—even accounting for the suppression of numerous protest actions and activities—of sustained debate and opposition, whether by a so-called opposition party, the Democrats, or by mass, grassroots uprisings and initiatives.[8] Despite worldwide popular opposition to US war policy, in other words, it is noteworthy that there is relative silence about the contradictions of contemporary forms of accumulation that it masks, except, of course, the concern with controlling oil production, reserves, and trade routes at any cost. As Barbara Ehrenreich would remind us in her comment on Piven's *The War at Home*, a 'brilliant and provocative theory of what's driving the new imperialism – and no, it's not the oil, stupid!'

Arguably, there is waning US popular support for the war in Afghanistan and Iraq. This is perhaps because the costs of militarization are beginning to reveal themselves in the everyday lives of people living in the US—declines in living standards and infrastructure as well as increased surveillance and curtailments of various assumed freedoms (Piven, 2004). Surely the sustained cutbacks in and privatization of education, health care, and social infrastructure, the poor quality of support for military personnel, and the increasing numbers of people giving their lives for a war that has no end is beginning to unravel support for current Bush policies and appointments (Giroux, 2005), including among the institutionalized political parties.

As for the development project per se, there is limited popular knowledge about United States Agency for International Development (USAID) practices and decision-making, about its working relationships with more than 3,500 American companies and over 300 US-based private voluntary organizations, or about its changing institutional structure under President Bush. Randall L. Tobias, for instance, was recently confirmed as USAID Administrator[9]—a position he holds concurrently with that of the nation's first Director of United States Foreign Assistance. In this position he reports directly to Secretary of State Condoleezza Rice and holds the rank of Deputy Secretary of State. This consolidation, along with shifting language and research funding under the umbrella of security—there is need for more people able to understand Muslim dominant populations—reveals the parallel, if not integration, of domestic and development-focused neoliberal policy reform. Let me begin, then, by summarizing two recent scandals to explore what they reveal about fissures in and interpretations of the current crisis.

A Current Scandal

I recently contributed to a discussion of the Danish cartoon scandal and agreed to share some thoughts on what followed in its wake. The scandal focused on the publication of anti-Muslim cartoons by the Danish right-wing newspaper, *Jyllands-Posten*. While the meaning of the cartoons and their publication were generally debated along established political lines, there was substantial support for the view that their purpose was not to engage debate but to provoke discord. This purpose was realized, in that they provoked what can arguably be understood as an overreaction by those offended as expressed in protests in Bangladesh, Indonesia, and Pakistan, as well as in Britain. Some of these protests turned violent but most, such as that in Hong Kong with more than 2,000 mostly South Asian Muslims, were peaceful (Ali, 2006).

In the American and European media the protests were portrayed as a vast uncontrollable uprising of Islamic militancy, a scourge on the landscape that demanded redress. This representation, which constructed Muslims not as individuals but as a collective enemy to be interpreted as an incident's cause, helped divert attention from the real tragedy of the contemporary moment, the war in Iraq and Afghanistan. According to Montero (2006), these portrayals ignore the conflation of religious fervor and inequality, the latter being the animation for many protest supporters and an indicator of the failure of development to reduce high levels of poverty despite a rhetoric of economic growth and the expansion of individual opportunity.

As I reflected on what to share, I was struck by the panel's title: 'Religious Sensitivity vs. Freedom of the Press?' While suggestive and open to varied interpretations, the title seemed curiously American, with explanation sought in the relationship between multiculturalism and difference on the one hand and individual freedom and choice on the other. *The Nation's* emphasis on freedom of speech added to the sense that individual rights and individual freedom were at the core of even popular left responses to the printing and subsequent reprinting of the clearly anti-Muslim cartoons.[10] It was also striking how this framing precluded engaging other possible interpretations of the scandal, interpretations that could lead to debate about the social construction of the other, historical interpretations of the war on terror, the reason why protests occurred where they did, and the place of cultural regulation in contributing to and diverting attention from the contemporary crises of development and of American political and economic hegemony. Moreover, this framing signals how political imagination in the US structures interpretations of the current crisis in ways that make sense of Pentagon claims of a just Iraq war as congruent with a non-imperial, neoliberal project to integrate the global economy in ways beneficial to all of its participants (Roberts et al., 2003).

There is no need to rehearse the role of the *Jyllands-Posten* position and its refusal to print caricatures of Jesus, or its call for cartoon submissions that were directed specifically at Muslims, from which were selected those published. Nor is it necessary to recount how the cartoon episode was manipulated for political purposes within the Muslim community, since the cartoons appeared months before various leaders resurrected them as a focus of mobilization. What is important are the stakes involved in the symbolic ritual of othering and its criticality for sustaining a particular neoliberal frame of development and security. Also important is the need to connect the disciplining and regulating of political contestation with the current practices of the economic-military nexus.

The connections between the cartoon scandal and the war on terror framed my remarks that evening and, as one colleague intimated, politicized the discussion as it built on an examination of the neoliberal project and its conditions of possibility within the US as well as between the US and its world neighbors. The connection between neoliberalism and the conditions that sustain it includes violence at home and abroad and an ideology that resurrects and continually reasserts civilizational difference and incompatibility. In order to understand the cartoon scandal and the protests that followed, I argued, it is crucial to connect the sustained loss of political, social, and economic rights and security and declines in standards of living worldwide to the reconfiguring and defense of universal claims of individual freedom, rights, and justice.

On the day of the scheduled talk, the Dubai Ports World episode surfaced. Dubai Ports World bid for the purchase of Peninsular and Oriental Steam Navigation, a British port operator. Dubai Ports World topped the purchase bid from Singapore's PSA International Pte. Ltd. and won the bid, which would generate an outcry of fear and Islam-baiting (Stone and Wang, 2006). The purchase completed the United Arab Emirates' rapid transformation from a local port operator to one of the world's largest operators, and positioned the company to take over the operations of six American ports—Baltimore, Boston, Miami, New Orleans, New York, and Philadelphia—as part of the $6.8 billion sale (Timmons, 2006).

As an economic decision of world players in the global economy, this purchase is hardly unusual, even if large. The result, however, both real and imagined, was a connection to September 11 and political disarray on the home front. Almost immediately, *The Wall Street Journal* (16 February, 2006) offered the headline 'White House Urged to Review Dubai Deal' and revealed that the chairman of the Homeland Security Committee was encouraging the White House to reconsider approval of a sale that would give the United Arab Emirates control over American ports, even while recognizing that about 75 percent of the containers that presently enter US ports go through terminals that are operated by foreign-owned firms, a point hardly mentioned at the time (Weisman and Graham, 2006). Neither is it popularly known that Singaporean, Danish, British, Japanese, and Taiwanese firms already manage American harbors. Was the news about foreign management a surprise to the American people, and did the fact that this was a Muslim firm only add to the surprise? As The *Nation* (2006, p. 8) made clear:

> Democrats and Republicans alike happily promot[e] corporate globalism with little regard for the public interests until the implications become too embarrassing: in this case, the control of the nation's ports being traded by transnational corporations even though the ports are policed by the Guard, Customs, and Homeland Security.

Dubai Ports World stated that it had won approval from a secretive US government panel that considers the security risks involved in foreign companies buying or investing in American industry. The US Committee on Foreign Investment 'thoroughly reviewed the potential trans-action and concluded they had no objection' (Bridis, 2006). The committee of representatives from the Departments of Treasury, Defense, Justice, Commerce, State, and Homeland Security could have recommended that President Bush block the purchase but, as Bridis notes, the Bush administration considers the UAE an important ally and the State Department describes the UAE as a vital partner in the fight against terrorism. In their defense, shipping experts noted that many of the world's largest port companies are not based in the US, and they identified DP World's strong economic interest in operating ports securely and efficiently: 'It's in Dubai's interest to make sure this runs well,' said James Lewis, who worked with the State and Commerce depart-ments. And Stephen E. Flynn of the Council on Foreign Relations noted that, even under foreign control, US ports would continue to be run by unionized American employees (Bridis, 2006).

But others, including the FBI, note that the UAE, a loose federation of seven emirates on the Saudi peninsula, was an important operational and financial base for the hijackers who carried out the attacks against the World Trade Center and the Pentagon. Moreover, the UAE recognized the Taliban as the legitimate government of Afghanistan, served as a key transfer point for illegal shipments of nuclear components to Iran, North Korea, and Libya and for money to the 9/11 hijackers, and has been accused of failing to cooperate in efforts to track down Osama Bin Laden's bank accounts (Weisman and Graham, 2006).

Senator Charles E. Schumer (D-NY), in a bipartisan letter to John W. Snow of the Department of Treasury, urged a complete and thorough investigation of this acquisition. 'America's busiest ports are vital to our economy and to the international economy, and that is why they remain top terrorist targets.' And, as he continued, 'just as we would not outsource military operations or law enforcement duties, we should be very careful before we outsource such sensitive homeland security duties' (Bridis, 2006). Curiously, Schumer remained unconcerned about the subcon-tracting of security forces, since he surely knew that neoliberal restructuring in the 1990s included 'downsizing and temping' military troops and subcontracting the guarding of Fort Bragg's huge ammunition dump to a private security firm (Lutz, 2002, p. 729). Moreover, he could hardly be unaware of the privatization of the US prison system and the incentives given to promote private and religious primary and secondary education.

Opposition to the port deal mushroomed, even among Republicans, and Bush's veto threat aggravated GOP allies. Surprisingly, even Bill Frist and Dennis Hastert, usually allies of the administration's projects, claimed threats to national security to justify their difference with Bush's initial position on the sale. The Army War College's 2004 report called the war in Iraq 'unnecessary' and the war on terror 'unrealistic', and reveals critical factionalism in the administration (Record, in Piven 2004, p. 127). The result: in a matter of weeks, Dubai Ports

World agreed to postpone its plans to take over management of the six US ports. 'We need to understand the concerns of the people in the U.S. who are worried about this transaction and make sure they are addressed to the benefit of all parties,' said Ted Bilkey, the company's chief operating officer. Accordingly, DP World delayed assuming management while it engaged 'in further consultations with the Bush administration and, as appropriate, congressional leadership and relevant port authorities to address concerns over future security arrangements' (*CNN.com*, 2006). By March 12, it bowed to pressure from Congress and announced a plan to sell its US operations to an American firm (Weisman and Graham, 2006).

These encounters suggest three observations. First, there is increasing fragmentation among US elites despite efforts to secure their allegiance along particular party lines.[11] The Dubai Ports World conflagration exposed both the complex face of capital and the contradictions constitutive of the decisions made by particular class factions. This factionalism was also revealed in the full-page *New York Times* ad (20 May 2006) with the headline: 'Ten CEOs call for this CEO to be canned.' The page frames a large photo of Donald Rumsfeld surrounded by commentary that identifies his sweetheart deals, wastefulness, lack of accountability, and squandered good will and trust.[12]

Second, the Iraq war and the war on terror exposes the interdependence of a rhetoric of neoliberalism built on exchange regardless of national origin but which in practice is revealed as the pleasures enjoyed by capital but not by labor. The latter face increasing strictures on mobility and personal security, whether, for example, Mexicans to the US or Bangladeshis to India. This suggests that the logic of development as a social practice presumes even as it constructs a racialized other; it constructs difference as a collective threat counterposed to an understanding of democratic liberalism that presumes substantive individualism.

Third, these contradictions play out and through neoliberal practices in individual nation-states and in the changing scenarios proposed for redress; they require us to take the world economy seriously. These incidents invite us to examine the development project, often focused on the effects of neoliberal discourses and economic restructuring on the people of the South, for the ways in which it reshapes cultural and political economies globally—that is, including people in the North. It is perhaps ironic that through everyday exchange people observe the very ordering they produce while reproducing themselves as its subjects.

Interpreting the Crisis

David Harvey and Giovanni Arrighi recently debated the social and political economy of what Harvey (2003) labels 'accumulation by dispossession' and Arrighi (2005a) calls 'global turbulence'. Their engagement appreciates the specificities of the current stage of capitalist development—its spatial unevenness, its future course, prospects, and organizational forms, and the economic blocs that establish its institutional context. Each attends to the creative capacities of capitalism and bourgeoisies to manage processes of accumulation in ways that condition the shift from embedded economy to neoliberalism.

Harvey (2003) argues that the transformation of the global political and economic order can be located in the early 1970s, when 'accumulation by expanded reproduction' was displaced by 'accumulation by dispossession'; this was a shift from policies and profits associated with mass industrialism to brute financial power and speculation. While Harvey acknowledges that oil played a role in the US decision to invade Iraq unilaterally, he argues for the region's importance in securing political and economic superiority. The military occupation of Iraq is therefore only the latest manifestation, if the most overt phase, of this capitalist strategy.[13]

Harvey (2003) builds this argument by drawing parallels between the New York City fiscal crisis of the 1970s and crises in dependent economies, such as Mexico, to show how private financial institutions came to mediate conditions for redress.[14] Here, he echoes Rosa Luxemburg in arguing that 'primitive' or 'original' accumulation is a continuous and persistent predatory practice, not limited to the early stages of accumulation, and 'entails appropriation and co-optation of pre-existing cultural and social achievements as well as confrontation and supercession, including the coercion and appropriation of skills, social relations, knowledges, habits of mind, and beliefs' (2003, pp. 146–148). Highlighting the privatization of social housing under Thatcher in the UK, and privatizations in Mexico, Argentina, and South Africa, he posits that finance capital and credit institutions backed by state authority constitute the 'umbilical cord' that integrates expanded reproduction and accumulation by dispossession. In the US, he connects these predatory practices to the costs of Vietnam and a failure to curb domestic spending, which led to a fiscal crisis privileging Wall Street, leading on to a transformation of loans and trade agreements underwritten by the International Monetary Fund and World Trade Organization. The result was a commitment to investment rather than productive capital in the creation of a transnational business class, which Gill (1995) refers to as 'market civilization'.

Harvey couples these changes to recognition of the European Economic Union's challenge to US strength, and to the increasing ability of China and India to absorb capital, a combination that unsettles the US as the world's economic and political hegemon and establishes the conditions for its turn toward naked military power. Military supremacy, he maintains, is what is available to a US ruling class threatened globally by European and Asian alliances, Islamic militancy, and challenges by Brazil, Venezuela, and transnational grassroots resistance. The militarized neo-conservatism that characterizes this shift is made explicit in the *Statement of Principles* of the Project for a New American Century, whose aim is to support increasing

> defense spending significantly if we are to carry out our global responsibilities today and modernize our armed forces for the future . . . [and accept] responsibility for America's unique role in preserving and extending an international order friendly to our security, our prosperity, and our principles. (New American Century, 1997, p. 1)

An organization informally organized immediately after the first Gulf War and formalized in 1996, the Project for a New American Century is supported by, among other notables, Elliott Abrams, Gary Bauer, William Bennett, Jeb Bush, Dick Cheney, Midge Decter, Steven Forbes, Francis Fukuyama, Lewis Libby, Norman Podhoretz, Donald Rumsfeld, and Paul Wolfowitz—all key players in the Bush administration, whether as members of the administrative bureaucracy or as a cultural production team of talking heads positioned to establish a particular interpretation of political decisions and practices. The Project promises to forge tighter ties among a particular fraction of capital, however unstable and tied to political party factions they remain. The growing instability of the factions of this cadre is noteworthy—Francis Fukuyama has deserted the group and others have begun to question the administration's reluctance to offer an alternative to the Iraq war if not to the war on terror.

The Project's emphasis on 'global responsibility . . . friendly to our security, our prosperity, and our principles' supports defense spending and modernized armed forces and contributes to the displacement of the Cold War by brute military force. For Harvey, this displacement by the militarization of everyday life is coupled with the privatization and commodification of public assets, financialization aided by reregulation, negative redistributions that include tax benefits on investment rather than incomes and wages, and support for corporate welfare through a vast array of subsidies and tax breaks. The consequences of these changes are social dislocations that disrupt stable patterns of employment and community formations and intensify the experience of insecurity, transience, and division.

Internationally, the deepening financial crisis unsettled the security of the Washington Consensus[15] and some of its key proponents, including Jeffrey Sachs (a prominent IMF consultant at the time) and Joseph Stiglitz (1998; Chief Economist at the World Bank), who eventually would acknowledge that financial market liberalization had actually contributed to instability. This discontent offers a liberal-individualist challenge to the architecture of development practices and reveals fractures within the contemporary imperial project. As Stiglitz (2002) elaborates, the management and manipulation of instability and crises forced dependent nations into bankruptcy and then demanded that they accept structural adjustment programs administered through the US Treasury, Wall Street, and the IMF. Harvey (2005) elaborates this by highlighting three decades of global ruling class assault instantiated in predatory practices.

For Harvey, neoconservatism is a response to the instability that neoliberalism fashions, a connection that links the costs of neoliberalism in the US and its bankruptcy as a development project to symbolic formations that legitimate or explain away its costs and failures. This is echoed in Makki's (2004, p. 163) insight that in accepting 'the claim that globalisation is a universal process propelled by its own interior logic, we give it a coherence it does not possess'. However, accepting it as fate serves as

> a convenient alibi for governments who willingly or unwillingly subscribe to the dogmas of market purism. The point here is not that there are no tendencies of actual globalisation, but that attributing to them an ineluctable logic conceals the fact that globalisation is also a project driven by private agencies of capital and transnational institutions. (Makki, 2004, p. 15)

Despite recognizing that these practices contribute to the current crisis, Harvey (2003, p. 28) remains optimistic about the rise of anti-capitalist social movements and union activity: '[I]f there is to be any kind of alternative to free-market neoliberalism/capitalism ... then ... collective action organized around the public interest is necessary.' This position is deeply rooted in the contradictory possibilities of social practice, whereby the conditions that underlie the crisis are also able to generate diverse and widespread resistances. Thus, for Harvey, these mobilizations are extremely hopeful,[16] as are the fractures in the class alliances that synergized interests in the 1980 and 1990s. Yet Harvey is also mindful of the response—disciplining New York City by taking advantage of the 1973 market crash that forced the City into the equivalent of a structural adjustment program, by requiring renegotiation of contracts with public sector workers, or disciplining Mexico in 1982, by requiring structural adjustment in exchange for a financial bailout. What remains elusive in these examples are the strategies and tactics that combine not only to censure but to enable capital accumulation under conditions that are visibly against the interests of its subjects, the relations that create either blind faith in the socially constituted inevitable or resignation. Harvey leaves little room to address how compliance is achieved, or how hegemonic interests are negotiated and serve as accomplishments of rule,[17] where the appearance of order is taken to attest to the existence of a natural order. This elides how through everyday exchange people observe the very ordering that they themselves produce and thereby reproduce themselves as its subjects.

Despite these limitations, Harvey appreciates the salience of contingency in ways that do not 'fix' states within a world system and do not conflate historical space with the reification of spatial distinctions. Importantly, his implicit critique of world systems theory acknowledges that relations of dispossession are not limited to the periphery, even as he makes clear that 'some of its most vicious and inhumane manifestations are in the most vulnerable and degraded regions within uneven geographical development' (2003, p. 173). For Harvey, the parallels between these unevenly situated spaces offer promising possibilities for collaboration in ways that link proletarian struggles at the point of production to struggles over the privatization of public utilities and services, forced mobilities and displacement, and depredations of natural resources and the environment.

Arrighi's opening remarks in 'Hegemony Unraveling' are directed at the intellectual project of Hardt and Negri: '[N]o nation-state, not even the US, can form the centre of an imperialist project' (2005, p. 23) Arrighi speaks from the large-scale, long-term change in the world system where systemic rather than national practices are relevant and war rescues declining military power. His discussion of power as the means to ensure hegemony is evocative, since it challenges the assumed overlap between territory and the conditions for its reproducibility, and between the capacity to rule and the presentation of rule as universal. The Project for a New American Century, he argues, was already formulated on September 11, with bin Laden providing both 'the popular mobilizing power and the targets' for an effective response (Mann, in Arrighi, 2005, p. 25).

Arrighi argues, *pace* Gramsci:

> [H]egemony is the *additional* power that accrues to a dominant group by virtue of its capacity to lead society in a direction that not only serves the dominant group's interests but is perceived by subordinate groups as serving a more general interest. ... If subordinate groups have confidence in their rulers, systems of domination can be run without resort to coercion. ... [However,] when such credibility is lacking or wanes, hegemony deflates into sheer domination, what Guha calls 'dominance without hegemony'. (Arrighi, 2005, p. 32)

This claim is not difficult to support, but it leaves undertheorized the conditions that generate confidence, translates the particular as universal, and helps to elide the costs of war that are clearly borne by subordinate classes. This translation is evidenced in the voice of a Vietnam veteran, who recalls President Johnson's June 1966 claim:

> "If we don't stop them [the Viet Cong] there, we'll be fighting them in San Diego and San Francisco.". . . In Vietnam I laughed my butt off. . . . I could just picture a group of Vietnamese in a boat, rowing across the ocean to attack San Francisco – amazing.' He then asks the pertinent question: 'Was I ever wrong in terms of thinking the folks "back home" had more smarts than to fall for a line like that! When I got back to the states in the late spring 1967, it took a very short time to realize that people actually believed the North Vietnamese and Viet Cong had the capability to cross the ocean and launch an attack on the U.S.' (Dalton, n.d., p. 1)

To be sure, we are no longer confident about our own abilities, or innocent about the abilities of 'distant enemies' to traverse the waters and launch an assault on American soil—9/11 ended that kind of innocence. But, curiously, we have avoided questions that did arise immediately after the 9/11 attacks: Why do they hate us and is the 'us' US capital or the American public? This reflective moment passed very quickly in the rhetorical climate of war, freedom, and democracy, and it also seems to have been eviscerated from many quarters of left critique. Answering this question requires an understanding of contemporary capitalism, with which Clinton's policies can be read in ways similar to those of the Bush regime—and Harvey offers us sufficient evidence for doing so.

However, to explain popular support or compliance requires more than the claim that 'the mixture of coercion and consent' involved in a range of challenges posed by processes of accumulation, such as bail-outs, 'varies considerably' (Arrighi, 2005, p. 45), lest we limit hegemony to the power of one state over another: 'how hegemony gets constructed through financial mechanisms in such a way as to benefit the hegemon while leading the subaltern states on the supposedly golden path of capitalist development' (Harvey, 2005, p. 151; also in Arrighi, 2005, p. 45).

The American *belle époque* of the 1990s, according to Arrighi, was based on the synergy of two conditions:

> the US capacity to present itself as performing the global functions of market of last resort and indispensable political-military power; and the capacity and willingness of the rest of the world to provide the US with the capital needed to continue to perform those functions on an ever-expanding scale. (2005, p. 65)[18]

The Bush decision to go to war troubled this synergy, leaving the administration with few options—it could not raise taxes, increase indebtedness, or secure enough oil to pay for an extended war itself—but to exploit US *seigniorage* privileges so that the dollar standard is not undermined. This may be but a short-term measure, although Arrighi is optimistic were the US to choose to work with, rather than challenge, China's growing leadership in East Asia and beyond.

How might exploiting such privileges challenge the hegemony between citizens and subjects rather than only between states? If we assume such a challenge, how might this turn our attention to the practices that enable rule by consent, coercion, or domination within particular territorially-based formations? How, in other words, might this focus offer a window on the ways that states secure hegemony? Surely an answer to this builds on the critical work of Harvey and Arrighi but also demands an exploration of the conditions for creating compliance. These conditions include, first, a standard of living that maintains the illusion that the economy is not under challenge or threat; this is premised on the assumption that compliance is generally linked to the prospect of privilege or security— increasingly unlikely as the US loses its foothold as a world leader. Second, media and information must be concentrated to construct knowledges and imaginations; this has been countered by librarians' refusal to share information on borrowers, which signals one of the most radical challenges to the current administration. Third, 'spin' and acts of concealment are used that justify institutional and policy decisions and interpret defeat and death in ways that foster support among politically disengaged subjects. Fourth, there is a shift from production to financialization that undermines secure employment and requires a complete overhaul of the Keynesian contract. Finally, new meanings are given to sovereignty and citizenship by altering rights and obligations between states and citizens; this entails imagining sovereignty as a status rather than as negotiated social relations.

These interests fall squarely within Abrams' astute observation that

> any attempt to examine politically institutionalized power at close quarters is ... liable to bring to light the fact that an integral element of such power is the quite straightforward ability to withhold information, deny observation and dictate the terms of knowledge. (1988, p. 62)

This view is grounded in Abrams' (1988) remarkable insight into the state as idea, and his astute observation that 'the presumption, and its effective implementation, that the "public sector" is in fact a private sector about which knowledge must not be made public is all too obviously the principal immediate obstacle to any serious study of the state' (p. 61) including its elected officials, policies, and programs. Under colonial domination or so-called democratic rule, the creative management of subordination requires moving towards assessing rule as an aspect of state–citizen/subject relations. This can illuminate how discourses of freedom, rights, and security are managed and manipulated in ways that build on yet transform law enforcement and rights, and reveal the changing meaning of the separation of powers, an independent Supreme Court, and international law as a guide to world order.

Contemporary discourses of freedom, rights, and security have been co-opted by a neo-conservative agenda that responds to the accumulation crisis by reframing fear and weakness in ways that disempower and exclude people from engaged public debate. This is evident in the examples discussed—the cartoon scandal and Dubai Ports World's attempted purchase— where the very formulation of the discussion was already constituted by a privately constituted public space. While the determination was not total, the increased concentration of information and images, and the declining transparency of democratic politics, constrained the drawing of connections between the crisis of capital accumulation and the role that war plays in its reproduction. One result, as Nancy Fraser (1999, in Sayer, 2003) frames it, denies people recognition. Sayer similarly argues that there has been a shift in the last two decades 'to expel normative questions and instead [to focus] on "engineering" questions', leading to a de-moralization of the political economy accompanied by a de-rationalization of values. The result is that, as people lose control over their economic lives, a philosophical discourse on ethics is made to appear irrelevant, relegating, in effect, moral-political questions to the private sphere (Sayer, 1998, p. 4). Sayer's (2004, p. 2) challenge is to distinguish between moral economy as an object of study and moral economy as a 'kind of inquiry'. Used as a kind of inquiry, he finds that in some cases, especially when they are compromised by economic forces, they 'represent little more than legitimations of entrenched power relations'. This interpretation links the moral and political economies in ways that interpret meaning as not 'merely reflective of social practice' but as constitutive of it (Sayer, 1998, p. 1), and recognizes that discourses and practices must remain attentive to indeterminacies, contingencies, cooptations, and reappropriations.

Notes

1   Most of the burgeoning literature on 'the terror of neoliberalism' and US militarization elides the politics of development. Piven (2004), however, does acknowledge the imperialist project.

2   Weber identifies these territorial distinctions as reifications. I stress political authority as historically constituted relations that build on the attendant consequences of these reifications.

3   Initial responses to the war were careful to separate the Bush administration from ordinary Americans, but after the Bush victory in 2004 voting citizens were considered complicit in this effort.

4   This racialization parallels the assumption of the collective African American who is assumed to speak for the collective rather than as an individual.

5   The index measures the ratio between the resources spent by governments arming themselves and those spent by private individuals making themselves comfortable.

6   Hall also identifies tensions between the free-market individual and the neoliberal emphasis on nation and family as cornerstones of patriotism.

7   I would be remiss if I failed to acknowledge those who have taken to the streets and wires to protest against the war, welfare reform, global sweatshops, immigration practices, and the lack of support for the Kyoto Protocol. But understanding the absence of a generalized response requires an understanding of the production of compliance and systems of rule that undermine and criminalize the democratic principles of debate. Moreover, in these discussions the connections between US imperial practice and the securing of capitalist accumulation remain invisible.

8   The 2006 elections changed what one might call the climate in support of extending US intervention in Iraq, but there is nothing to indicate a link between the war and the crises of accumulation—crucial for locating the contemporary crisis beyond the personalities of the Bush administration or party politics.

9   The US Senate confirmed Tobias on March 29, 2006. Other changes include regular meetings with faith-based organizations to provide technical assistance to USAID. USAID's Volunteers for Prosperity Office has recruited nearly 200 non-profit and for-profit organizations, representing a pool of at least 34,000 skilled US professionals (see http://www.usaid.gov/about_usaid/presidential_initiative/).

10   *The Nation* editorialized: 'This magazine has historically been committed to freedom of speech, an essential principle that democratic societies have established over years of struggle, and we remain vigilant in its

defense' (2006, p. 8). The issue's cover page read: 'The Cartoon Bomb: Free Speech and the Furor in the Muslim World'. See also Scheer (2006).

11 McCain's shifting support for the president reveals the pressure of the party machinery and its failure to control disagreement within the military. General Peter Pace, chairman of the Joint Chiefs of Staff, was reported not to favor the invasion of Iraq. Hillary Mann, the National Security Council's Iran expert until 2004, said Pace's repudiation of the administration's claims was a sign of grave discontent at the top. 'It is extraordinary for him to have made these comments publicly, and it suggests there are serious problems between the White House, the National Security Council and the Pentagon' (http://www.timesonline.co.uk/tol/news/world/iraq/article1434540.ece).

12 Many of the signatories represent liberal companies, such as Ben & Jerry's and Working Assets, but others represent established conservative companies such as Eastman Kodak, Phillips-Van Heusen, and Burlington Industries. Working against the intolerance of dissent and the silencing of criticism they have organized 'Priorities!' to remove Rumsfeld from office (see http://www.sensiblepriorities.org).

13 Arrighi (2005, p. 83) argues to the contrary that, far from laying the foundations for a second 'American Century', the occupation of Iraq jeopardizes the credibility of US military might, undermines the centrality of the US and the dollar globally, and strengthens the emergence of China as an alternative to US leadership in East Asia and beyond. Harvey also interprets the invasion of Iraq as a sign of US economic and political weakness displaced by military force.

14 In the 1970s New York faced a fiscal crisis that left them with no ready access to credit and led to the issuing of bonds that were backed by a dedicated portion of the city's sales tax. This reveals the underside of the wealth that we associate with New York; a deep poverty that depends on large assistance programs including support for healthcare, education, and public housing. The potential bankruptcy, parallel to that in Mexico, threatened the very core of the city's sustainability.

15 The Washington Consensus is a term introduced in 1989 by John Williamson to describe a set of economic policy prescriptions thought to constitute a reform package to be used by Washington-based institutions (International Monetary Fund, World Bank, and the US Treasury) to support institutional reform in Latin America (Williamson, 2000). The term has since been used as interchangeable with the terms neoliberalism or market fundamentalism, whose reach now extends beyond Latin America.

16 He does caution that old social solidarities are increasingly superficial and thus dampen a general sense of optimism.

17 Training Southern bureaucrats and leaders in American institutions undoubtedly contributes to compliance among them, as does the recruitment of foreign students to US business and law schools.

18 I share Arrighi's discomfort with Harvey's presumed synergy between neoliberalism and neoconservatism, whereby the latter stands in for the values and moral compass of the neoliberal project. However, both Harvey's formulation and Arrighi's (2005, p. 47) critique elide how 'belief that free markets in both commodities and capital contain all that is necessary to deliver freedom and well-being to all and sundry' actually comes to be believed. By what processes do such assessments gain legitimacy? Arrighi's reply is to look to inter-state responses, both from potential Northern allies and from those of the global South who are likely to experience an increase rather than a decrease in ferment against forms of dispossession. This is suggested by the location and range of responses to the cartoon scandal; violent protest often occurred in situations of extreme poverty, such as among the poor and marginal in Bangladesh, Pakistan, and Indonesia.

References

Abrams, P. (1988) Notes on the difficulty of studying the state (1977), *Journal of Historical Sociology*, 1, pp. 58–89.

Ali, T. (2006) This is the real outrage, *The Guardian*, 13 February.

Althusser, L. (1971) Ideology in ideological state apparatuses, in L. Althusser (ed.) *Lenin and Philosophy and Other Essays* (London: New Left Books).

Arrighi, G. (2005a) Hegemony unravelling I, *New Left Review*, 32(March–April), pp. 23–79.

Arrighi, G. (2005b) Hegemony unravelling II, *New Left Review*, 33(May–June), pp. 83–116.

Bridis, T. (2006) United Arab Emirates firm may oversee 6 U.S. ports, *The Washington Post*, February 12.

CNN.com (2006). Ports company will delay takeover, 24 February, http://edition.cnn.com/2006/POLITICS/02/23/port.security/.

Corrigan, P. & Sayer, D. (1985) *The Great Arch: English State Formation as Cultural Revolution* (Oxford: Basil Blackwell).

Dalton, J. (n.d.) No matter how much things change, they seem to remain the same, in *Statement of Principles*, Project for the Old American Century, http://www.oldamericancentury.org/dalt1049.htm.

Gill, S. (1995) Globalisation, market civilisation, and disciplinary Neoliberalism, *Millennium: Journal of International Studies*, 24, pp. 399–423.

Giroux, H. A. (2005) The terror of neoliberalism: rethinking the significance of cultural politics, *College Literature*, 32(1), pp. 1–19.

Gross, D. (2006) Obscure economic indicator: the guns-to-caviar index, good news! It's going down, *Slate*, 14 December, http://www.slate.com/id/2155445.

Hall, S. (1979) Culture, the media and the ideology effect, in J.M.G. Curran, J. Woollacott, J. Marriott & C. Roberts (eds.) *Mass Communication and Society* (Beverly Hills, CA: Sage).

Hall, S. (1988) The toad in the garden: Thatcherism among the theorists, in C. Nelson & L. Grossberg (eds) *Marxism and the Interpretation of Culture* (Champaign: University of Illinois Press).

Harvey, D. (2005) *A Brief History of Neoliberalism* (New York: Oxford University Press).

Harvey, D. (2003) *The New Imperialism* (Oxford: Oxford University Press).

Johnson, C. (2004) *The Sorrows of Empire: Militarism, Secrecy, and the End of the Republic* (New York: Metropolitan Books).

Lutz, C. (2002) Making war at home in the United States: militarization and the current crisis, *American Anthropologist*, 104(3), pp. 723–735.

Makki, F. (2004) The empire of capital and the remaking of centre–periphery relations, *Third World Quarterly*, 25(1), pp. 149–168.

Midnight Notes (1990) *The New Enclosures*, http://www.midnightnotes.org/pdfnewenc1.pdf.

Montero, D. (2006) Pakistani riots about more than cartoons: violent protests may have been influenced by poverty as much as religious fervor, *Christian Science Monitor*, 17 February.

The Nation (2006) Editorial, 27 February, p. 8.

New American Century (1997) Statement of principles, 3 June, p. 1, http://www.newamericancentury.org/statementofprinciples.htm

Piven, F. F. (2004) *The War at Home: The Domestic Costs of Bush's Militarism* (New York: New Press).

Roberts, S., Secor, A. & Sparke, M. (2003) Neoliberal geopolitics, *Antipode*, 35, pp. 886–897.

Robinson, W. I. (1998) *Promoting Polyarchy: Globalization, US Intervention and Hegemony* (Cambridge: Cambridge University Press).

Sayer, A. (2003) *Critical and Uncritical Cultural Turns*, Lancaster University, http://www.comp.lancs.ac.uk/sociology/papers/sayer-critical-and-uncritical-cultural-turns.pdf.

Sayer, A. (2004) Moral economy. Department of Sociology, Lancaster University, http://www.comp.lancs.ac.uk/sociology/papers/sayer-moral-economy.pdf

Scheer, R. (2006) In defense of free thought, *Truthdig*, http://www.thenation.com/doc/20060306/scheer0222.

Schneider, K. G. (2002) The patriot act: last refuge of a scoundrel, *American Libraries Association*, http://www.ala.org/al_onlineTemplate.cfm?Section2002columns1&Template=/ContentManagement/ContentDisplay.cfm&ContentID=12585.

Smith, M. & Baxter, S. (2007) US generals 'will quit' if Bush orders Iran attack, *The Sunday Times*, 25 February.

Sparke, M. (2003) American empire and globalization: postcolonial speculations on neocolonial enframing, *Singapore Journal of Tropical Geography*, 24(3), pp. 373–389.

Stiglitz, J. (1998) More instruments and broader goals: moving towards a post-Washington Consensus. WIDER Annual Lectures, No. 2, Helsinki.

Stiglitz, J. (2002) *Globalization and its Discontents* (New York: W. W. Norton & Co.).

Stone, R. & Wang, M. (2006) P & O takeover battle heats up, *The Wall Street Journal*, 27 January, p. C4.

Timmons, H. (2006) *The New York Times*, November 2.

Wallerstein, I. (2000) Globalization, or the age of transition? A long-term view of the trajectory of the world system, *International Sociology*, 15, pp. 249–265.

Weber, H. (2004) Reconstituting the 'third world'? Poverty reduction and territoriality in the global politics of development, *Third World Quarterly*, 25, pp. 187–206.

Weisman, J. & Graham, B. (2006) Dubai firm to sell U.S. port operations, *Washington Post*, 12 March.

On the Critique of the Subject of Development: Beyond Proprietary and Methodological Individualism

MARTIN WEBER

The Subject of Development: Normative Underpinnings, Normative Problems

The concept of development has been understood to involve inextricably an integral commitment to teleology, whether in its weak form, as in those parts of the literature emphasising emancipatory social and political change, or in its stronger form, as for instance in modernisation theory and the technocratic or authoritarian strands of thought it has spawned. As a concept it has been applied universally, although with different connotations, to both the 'developed' and the 'developing' world—there is, in fact, no human society without development. It is hence appropriate to conceive of development in the broadest possible way, as an inherent category of the socio-political imagination of people or peoples, where such imagination centres around the accounts people give of 'how should we live', both in spatial and temporal terms.

To be sure, not much follows from such a broad and formal background conception of what structures the content of development. In order to arrive at the modern, common-sense notion of 'development', with its entailed corollaries, we must reconstruct a number of moves, which progressively constrain both the meaning of development and the socio-political moves accorded to practicing development 'legitimately'. One ineluctable part of such a project, and, I believe, an important one, concerns the reconstruction of the normative resources according to which the contemporary (that is, the modern) development project is presented as authoritative, and hence from which draws its political strength.

The normative resource I focus on in this paper is the 'developmental subject', part of the success-story of the modern project, yet at one and the same time increasingly seen as a crucial constituent of its problematic and contradictory implications. Unpacking the subject of development, and its subjectivity, remains one of the most challenging aspects of broader attempts to inaugurate a rethinking of development.

In what follows I consider two sets of implications of 'modern subjectivity' for development thinking. The first set concerns the continuing substantive salience in the development discourse of the proprietary conception of subjectivity associated with classical liberal thought. The second raises the related, yet distinct, issue of methodological individualism, through which the contemporary development discourse maintains its ties with disciplinary economics, but which increasingly distances it from progressive reconceptualisations in social theory. Rather than discussing these two sets separately, I want to proceed by way of illustration, reconstructing their common background in the modern liberal tradition, and tracing them through two sets of criticisms with which this tradition, despite some of its undeniable achievements, can be confronted.

Hence, I reconstruct first the classical notion of the modern subject, in the context of a discussion of shifts in time-space apprehensions, as well as with regard to the egalitarian implications it had for the unfolding of modern institutions of social and political order. Although the one-sidedness of the liberal conception of subjectivity which would emerge from the period of consolidation of enlightenment thought was sensed and, to some degree, theorised early on, the onset of the academic division of labour prevented a wholesale reappraisal, which may have been plausible for the first time in the beginning of the twentieth century. The consolidation of liberal thought is thus shown to cement the two complexes of substantive proprietary subjectivity, and methodological individualism.

With this reconstruction in the background, I then turn to attempts to reconnect conceptions of subjectivity with 'developmental' issues, with conceptions of weak teleology conceived to counter both strong versions of a philosophy of history and technocratic determinism. In this section, I am aided by the work of McPherson (1971, 1973), for whom the liberal tradition had bifurcated early on in its rise through the context of consolidating modernity. MacPherson launched a plausible and still telling challenge against the paucity of negative conceptions of liberty, and connected this critique directly with a diagnosis of the foregone developmental possibilities inherent in human association and the pursuit of common purposes. After reconstructing what remains plausible and important of MacPherson's critique of the liberal subject, I turn to the limits of his argument, which I show are linked to his adherence to a particular idiom of political theory. My argument here is that while MacPherson succeeds in his critique of the proprietary 'abridgement' of liberal subjectivity, his proposed alternative remains too closely tied to the other issue under consideration: methodological individualism. His account of 'developmental subjects' would today have to be contextualised within the insights of the intersubjective turn, and would have to be complemented with a critical social theory, in accordance with which MacPherson's demands for redistributive and mutually assured realisations of the conditions of freedom can be given the appropriate normative weight.

In the final section, I turn to recognition theory as fleshed out in the work of Axel Honneth (1996, 2000, 2001, 2004), and suggest that it provides a more adequate framework for thinking through the contradictions of modern subjectivication in the context of continued patterns of subalterneity and domination in the global politics of 'development'. Honneth's work offers the prospect of substantive accounts of recognition, necessary for the development of positive relations to self at the individual and collective levels, substantive also with regard to the redistributive requirements which can be further elaborated through recognition-theoretically inflected theories of justice (see, e.g., Forst, 2001). Thus the subject of development can today be reconfigured so as to enable emancipatory social and political struggles to be practiced, as well as understood with regard to their normative implications, without succumbing to the problem of 'imperial' or 'hegemonic' accounts of the subject, or 'development'. In such an approach, the twin concerns known from postcolonial studies, the 'politics of identity and difference' and the 'politics of inequality', are integrated from the perspective of a normatively demanding and sensitive critical social theory.

Developing Modern Subjectivity

The emergence of the modern conception of subjectivity, and of the modern subject itself, has come to be represented under a number of rhetorical ciphers, which emphasise a break with the doctrines of personhood and socio-political standing which had dominated in the European context until the Renaissance. Moreover, the coordinates of cultural experience in general, as well as aesthetic perception in particular, are held to have undergone significant transformations during that period. A text often invoked to signal this shift is Petrarca's letter to Dionigi, written after his ascent of Mont Ventoux. It communicates, according to the modernisation discourse of art history and literary studies, a novel experience of space-time, focussed on the gaze of the individualised self. This experience of the individuated juxtaposition of the solipsist observer and the surrounding world for which her/his standpoint becomes also the vanishing-point, the point at which all axes of vision and time syncretise, is generally interpreted to signal the emergence of qualitatively new possibilities of human social being.

As Charles Taylor demonstrated in *Sources of the Self* (1992), the nature of the transition thus inaugurated proved to spell the end of the institutional orders of the Middle Ages, the erosion of the 'ethics of honour' together with the doctrines of social estate to which it belonged, and the inauguration of new and more inclusive conceptions of social order, for instance in the form of an entrenchment of notions of natural law. How these moves congealed with the emerging and consolidating doctrine of scientific knowledge and the purposeful control of nature, as advanced between the two philosophical doctrines of empiricism (Bacon) and rationalism (Descartes), is well documented, and requires no further elaboration in this context.

The crucial abstraction-achievement involved in the social institutionalisation of the subject as the source (rationalism) or focal point (empiricism) of knowledge and world-disclosure, together with the universalistic presumptions upon which it comes to rest (in principle, both Bacon's methodologies and Cartesian self-reflections are understood to be available to any human individual), pave the way for egalitarian positions both in thought and in socio-political practice. The cost, however, is that any insight is forgone into how the subject comes to be what it is conceived to be for the purpose of the modern conception of the self. Beginning with Hobbes' (preliberal) conceptualisation of the state of nature as the condition of absolute freedom in which 'everybody has the right to everything, including everybody else', the modern social and political subject is posited in static terms. Hobbes' theory of formal equality, and Locke's expansion towards natural rights (and law) prepare the way for the liberal conception of privatist interests, held and pursued by individuals for particularist reasons—that is, reasons strictly of their own (e.g., desires or needs, perceived or real).

Advancements of Modern Liberal Subjectivity

Before pursuing a critical inquiry into the legacy of this conception for the formation of the developmental subject, and preparing to insert it into the development debate, it is now important to take stock briefly of the contradictions which arise in the context of the advancement of individual liberties and concomitant duties. For, as should be clear despite the critical narrative gesture I have adopted above, the implications of this entrenchment of methodological individualist premises and their normative implications are not appropriately captured if one detracts from the historical, social, and political advances they constitute when viewed in a wider context.

In the social-political fabric, the advance of the modern subject erodes the binding force of the order of societies into estates—social hierarchies to which one belongs, as it were, by being born into them—and the accompanying determinism which constrained the prospects and identities any person may have plausibly wished to pursue. From education to employment, social networks to modes of interaction, this older prescriptive order became progressively unsustainable as the notion of individual capabilities, which transcend such pre-loaded social identifications, took hold. In this regard, the degree to which the institution of modern subjectivity increased the potential for experiences of freedom and autonomy should not be detracted from. Likewise, in the arena of individual legal representation, in which culpability was similarly asymmetrically apportioned with regard to both victim and perpetrator social standing, there has been a determinate advance.

Finally, the facilitation of religious autonomy, and the separation of religious from political authority has, at least in some important respects, the effect of raising the profile of minorities, and promoting conceptions of the common good in which exclusionary doctrines involving church or cult membership can no longer assume the status of 'legitimate public policy'. Understood from these premises, it becomes possible to understand and defend aspects of the evolving modern conception of subjectivity as definite advances over previous orders. It also becomes possible to appreciate that, to a degree, the potential for executing meaningful choices is enhanced in the process, although, as we shall see below, this is not necessarily good news for the dominant liberal ideal of freedom as 'freedom of choice'.

The Subject Without Development as the Subject of Development: MacPherson's Critique of the Substantive Implications of Liberal Thought

This is the thread which C. B. MacPherson admirably picked up in his collection of essays, *Democratic Theory* (MacPherson, 1973). He diagnoses a gap in liberal political thought between the constitutive assumption of rational individual agency and freedom, against which liberalism assesses the intrusions of government and state, on the one hand, and on the other, the insight that this rational individual agency is, in the context of each individual biography, to a significant degree acquired. Moreover, MacPherson implicates in his arguments the very quality of social and political organisation in constraining or sustaining the development of individual capacities for freedom, autonomy, and social responsibility. This revision of the implications of the social-ontological undercarriage on which the liberal conception of individual autonomy must, tacitly, rely raises a whole set of questions regarding justice and equality not present under the premise of rational self-satisfaction. The latter compels the assumption that individual needs and desires constitute genuine expressions of autonomous wills, and are therefore only susceptible to legitimate limitations where their pursuit impinges directly on congruent claims to self-realisation by others.

In his critique of this conception, which he develops in a discussion of Berlin and Hardy's (2005) distinction between positive and negative liberty, MacPherson uses the concept of 'developmental liberties' to problematise the choice-egalitarian norm, which underpins the unreformed liberal individualist stance (MacPherson, 1973, pp. 95–119). The latter is both a methodological problem and a normative one.

Methodologically, reliance on individual self-reported preferences, desires, or goals requires abstractive social ontology, the limitations of which we have already seen; the formation of individual preferences, needs, or desires is thus not accorded any significance, and neither is what they and their pursuit mean for the actors themselves, or for those around them. The implications of this methodological individualism can be tentatively grasped in a general fashion if one considers that, from this perspective, distinctions between altruistic actions and selfish actions do not matter *sui generis* (i.e., as characteristics of the actions and the actors themselves), but only insofar as they represent individual choices with either legitimate or illegitimate consequences. The identity of the hypostatised individuals as social actors, who are significantly socialised, is removed from the account, which thus institutes the ideal of legal limitations to transgressive choices as the license for the political. The latter hence consists in the observance, sanctioning, and enforcement of rules regarding the scope of individual choice-acts.

The normative consequences of this conception can be grasped along similar lines. Since the focus on the choice-act disregards the social identity of the chooser (a feat which, for liberals, guarantees an egalitarian notion of fairness), motives are ignored for the purpose of the arbitration of the question of unnecessary constraints on executing choice. This can only be sustained by complementing the neutral account of choice-acts with either a deontological conception of absolute duties, or the contract-theoretical constitution of the political authority which is to adjudicate the competing claims of individuals. The advance of the latter requires an account of a second-order interest by individuals in rationally choosing an institutional structure which guarantees a maximum of choice freedom while constraining its excesses in the intersubjective world of competing needs, desires, and demands.

This is guaranteed through formal law, which ostensibly applies to each entity with legal subjectivity equally at the level at which such subjectivity is constituted. Hence, we have 'corporate' subjects, and cases in which collectivities may be culpable not as the collectivities as such, but in the form of the legal subject through which they are represented. Consider as an example the difference between criminal negligence in the case of an individual manager's failure to provide adequate safety training for employees, and the charge of corporate manslaughter against the firm as a whole for systematic failures in safeguarding its employees' welfare.

MacPherson's Critique of the Liberal Subject: The Missing Developmental Substance

The difficulties with the liberal tradition that MacPherson notes are, however, not understood by him to be undermining core features of the advantageous contributions which the modern orientation to subjectivity has facilitated. Rather, his criticism is directed at an undue and, in his argument, unnecessary skewing of the latter in individualist terms, where this is not, in fact, necessary, but rather has the characteristics of ideology (i.e., a systematic distortion).

MacPherson's discussion of the developmental deficit in liberal political theory focuses on two key aspects. First, he examines the abstractive assumption of fully-formed individuality, on which the liberal conception of rational choices, and their qualitative equivalence, hinges ('all things being equal'). Second, he considers the social and political power relations, and their expression in institutions, which arise from the narrowed and abstracted conception of individuals as rational agents.

The first set of concerns proceeds through an immanent critique of the liberal discourse of equality of opportunity, which underpins the justification of negative liberties not only in Berlin's work but symptomatically throughout the liberal tradition (including the 'social democratic' liberalism of Rawls). MacPherson demonstrates that the omission of an account of how the rational agents of the liberal political universe become established leads to the theoretical preclusion of dealing with the differential positions of individuals within the social and political power relations into which they are thrust without the involvement of any agency on their part. This argument, which is in the first instance a minimalist defence of an active involvement of the public institutions of the state in addressing and redressing social and material inequalities by making available programmes targeted at the systematically disadvantaged, has made a comprehensive appearance in revisions of liberal political philosophy over the last two decades, and has generally been held to be consistent with an amended form of liberal political theory, although not with the 'nightwatchman' liberalism of Hayek or Friedmann (MacPherson, 1973, pp. 143–156). MacPherson adds, however, an in-depth consideration of the institution of private property.

In *The Political Theory of Possessive Individualism* (1971), MacPherson traces the evolution of liberal political thought from Hobbes through Locke to the twentieth-century versions defended *inter alia* by Berlin, Dahl, and Schumpeter. His inquiry leads him to a critique of the way in which Locke took the egalitarian doctrines of Hobbes' absolutism and inserted them into his account of representative government, which was to become the foundation of liberal political thought. Hobbes had identified individual rational self-interested agents in a state of absolute equality as the asocial basis of any human consocial arrangements, and argued that the latter could only be sustained through the institution of sovereign absolute rule, which would institute the rights, laws, and duties according to which the rules for coexistence would become adjudicated and enforced. Because it was in the individual self-interest of any rational agent to avoid living under a condition of generalised paranoia (the 'state of nature'), this sovereign absolute rule could be understood as sanctioned by the will of each and every individual to be 'lifted' out of the conditions of mutual permanent suspicion. However, according to Hobbes, this 'contract', which establishes sovereign absolute rule, is an ideal construct insofar that its validity transcends context, consent, and indeed any agent's perspective on it. The implicit agreement of all by virtue of their rational agency is just as absolute and irrevocable as the rule of the sovereign, which he envisaged in its institutionalised (i.e., depersonalised) form.

Locke's discontent with this is well known. With Hobbes, he departed from the state of anarchy, the presumption of equality among individuals, and the conception of the latter as rational agents. Against Hobbes, he argued that actual sovereign rule should be seen as contingent upon the rulers' observation of individual rights. For, also contrary to Hobbes, Locke argued that the equal individuals in the state of nature were, as subjects, bearers of natural rights, and that the latter's observance would be decisive for the legitimacy of political rule (see, e.g., Locke, 1988, 'Second Treatise on Government', §123). Locke therefore introduced the notion of representation into the relationship between ruler(s) and ruled, as well as (again in sharp distinction to Hobbes) the right to resistance where rule arbitrarily or systematically denigrates the integrity of individuals' natural rights.

MacPherson reconstructs Locke's argumentative move, highlighting its inherent democratic potential, and the significance it had for the development of democratic rule and institutions. However, in his appraisal of Locke's list of natural rights, he considers in particular the prominent place given by Locke to the right to (exclusively) own property. This right, according to MacPherson, lacks the argumentative clarity and logical stringency accorded in Locke's treatise to each of the other rights. MacPherson then seeks to demonstrate that the inclusion of the right to property is, in fact, an analytically unjustifiable inclusion of a second-order right into the canon of first-order natural rights, and that, as a consequence, Locke's political theory imposes unnecessary and distorting limits on the emerging commitment to the democratic provision. According to MacPherson, the arguments in Locke's treatise which sustain the inclusion of the right to private property conceived in exclusionary terms manipulate what would be a derivative conception, that of property, into the status of a constitutive social and political institution. Locke is here indicted for dressing up ideological preferences—those of the rising bourgeoisie—in the garb of philosophical truth.

This gives MacPherson an opportunity to consider the abstractions on which Locke's arguments rely as steps in a reproduction of fundamental inequalities of power and political influence. Locke's liberal conception of the individual with absolute rights to appropriation and exclusive ownership leaves no room to problematise the unequal starting points from which individuals enter into social and political relations. Because of these 'pre-theoretical' and disarticulated inequalities, the prospects for individual autonomy, which is, after all, the standard of freedom which Locke too seeks to defend, differ greatly, depending not so much on talents or 'hard work' but rather on the relative wealth with which one is endowed from birth. Locke, who is of course aware of this problem, solves it through infinitesimalism (Locke, 1988, 'Second Treatise on Government', §36). He suggests that, since there are limitless things in the world to appropriate, it is down to the enterprising spirit of individuals to seek the expansion of their property by, for instance, means of colonial settlement. It is doubtful whether the infinitesimal solution was proposed by Locke in good faith, but it serves in any case as the means by which the life chances of individuals are again equalised only in the abstract. The result is what we might call 'deferential liberalism', a political theory premised on promises which always seem to be redeemable in the near or medium-term future, subject to individual self-reform. Locke's proprietary liberalism, ultimately based on the conception of 'self-ownership', which is itself a pre-condition for the 'instrumentalisation' of the self in the context of exchange in the labour market, is thus shown by MacPherson to be a deficient and no less than contingent conception of 'autonomous' selves (i.e., selves capable of exercising freedom).

MacPherson thus offers us a critique of the substantive assumptions of the liberal conception of subjectivity, with the aim of restoring a substantively conceived account of the individual interest in development, understood as a facilitation of reducing heteronomies and increasing autonomy. The latter, in MacPherson's reasoning, involves a critical orientation to redressing inequalities inherent in persistent social structures, which he shows to be linked to the predominance in liberal thought of proprietary subjectivity.

MacPherson's Concept of the Developmental Subject, and its Limitations

MacPherson's critique, as we have seen, is directed straight at the heart of the institutional set-up to which classical liberal political theory gives rise through its abstractive moves.

Liberalism abstracts first from the content of the choices individuals make, and denies these any intrinsic value or moral weight. Through this move, liberal theory obtains the neutrality of public/ political bodies *vis-à-vis* the desires, wishes, and projects of individual members of society. Instead of considering the content, only the effects of individual agency through which choice is enacted come into consideration, and only insofar as they have (potential) freedom-limiting consequences for others.

Liberalism abstracts second from the context in which individual choices are made, considering again only the expressions of desires, wishes, and individual projects as socially and politically relevant and administrable facts.

This twin move brackets out what MacPherson tries to capture with his notion of developmental freedoms: because the property form is not included within the forms of social agency which potentially limit the (negative) freedoms of others, the social and political 'space' for individual flourishing is constricted to the degree that the infinitesimalist assumption mobilised in its defense turns out to be a fiction. Instead, we are confronted with the reproduction of social relations through which 'free' individuals are effectively forced to sell their labour time in competitive markets (see both Hegel and Marx, and, for an analysis of the implications of this, Rosenberg, 1994). The invocation of 'freedom' only sparsely covers up the real relations of coercion and domination involved in this setting.

These moves bracketing out content and context are, according to MacPherson, lodged in the underlying conception of freedom as 'self-ownership', and the latter's operationalisation within the context of a rising market society. MacPherson demonstrates that this notion of self-ownership—a proprietary relation to 'self'—pervades Hobbes' psychological approach to political theory, and remains dominant through Locke's meliorist inclusion of negative liberties, as well as the levellers' socio-political reform project. It defines the heritage of liberal political thought to such a degree that by the time John Stuart Mill (1991) began to engage what MacPherson calls 'developmental freedoms'—those conceived of in terms of becoming an individuated person, and in terms of achieving a degree of autonomy *vis-à-vis* one's appetitive drives, as well as the influence of others—he could do so only by leaving the proprietary basis of the conception of freedom untouched.

The paradoxical outcome of this historically embellished development of the substance of freedom in liberalism is, according to MacPherson, the systematic inability by liberal political thought to comprehend the struggles of subordinate classes or groups as expressions of a political will to emancipation. Because of the generalised abstractive fiction of proprietary self-ownership, the basic conception of social equality becomes that of the right to engage in contracting proprietary possessions: The sale of labour-power is stripped of any insight into the potentially coercive element which arises under social conditions of 'having to work' (and having to do so at rates determined by the 'market'), and instead becomes presented as the expression of the merely formal freedom to enter into contractual relations, or to refuse to do so.[1]

The Problems of MacPherson's Argument

MacPherson's Marxist-inspired critique of liberal political theory leaves us with fundamental insight into the unevenness of the institutionalisation of the conditions and conceptions of freedom, which today are marketed (Steger, 2005) or promoted (Kaldor, 2003) on a global scale. Indeed, the proprietary aspect of the global individual rights culture presses to the fore in all contexts, for instance in global health governance, the current anti-poverty campaigns, or questions over humanitarian intervention. In addition, MacPherson restores the notion that freedom is fundamentally a qualitative concept, and that its experiences have to be real, lived, and substantiated in a way which is non-trivial with regard to its contents. MacPherson's conception of developmental freedoms, which he explicates with regard to education and the role of society within it, makes clear that the qualities of freedom enjoyable by any individual rely on relational circumstances through which individuals first achieve those forms of autonomy which become experienced as freedoms (MacPherson, 1973, pp. 40–52).

With these criticisms in place, it becomes clear that the contradictions built into the classical liberal approach are so severe that the social institutions of the liberal order, which are to occupy a supposedly neutral position for the arbitration of claims and counter-claims by free (proprietary) agents, are thoroughly implicated in the extension of asymmetric relations of power, wealth, and influence. The *Empire of Civil Society* (Rosenberg, 1994), to which liberalism commits in reserving the authority of state power to the securing of individual property rights, shows itself as the exclusionary realm of negative sociality as Hegel had already identified it: civil society produces poverty.[2] This ideology-critical deconstruction of the proliferating liberal democratic order is then used by MacPherson to clarify the substantial implications of democratic self-rule. For MacPherson, the social and political institutions of liberal democratic states have to be reformed so as to make possible the pursuit of collectively secured conditions for expanding the realms of freedom for everyone. MacPherson sees this to be the intrinsic promise of democratic self-governance, and liberalism's development as foreclosing the realisation of its initial promises.

However, viewed in the context of our concern with the developmental subject, MacPherson's argument requires significant correctives today. In the first instance, when confronted with the global organisation of the institutionalisation of proprietary freedom, the problems which MacPherson diagnosed for liberalism within liberal democratic states are played out on a different scale, and with different consequences for the political solutions he implies. His argument does not envisage the extension of sanctionable proprietary individual claims through consolidated forms of global governance, which, with regard to the socio-politically rich conception of agential citizenship underpinning MacPherson's turn to the inclusion of developmental freedoms, only exacerbates the democratic deficiencies he diagnoses in the context of 'state-societies'. Furthermore, it does so without compensating with commensurate political discourses focussing on the expansion of the democratic provision. His account hence omits a social theoretic component with which the normative implications of the political theoretic abstractions of liberalism can be captured along the social realities of its extension.

The processes by which the liberal developmental subject becomes globalised can be gleaned through progressive societalisation of institutional formations which realise its substance in different functional domains. The constitution of corporate agency in terms of proprietary subjectivity propels the advancement of sanctionable property rights, which are enforced through the extension of the coercive administrative capacities of modern states to the supra-territorial level; states' powers and prerogatives become coordinated to the degree that it becomes possible to speak, in political terms, of 'global constitutionalism' (Gill, 2003). The flip-side of this social-theoretically visualised problem enters onto the horizon of MacPherson's analysis only in the most indirect way—as 'global' social integration, which brings with it new forms of exclusion, and selection against forms of life not compatible with the elementary institutional premises on which it comes to rest. The experiences of heteronomy engendered by these processes contradict the progressivist framing to which liberalism lays claim, predominantly in the idiom of human rights. Only by considering the full implications of this from the participants' perspectives can the critique of liberalism aspire to take adequate account of its own situatedness, not least *vis-à-vis* post-colonial experience.

The second limitation to MacPherson's argument concerns the anticipated political content of the forms of redress he has in mind for instituting the appropriate attention to the objectives of developmental liberties. MacPherson stays more or less within the framework of the division of labour between political theory (and philosophy) and social theory or sociology. Thus, while his arguments are clearly underpinned by a strong commitment to conceiving of society in terms of differentially empowered strata (if not 'classical' classes), the egalitarian normative element of his account targets only the organisation of government-instituted public services. The latter are understood to have to develop the capacity for providing, in an egalitarian way, an enabling environment for the individual development of skills, traits, and identities, before the experience of autonomy can have any reality at all. The implicitly invoked standard in normative terms here is, to borrow a phrase from Axel Honneth, the collectively organised provision of 'the conditions for positive relations to self'. MacPherson's argument, however, does not break through to articulating this normative commitment in such terms as to make it plausible as a critique of the social-ontological premises of the liberal position. *With* liberal political theory, he too conceives of individuals mainly as bearers of—potentially conflicting— interests; the chances of realising them remain unequal unless public policy intervenes for redress. This adherence to the premises of interest-mediation explains why MacPherson doesn't seem to see the need to address the nature of the institutional forms of liberalism, but rather argues for extending their scope. While he thus delivers a critique of possessive individualism, it is less clear to what degree he carries through a more full-blown critique of methodological individualism, in which the possessive institutional aspect may be dominant in the expanding liberal political form but remains only an aspect.

MacPherson's argument thus points us in the right direction, but gives us no further criteria with which to investigate critically the distortions which arise in the contemporary context of the institutionalisation of the developmental subject. In particular, his argument leaves us short of the required normative vocabulary with which to grasp the dimensions of 'self-development' today associated with the 'politics of identity'. Particularly with regard to recent post-colonial scholarship, then, MacPherson's critique of the proprietary notion of selfhood falls short of providing criteria with which the social and political implications of developmental subjectivity can be understood better.

From Political Theory to Critical Social Theory: Taking MacPherson's Argument Further

The developmental subject is constituted formally in terms of interests which can find institutionalised expression in the language of rights. The modernisation process implied in the development project is premised on these factors, which therefore can be appropriately conceptualised as being part of a push for the globalisation of liberal order. The prescriptions of multiparty democratic governance for the development of an effective and efficient state-administrative complex, together with the demand for accountability, are the flip-sides of the basic idea that the organisation of general prosperity relies on the entrenchment of the 'liberal subject'.

Not only is the expansion of property rights regimes integral to this process, it is also the means by which ostensibly ossified, inflexible, and inhibitive socio-political relations are transformed in line with the formal creation of a new, stratified social universe of 'ownerships'. From the minimalist, residual notion of self-ownership, which enables individuals without any further proprietary resources to sell their labour-power, to the exclusive subject-bound ownership of financial means, which can be deployed via contracts in the search for profit-margins and returns, the institutionalised notion of individual subjective freedom, expressed in terms of the possessive individualism which MacPherson criticises, pervades the reform plans extended for the purpose of 'development'.

The human security agenda plays a part in the consolidation of this expansion of classical liberal politics, insofar as its proponents remain committed to an unproblematised and unsubstantiated conception of individual experience as the basis for claims to human security violation. Although not necessarily intended, this stance leads more often than not directly to the proposal of further liberalising measures, through which the injured integrity or dignity of individuals could be restored. Such tendencies can be observed, for instance, in the context of global health governance, where the securitisation of the HIV/AIDS problem in sub-Saharan Africa has ultimately lead to a more comprehensive effort to ensure that any solutions to the individualistically conceived problem of 'access to drugs' comply with, rather than challenge, the proprietary interests of major pharmaceutical corporations (Thomas and Weber, 2004). The individualised instances of illness and disease, coupled with images circumscribing the loss to economic livelihoods and development potential, let any measure appear cogent which in the immediate context ameliorates the conditions, and which promises efficiencies in large-scale interventions.

The interventionist appeal, which calls for the implementation of development schemes in such contexts, rests for its normative force on the unquestioned conception of autonomy as individual(ised) self-ownership. The upshot is the push towards the institutionalisation of a 'pluralism of the smallest possible unit': the individual subject among other individual (and individualistic) subjects. Viewed critically from this perspective, we arrive at a plausible conception of what is *correct* about the critique of inherent power-relations in the expansion of 'Western' human rights culture, and the asymmetries and distortions it entails, without having to resort to the implausible and overall unattractive ideals of simplistic cultural relativism. Recall that the latter's critical intent has been focused on the suppression of identitarian concerns, which were seen to have been undermined by the imposition of liberal individualism. When we view the latter in terms of the substantive framing of social and political institutions, we can generalise this critique, which equally applies in contexts where these institutional settings have become entrenched (e.g., 'the West' insofar as such geographical identifications continue to have currency against the insights of more thoroughly relational analyses).

Now, it appears that the gains accrued by the universalisation of the liberal individual rights culture are potentially undermined by the subordination of substantive inter-subjective experiences and engagements. The latter, however, are constitutive of the capacity to experience freedom: The development of subjectivity itself is advanced, after all, intersubjectively, and relies qualitatively on social environments characterised significantly by care, love, the mutually experienced recognition of rules and conventions of social conduct, and the equitable extension of rights (Honneth, 1996). It should be clear from the above reconstruction that the target of criticism here is thus not the concept of individual rights as such, but much more specifically the liberal individual rights culture with the proprietary provisos already identified by MacPherson. The 'colonisation' of the subject of development occurs through this form, which at one and the same time elides any account of the subject's own development (formation through inter-subjective relations), and, through the conception of self-ownership, offers a social action-space framed in terms of exchange/compensation or trade.

In the concrete development context the results of this can be seen where socially guaranteed forms of autonomy are torn asunder through the often state-enforced imposition of exchange systems based on money. Subsistence communities, unless their ecological circumstances are exposed otherwise to radical deteriorating change, experience the arrival of the monetarised exchange paradigm, with concomitant compensation policies, quite plausibly as a loss of autonomy, where the latter implies substantive conceptions of freedom. The 'compensation culture' exacerbates the loss of social autonomy, which occurs as subsistence farmers are displaced into urban shanties. Any experience of social injury thus must be translated first into the individualist idiom. Again, this is not a problem *per se*—only to the degree that such a translation involves a switch to the proprietary individualist frame of reference, forcing the abstraction from concrete experiences of misrecognition and moral injury according to which lack of social esteem is compensated for in terms of the medium of exchange (money, or the legally sanctioned expansion of purely 'private' space). In the latter case, the compensation offered for the loss of socially guaranteed and achieved autonomies, when it is rendered through the form of the exchange medium of money, can only fail with regard to the scope and experience of the injury inflicted. In addition, the compensatory act takes on the character of a form of denigration, in which the recipient is offered an 'equivalent' which is directly experienced as an insult.

The problem of liberalism is that on its premises one cannot register this, or any other of the foregone experiences of inter-subjectively constituted autonomy. On the basis of the 'pluralism of the smallest unit' mentioned above, liberal thought robs itself of criteria with which to judge that where a morally satisfactory resolution of a dispute between (ostensibly) autonomous people is achieved without recourse to the institutions of law and state, this may be a superior socio-political event. Again, the suggestion is not that recourse to the institutions of law and state is always a morally and practically inferior move, but rather that the institutionalisation of proprietary individualism incentivises towards a comprehensive instrumentalisation of legal provisions as the privileged mode of engagement in the context of social conflict.

Viewed from this critical perspective, it becomes clear why the extension of liberal institutions premised on the proprietary conception of the subject leads to experiences of 'nautonomy'[3] in cases where people are not already socialised into the context of the formal social and political relations this entails.

Recognition Theory: Plausible Pathways

The critical perspective sketched above with the help of a few general examples is developed today nowhere clearer and more comprehensively than in the work of Axel Honneth. He developed his recognition-theoretic approach explicitly to work towards an understanding of human development, with consideration of both the formal requirements which ground the institutions of societalisation through which rules and norms are extended and the substantive requirements of the 'ethical life' through which individuals can come to positive relations with themselves and others. The theory of recognition thus aims at nothing less than providing a way not only to side-step Berlin's dilemma of positive and negative liberties, but also to arrive at a reconceptualisation of their implications from the perspective of an inter-subjectivist theory of the formation of personhood.

The critical element in this reconstructive effort comes into its own when Honneth considers the tension field opened up between the 'struggle for recognition', in which individuals are involved as both differentiating themselves from and simultaneously relying upon others, and the denigration of demands for recognition as the deficient form of interaction. In keeping with his reworking of Hegel, Honneth traces these tensions from the 'ontogenetic' level of individual face-to-face recognition in the development of subjects in family/friendship relations, through the formal recognition of legal subjectivity, to the level of general social recognition beyond formal obligation comprised by the recognition affirmed by relations of solidarity.

Love, rights, and solidarity thus stand in triplicate complementarity to one another as the markers for relations of recognition/denigration.

The advantage of Honneth's conception is that it makes substantial points about the conditions for successful development—understood in a comprehensive fashion— without incurring either a cultural-imperialist normative load or, conversely, a form of cultural relativism which would constrict critical engagements in the mode of normatively demanding theory. His theoretical construct, by keeping individuals, societalisation, and ethical relations in view simultaneously, offers a more adequate point of departure for asking explicitly normative questions about development and its projects than those offered from theoretical traditions forcing a choice between methodological individualism or, conversely, holism (the latter comprising nationalist ideologies, but also some strands of socialist ideologies).

From Honneth's perspective, it becomes possible to ask of social and political arrangements whether they are 'good' or 'bad' in sustaining relations of recognition, as well as positive relations to self. In his own work, this has meant that he has progressively pushed one question more and more into the foreground. This question animated his work from the outset in the 1970s, and demonstrates some continuity with the core project of the Frankfurt Schools critique of the dialectic of modernity: To what degree are capitalist societies capable of sustaining conditions under which relations of recognition can expand?

That Honneth means his recognition theoretic approach to be capable of delivering an intersubjectivist critical social theory, which captures both the politics of identity and the politics of distribution/redistribution, is evidenced in his exchange with Nancy Fraser (Fraser and Honneth, 2003), where he argues that the recognition theoretic approach allows the identification of material injustices as well as the patterns of denigration affecting peoples' identities. Honneth argues that social esteem, which is necessary for the development of positive relations to self, and hence the capacity for freedom, requires that self esteem be experienced from the perspective of each participant. The recognition theoretic conception of a 'moral grammar of social conflict' then brings into view the problematic of socially reproduced poverty, unemployment, or heteronomies, under the premise of the explicit inclusion of their experience as morally relevant, and relevant from the perspective of the experience of those making up these social relations.

Such an approach, then, moves beyond the limitations we have explored with reference to the political theory of MacPherson, strengthening the critique of persistent inequalities, denigration, and imiseration through a relational perspective in which the actors themselves are central (see also Forst, 2001). This actualisation of critical theory, which is combined with ambitious and incisive reconceptualisations in the field of theories of justice (Honneth, 2004), holds perhaps the greatest potential for thinking inclusively about social relations of inequality and difference in the global space.

Tentative Conclusions

We have arrived at a point where the colonising aspect (and with it the colonialist attitude) of the expansion of the institutions built on the normative bedrock of a proprietary conception of liberal individualism can be appreciated in moral terms, and hence open a perspective on the moral motivation for struggle and resistance through which these modes of social action receive their dignity. This, of course, is only groundwork for any attempt to conceive of institutional arrangements through which promises of development may be realised in political processes not premised on the form of domination and coercion identified in the contradictory conception of freedom and autonomy promulgated under the advancement of liberal capitalism. The more these contradictions become manifestly felt, and the more it becomes possible to give voice to the ways in which they are socially and politically experienced, the more the whole normative edifice through which capitalist social relations are sustained comes under pressure. Development, and the contest over its meaning, marks a crucial site in which these struggles play out.

Notes

1   One of the moral scandals of the 'liberal abstraction' can be captured with the help of the example of the fiction of the 'freely entered into' labour contract; from this perspective, there is simply no difference between a marginalised human being entering into the contractual relations of prostitution in order to pay for the education of a child and the freelancing business consultant contracting on a report for the purpose of adding another super-car to the fleet. Power, need, and heteronomy are simply 'disappeared' from the story under liberalism's proprietary individualist abstraction.
2   See Hegel (1991, pp. 553–554). I trace outlines of a Hegelian critique of current progressivist appeals to 'civil society' as an emancipatory global political force in a forthcoming article, 'Hegel Beyond the State?' (unpublished paper, available on request from author).
3   See Held, who uses this concept to capture the obverse of 'autonomy' (1995, p. 171).

References

Berlin, I. & Hardy, H. (2005) *Liberty: Incorporating Four Essays on Liberty* (Oxford: Oxford University Press).

Forst, R. (2001) Towards a critical theory of transnational justice, in T. Pogge (ed.) *Global Justice* (Oxford: Blackwell).

Fraser, N. & Honneth, A. (2003) *Recognition or Redistribution* (London: Verso).

Gill, S. (2003) *Power and Resistance in the New World Order* (Basingstoke: Palgrave).

Hegel, G. F. W. (1991) *Elements of the Philosophy of Right* (Cambridge: Cambridge University Press).

Held, D. (1995) *Democracy and the Global Order* (Cambridge: Polity).

Hobbes, T. (1982) *Leviathan* (London: Penguin).

Honneth, A. (1996) *The Struggle for Recognition* (Cambridge: Polity).

Honneth, A. (2000) The possibility of a disclosing critique of society: the 'dialectic of enlightenment' in the light of current debates in social criticism, *Constellations*, 7(1), pp. 116–127.

Honneth, A. (2001) Recognition or redistribution? Changing perspectives on the moral order of society, *Theory, Culture & Society*, 18(2–3), pp. 43–55.

Honneth, A. (2004) A social pathology of reason, in F. Rush (ed.) *The Cambridge Companion to Critical Theory* (Cambridge: Cambridge University Press).

Kaldor, M. (2003) *Global Civil Society: An Answer to War* (Cambridge: Polity).

Locke, J. & Laslett, P. (1988) *Two Treatises of Government* (Cambridge: Cambridge University Press).

MacPherson, C. B. (1973) *Democratic Theory: Essays in Retrieval* (Oxford: Oxford University Press).

MacPherson, C. B. (1971) *The Political Theory of Possessive Individualism* (Oxford: Oxford University Press).

Mill, J. S. (1991) *On Liberty and Other Essays* (Oxford: Oxford University Press).

Rosenberg, J. (1994) *The Empire of Civil Society* (London: Verso).

Steger, M. (2005) American globalism "Madison Avenue style", in P. Hayden & C. el-Ojeili (eds) *Confronting Globalization* (Basingstoke: Palgrave).

Taylor, C. (1992) *Sources of the Self* (Cambridge, MA: Harvard University Press).

Thomas, C. & Weber, M. (2004) Whatever happened to health for all by 2000? *Global Governance*, 10(2), pp. 187–206.

'Failed States' and 'State Failure': Threats or Opportunities?

MORTEN BØÅS & KATHLEEN M. JENNINGS

Introduction

In the aftermath of the terrorist attacks of September 11, 2001, the Western world has become increasingly concerned with 'failed states' in the global south. The debate around such states takes place on both a policy and a critical level (see, e.g., Armstrong and Rubin, 2005; Bøås and Jennings, 2005; Chabal and Daloz, 1999; Clapham, 2000; Herbst, 1996; Mayall, 2005). However, the degree to which the latter informs the former is questionable. Especially since 9/11—and much to the detriment of effective policymaking—the critical genesis and development of the concept has been largely overshadowed by its political and rhetorical uses. Reframing existing conflicts, humanitarian crises, or pockets of instability according to a failed states framework—building on a presumed link between failed states and terrorism—has provided a basis for Western policymakers, analysts, and advocates to access, re-channel, or increase military and financial resources. Some leaders of countries considered failed or failing have similarly exploited the concept in ways intended to buttress regime security (Bøås, 2007; Bøås and Dunn, 2006).

However, the way in which the failed state concept has been understood and operationalised, especially since 2001, is problematic. From an analytical standpoint, the concept's usefulness to effective policy formulation is in fact sharply limited. The concept is based on flawed assumptions about state uniformity, which enables crucial differences in state formation and recession to be smoothed over and obscured, while elevating analytically superficial similarities that both inform and perpetuate misguided policy responses (Bøås and Jennings, 2005).

It is difficult to gauge the extent to which the failed state concept is used pretextually; that is, not to guide policy formulation, but to justify and defend policy interventions by recourse to the security, governance, or humanitarian crises of a 'failed state'. Perhaps more interesting than untangling this knot, however, is examining the circumstances under which the failed state label is—or is not—applied. After all, many states experience at least some of the security, humanitarian, and governance crises commonly associated with failed states, but it is only to some that the label is attached.

We argue that the use of the failed state label is inherently political, and based primarily on Western perceptions of Western security and interests. This argument expands upon our previous observation (Bøås and Jennings, 2005) that, in order to bring meaning to the failed state concept, one must first ask: For whom is the state failing, and how? Such questioning enables the realisation that the structures and power relations generally considered the consequence of state failure may in fact be deliberate. Indeed, assuming that the recession and informalisation of the state—to the extent that decisions about distribution and redistribution occur outside and in-between official state structures—constitutes failure overlooks the fact that, for those in power, such conditions may be their objective, consolidating elite networks and reinforcing regime security (Bøås and Jennings, 2005; see also Reno, 1998). Building on this contention, therefore, we maintain that states called 'failed' are primarily those in which this recession and informalisation of the state is perceived to be a threat to Western interests. In other states, however, this feature of state functioning is not only accepted, but also to a certain degree facilitated, as it creates an enabling environment for business and international capital. These cases are not branded failed states. Crucially, labelling states as failed (or not) operates as a means of delineating the range of acceptable policy responses to those states.

Below, we argue that Afghanistan, Liberia, and Somalia illustrate the 'failed state as security threat' scenario, which entails more offensive policy responses once the situation in the state in question generates sufficient alarm among Western powers. Conversely, Nigeria and Sudan highlight how similar attributes of state functioning are overlooked—the 'failed state as good for business' model. First, however, we will briefly outline the case against the failed state concept as a useful policy and analytical tool.

Limitations of the Failed State Concept

The orthodox interpretation of failed states is closely tied to a view of the modern state system that assumes that all states are essentially alike and function in the same way. States control their borders, have a monopoly on the use of force, and generally supervise the management and regulation of economic, social, and political processes in accordance with Western standards (see Duffield, 2001); failed states, on the other hand, are characterised by an inability to control territory, borders, and internal legal order and security, and lack the capacity or will to provide services to the citizenry (typically due to some kind of large-scale institutional collapse; Jennings, 2007; see also Krasner, 2005; White House, 2002). States considered to be functioning are perceived as legitimate actors and worthy recipients of Western donor assistance, whereas those unable or unwilling to function according to the template tend to be regarded with some suspicion, and/or are assumed to represent a security threat to the Western world.[1] This tendency is particularly evident in the 2002 US *National Security Strategy* (White House, 2002), the 2005 US Agency on International Development (USAID) paper on failed states, and the 2003 European Security Strategy (European Union, 2003). Although the explicit emphasis on failed states has been reduced in revised versions of these key documents, this does not imply that such dichotomisation has disappeared, but rather that it has been thoroughly mainstreamed.

Unfortunately, this categorisation, by donors and policymakers, of states as functioning or failing is reductive, non-contextual, and ahistorical. The notion that states can be divided into those that are worthy and those that are suspicious stems from the assumption that all states can and should function in essentially the same way, and can therefore be located on a spectrum from good to bad (Bøås and Jennings, 2005). This is simply untrue. Every state is a culmination of unique historical processes. Problematising them not on the basis of their own merits, needs, and particular pathologies of state and regime formation, but against the norms and standards of a specific type of advanced, northern state results in misguided and self-referential policy responses.

Furthermore, the corollary of the assumption that states can and should function the same way—namely, that poorly functioning states can be 'fixed' using technocratic solutions, such as good governance programmes or security sector reform—ignores the issue of why it is these states function as they do.[2] As noted above, we argue that most policy interventions and analyses overlook the deliberate aspect of state failure: the extent to which regimes allow and enable state recession in order to serve their own financial and security interests, regardless of the best interests of the people. Conversely, good governance and institutional reform agendas are predicated on the self-referential notion that modern, Western, 'liberal market democracies' (Paris, 2004, p. 5) are the normative goal, and that mimicking their structures is the only viable option to overcome the decrepitude that enables criminality, terrorism, and poverty to flourish. These states are thus severely compromised, insofar as they are trying to 'fix' that which is probably broken for a reason. Even where this programming occurs in the context of post-conflict peacebuilding operations, the fact of conflict (and probably regime shift) does not necessarily change the incentives for continued state recession and informalisation, as the pathologies that created these incentives typically remain intact.

The failed states concept thus seems to privilege ill-informed and unhelpful analyses and policy interventions. Much of the policy thinking and rhetoric around state failure is based on analytically superficial similarities (reinforced by early warning and indexing exercises, such as the 'Failed States Index' compiled annually by *Foreign Policy* and the Fund for Peace); this perhaps explains the tendency to conflate failed states with conflict, despite the fact that countries with relatively robust institutions also experience conflict (see Einsiedel, 2005; Ignatieff, 2002; Jennings, 2007).

Interestingly, however, the currency that the failed state idea has recently had in European and American policy arenas has not been borne out in implementation. This contradiction has been most evident in the Bush administration. In its 2002 *National Security Strategy* (p. 1), the administration declared: 'America is now threatened less by conquering states than we are by failing ones.' However, it proceeded to populate its 'axis of evil' with three states that, at least according to the metric of maintaining a monopoly over the use of force, were strong indeed: Iraq, Iran, and North Korea. Iraq even managed a reasonable amount of service provision to its citizens until the US-led invasion in 2003—an invasion and occupation that, by straining US military, financial, and diplomatic resources, has arguably strengthened the hand of the governing regimes in the other 'axis of evil' states, while compromising the ongoing multi-dimensional operation in the most high-profile of 'failed states', Afghanistan (see, e.g., Cordesman, 2006).

Threat or Opportunity?

The disjuncture between strategy, rhetoric, and implementation manifest in the Bush administration's foreign policy returns us to a point raised above: that it is difficult to trace the extent to which the thinking on failed states actually guides policy, or is used merely as a pretext for more-or-less intrusive interventions. Ultimately, this may not be discernible to those outside the immediate policy circle.

However, the use of 'failed states' as pretext has an interesting converse, which is that states not facing punitive or intrusive policy interventions are typically not referred to as failed, even when they share some or all of the characteristics ascribed to those so labelled.[3] This suggests that determinations of state failure have less to do with a particular state's functioning and more to do with its ability and willingness to be a relevant partner for Western countries in their efforts to guarantee their own security, access to resources, and support for their interests. It expands our original question on state failure—for whom is the state failing, and how—from the domestic to the international stage, with the revision: Who does a state's failure help or hurt, and how? Thus, Afghanistan (post-9/11, pre-invasion), Liberia, and Somalia are failed states; Nigeria and Sudan (post-1998, the year the Clinton administration bombed Sudan and the year before oil exporting began) are not.

Labelling states 'failures' is not just a rhetorical exercise. Rather, we argue that it is used to delineate the acceptable range of policy options that can then be exercised against those states. In Afghanistan, Somalia, and to a lesser extent Liberia, state failure has been defined as a security threat to be handled militarily. It also implies, in the Liberian case, a subsequent level of international involvement that greatly and overtly diminishes state sovereignty, which is predicated on the same assumptions about state functioning criticised above. Similar scenarios in the oil-rich Niger Delta in Nigeria and Sudan, although clearly causes of concern, have not been so defined.

It is important to note, moreover, that the situations in Afghanistan, Somalia, and Liberia only became cases of actionable state failure when Western security or other interests became threatened. In Afghanistan, the Taliban was in power for several years prior to 9/11, without generating much outrage over its human rights abuses or practice of harbouring terrorists; indeed, as seen below, by many inside and outside Afghanistan the Taliban were tolerated because they managed to bring stability to the country. In Liberia, it took the combination of al-Qaeda rumours and Charles Taylor's connection to rebel groups in Sierra Leone before the situation merited a more vigorous response. Similarly, it was only when Somalia retained some few degrees of statehood under the rule of the Islamic Courts Union (ICU)—in effect moving away from the failed state category—that it became a security threat to be urgently addressed by the United States and its regional allies. On the other hand, although there is little to suggest that the level of state failure and human suffering is comparatively less in the Niger Delta of Nigeria or in Darfur in Sudan, few if any Western leaders would dare to describe Nigeria as a failed state, much less consider an intrusive or unwelcome intervention in either country. We elaborate further on these cases below.

The 'Failed State as Security Threat' Scenario

Afghanistan's recent history exemplifies the 'failed state as security threat' scenario, and how this has been acted upon by Western powers. Significantly, the rise and fall of the Taliban also indicates that the intervention in Afghanistan—despite rhetoric to the contrary—had little to do with any humanitarian or governance-based conception of state failure. Institutionally, Afghanistan was less a failed state under the Taliban than under preceding regimes: the Taliban re-established a central government, restored some law and order—albeit based on a brutal interpretation of *sharia* law—and even decreased poppy cultivation, a feat that has not been replicated by Western forces despite concerted efforts. Meanwhile, their many human rights abuses were, as noted below, deemed insufficiently important to justify international involvement before 2001. What eventually brought down the Taliban, of course, was not state failure but that they harboured Osama bin Laden, who moved to Afghanistan from Sudan in 1996. When they came to power, bin Laden established an alliance between the Taliban and his al-Qaeda organisation, which persisted even after the 1998 bombings of the US embassies in Nairobi and Dar es Salaam.

The Taliban's arrangement with bin Laden was not, however, the extent of the Taliban's interaction with the Western world, including the United States. With the collapse of the Soviet Union, major US oil interests, led by UNOCAL, searched for ways to get oil and gas out of Turkmenistan and other former Soviet republics without passing through Russian or Iran. It soon became clear that the only viable route for such a pipeline was through Afghanistan (Rashid, 2001). When the Taliban came into power, the US administration duly entered into discussions with them. However, relations deteriorated over time, particularly after 1998, and by the end of the Clinton administration, communications were essentially terminated. When Bush took over, discussions with the Taliban restarted, with the aim of persuading the Taliban to sign an agreement with the opposition Northern Alliance in order to facilitate the construction of the pipeline. These discussions continued almost until the attacks on 11 September 2001 (Brisard and Dasquie, 2002).

In this period, the language of the relationship did not dwell on the extent to which Afghanistan was a failed state—which would have provoked discussion about the many human rights abuses of the Taliban, especially related to women and girls—but rather centred on the gospel of oil and geopolitics. The 2001 terror attacks radically altered this dynamic. However, it is interesting that during the period immediately preceding and following the subsequent invasion, the human rights situation under the Taliban (especially the plight of women) suddenly received a great deal of lip service as an additional humanitarian justification for offensive intervention. This is not to say that the humanitarian-based argument for overthrowing the Taliban was necessarily wrong or specious, but rather to point out that this argument was never seriously considered (or even voiced) before the 9/11 attacks changed the equation of the Western relationship to Afghanistan.

It is further noteworthy that on 30 May 2002—little more than six months after the signing of the Bonn Agreement—President Hamid Karzai signed an agreement with Pakistan and Turkmenistan, concerning a pipeline from Turkmenistan to Pakistan through Afghanistan. Thus, although the intervention in Afghanistan was driven more by revenge and fear than oil, postwar priorities clearly reflected specific Western interests. This continues today, as evidenced by unpopular poppy eradication programmes without alternative livelihood provision (Barnes Higgins, 2007; Tisdall, 2007).

The Somalia case shares some of the features of the Afghanistan story. Like Afghanistan, Somalia is often considered an archetypal failed state and terrorist safe haven (see, e.g., International Crisis Group, 2002). Since the overthrow of long-time Somali leader Siad Barre in 1991, Somalia has experienced failed international interventions, large-scale refugee flows, and the ongoing absence of even rudimentary state services and institutions; Somalis live in an environment of predation and pervasive insecurity and deprivation (Bakonyi and Stuvøy, 2005; Kapteijns, 2001; Samatar, 2000). There is no real central authority, and neither are there many of the other characteristics generally associated with a sovereign state.

This does not mean, however, that total anarchy has prevailed. Instead, existing religious and social/familial (clan-based) structures have attempted to fill some of the space left by the government's collapse. For example, Koranic schools have taken on a social function in addition to their religious role, while a system of *sharia*-based Islamic courts has evolved since 1991 to become the main judicial system. This was the genesis of the ICU, which, over the course of 2006, took or consolidated control of the country from the ineffectual, opportunistic, and externally constructed Transitional Federal Government (TFG). The ICU's primary appeal was that it brought stability and predictability to areas under its control, even managing to reopen Mogadishu international airport, which had been closed since the UN withdrawal in 1995.

It is therefore interesting that the failed state rhetoric which has been used to describe Somalia for years only became actionable when a unifying Islamic force brought some degree of statehood back to the country. The Ethiopian and US actions against the ICU in December 2006 and January 2007 were intended to depose the ICU, shore up the TFG, and take out some top US terrorist targets. Since then, however:

> There is no reliable security [in Mogadishu] ... random attacks have created fear among the civilians who had enjoyed relative safety under the Islamists' six-month rule ... Meanwhile, the warlords that terrorised the capital before the rise of the Islamic courts are back ... [and] many fear that the clan-based warlords could organise themselves again if the lawlessness and insecurity persists. (Hassan, 2007 para. 1–2)

This again illustrates that the application of the failed state concept does not necessarily reflect what is in the best interests of human security, but it does consistently reflect the best interests of Western powers and their allies.

The last case in this section, Liberia, illustrates another facet of the acceptable range of policy responses to failed states. The primary international response to the Liberian civil war, which began in December 1989, was apathy, followed eventually by a UN sanctions regime (beginning in 2001). The sanctions regime exacerbated the effects of long-term economic mismanagement, non-functioning institutions, corruption and predation, and the widespread destruction of infrastructure (Bøås, 2005; see also Ellis, 1999). Only in the summer of 2003, when President Charles Taylor went into exile in Nigeria, was a UN peacekeeping mission agreed.

The Liberia case is interesting because it brings to the fore the governance aspect rather than the security aspect of the failed state concept and implementation. Certainly, regional and international security considerations played a role in the eventual international intervention, including the US's subdued show of force in mid-2003 (International Crisis Group, 2003). However, more notable is that what is happening in Liberia now is a concrete manifestation of one of the flawed assumptions we identified above: that poorly functioning states can be 'fixed' using technocratic solutions, such as good governance and other institutional reform programmes, regardless of the reasons why they were 'broken' in the first place. It also shows the extent to which failed states, once they become the object of wider attention, are considered to have ceded most or all of their sovereignty.

In the early phases of the UN Mission in Liberia (UNMIL), the international community was quite optimistic about what the cobbled-together National Transitional Government of Liberia (NTGL) could achieve in the designated two-year transition period. Unfortunately, the NTGL exhibited much the same behaviour as previous Liberian governments—it was more interested in fleecing than in rehabilitating state institutions. Policymakers eventually began to realise that Taylor's flight was not the magic bullet they expected, but that Taylor was simply a manifestation of larger underlying problems in Liberian society (see Bøås, 2005).

The consequence of this rethinking was the Governance and Economic Management Assistance Programme (GEMAP), a plan intended to combat corruption and theft, which included placing international experts in key administrative positions for at least three years. The NTGL was forced to accept GEMAP, and it has been impossible for Ellen Johnson-Sirleaf's democratically elected government to refuse or re-negotiate its terms. The Executive Director of the Bank of Liberia is therefore obliged to have all operational and financial matters co-signed by an international expert selected by the International Monetary Fund (IMF), and the heads of five other governmental agencies also have to pass all decisions through a non-Liberian counterpart with co-signatory powers. Although most Liberians are in favour of mechanisms to curb corruption, nevertheless there are critical questions that should be asked. Is the international community turning the state into what Thandika Mkandawire (1999) has called a 'choiceless democracy', especially when Liberian priorities and the international economic orthodoxy conflict? Does GEMAP have a chance to create sustainable outcomes, given that countervailing incentives and power structures remain largely intact and can re-surface when the international minders have gone? And to what degree does the programme facilitate its aim of good governance in Liberia, as opposed to increasing dependence on international experts? Finally, because few attempts have been made to include the re-emerging Liberian civil society in the programme, it runs the risk of creating an unholy alliance between those opposed to GEMAP because it is a threat to their livelihoods (e.g., corrupted elites) and progressive forces in civil society opposed to it for principled reasons. Already dependent on a large UN peacekeeping force for security, Liberia is now essentially an international protectorate in economic matters as well.

Other countries share many of the features identified in these failed states, but do not face the same sorts of interventions. The cases of Sudan and Nigeria illustrate this point.

The 'Failed State as Good for Business' Model

International interventions involve several considerations, but power and interest are always important factors. Power has to do with the rules of engagement in the international community, and here the former great powers have a special role, reflected among other things in their special position in the Security Council of the United Nations (see also Sørensen, 2006). This anodyne observation helps explain why Sudan escapes being treated according to the 'failed state as security threat' scenario outlined above. The crisis in Darfur, regardless of the attention it has garnered in Western media, is hardly forced by Western powers (Flint and Waal, 2005); in fact, the only action resembling the 'failed state as security threat' response was made back in 1998, when the Clinton administration bombed a factory in Sudan in retaliation for the terrorist bombings of the American embassies in Nairobi and Dar es Salaam. Since then, the approach from the West has been much gentler. The reasons are oil and China (see also Kessler, 2007).

China is currently Sudan's biggest trading partner, and has invested heavily in its oil sector. Sudan is one of Africa's most rapidly growing economies—enjoying 7–8% growth in 2006—and much of this is owed to its relationship with China. In the 1980s and 1990s, when the North–South civil war forced Western companies to pull out, China stepped in, helping Sudan become an oil exporting country in August 1999 (approximately a year after the US bombing raid; Johnson, 2003).[4] China's involvement, and the subsequent transformation of the Sudanese economy to an oil economy, changed the nature of the Western powers' engagement. Substantively, Sudan may still have been a failed state, but it was no longer in the category of states that could be the target of an intervention. As Sudan's primary investor and key trading partner, China could have played a vital role in trying to resolve the war in Darfur. Instead, it has blocked tough resolutions at the Security Council and refused to push for a more robust peacekeeping force, preferring a joint UN–African Union force.

The Sudan case shows that having strategic resources and great power allies is an efficient shield against being included in the 'failed state as security threat' category. The application of this category is not about stopping human suffering, but about Western perceptions of Western interests coupled with what is seen as possible. Even great outrage among Western publics over the Darfur situation—which hasn't happened—would not prompt these powers to intervene and risk upsetting the apple cart with China, or the future commercial interests of their own companies. Instead, the response to the Darfur crisis has been half-hearted and repeatedly thwarted by the obstructionism of a Khartoum government seemingly sanguine about the consequences of its actions.

The Nigerian case illustrates many of the same dynamics. The Niger Delta currently comprises a dangerous combination of poverty, marginalisation, and underemployment, combined with environmental problems, crime, corruption, and local communities who see few benefits from oil production. This has fuelled a militant uprising, which not only threatens Nigeria's oil production but also the country's fragile democratic transition (see Human Rights Watch, 2007; Omeje, 2006). In effect, this region of Nigeria displays all the features of a failed state. However, although the rebellion in the region is reducing the world output of oil—Nigeria's oil production has fallen by at least 20% in recent years (USIP, 2005)—it is notable that the failed state concept has no traction in the policymaking and rhetorical arenas relating to Nigeria. Commercial interests and power politics—particularly Nigeria's leading position in the volatile West African region—are again key elements.

Ongoing internal crisis or not, Nigeria is a regional superpower the West needs. Oil is a crucial factor, as is the fact that oil extraction becomes cheaper and more attractive to Western companies when its extraction is loosely regulated or unregulated (as in the Niger Delta). The environmental havoc now seen in the Niger Delta is the inevitable result. Moreover, the corruption deemed sufficiently disabling to require 'shared sovereignty' (Krasner, 2005) in Liberia is seen more as a cost of doing business—perhaps even an enabler—in the Niger Delta, as is the hiring of private security companies to protect oil company employees and subcontractors. Finally, Nigeria is not only a superpower with regard to energy: it is also a regional superpower in military terms, and thus a regional powerbroker. It has come to be regarded as a useful ally in the West African war zone, due to the roles it played in the ECOMOG interventions in Liberia and Sierra Leone (see Bøås, 2001, 2005).

These are the dimensions that determine whether or not the failed states card is played: a combination of self-referential security, commercial interests, and the perceived risk of intervening. This shows how shallow the political use of the failed state concept is.

Concluding Remarks

The Western world has become increasingly concerned with failed states in the global south. However, the way in which the failed state concept has been understood and operationalised, especially since 2001, is problematic. Although the concept's usefulness to policy formulation is low, it is used to justify and defend policy interventions. And as we have argued, while many states experience some of the security, humanitarian, and governance crises associated with failed states, it is only to some that the label is attached.

This matters because labelling a country as a failed state is more than merely a rhetorical exercise. It delineates the acceptable range of policy options that can be exercised. States called 'failed' are therefore primarily those in which such crises are perceived to threaten Western interests; in other cases, conversely, these features of state (mal)functioning are not only accepted, but sometimes almost encouraged. Above, the former scenario is illustrated by Afghanistan, Somalia, and to a lesser extent Liberia, and the latter by Nigeria's Niger Delta region and Sudan. Failed state situations are sometimes defined as threats and sometimes not: the crucial point is that the concept and term itself does not shed any light on the human security situation in the countries in question.

There is little to suggest that the levels of state failure and human suffering differ much in the five countries discussed. However, few would dare to describe Nigeria as a failed state, or argue for an intrusive intervention in Sudan without a UN Security Council mandate. Countries with superpower protection, or those seen as useful regional allies in possession of strategic resources, are not given the failed state treatment. This demonstrates how shallow the political use of the failed state concept is—an observation further strengthened by the Afghanistan and Somalia cases, in which intervention occurred not when they were most 'failed' but after regimes considered threats in the Western world started enhancing their levels of statehood in these countries. The failed state concept, as currently understood and operationalised, does not relate to human suffering, and its value to thoughtful analysis and effective policy planning is questionable.

Notes

1 Most of these states do not pose direct military or security threats to the West. Their main source of menace is indirect—for example, these states may harbour terrorists that attack Western interests (this is somewhat disingenuous, considering that the worst terrorist attacks in US history were carried out by men residing in the United States, and planned and funded by a person from Saudi Arabia believed to be currently living in Pakistan, which are both US allies). Another indirect threat often cited as coming from failed or failing states is that of illegal narcotics and associated organised criminality (European Union, 2003). This rather ignores the demand-side of the equation: illegal narcotics would not pose such a threat to Western society if there were not so many Westerners abusing them. Migrants are also increasingly seen in both the United States and Europe as posing a threat; this is intensified by irresponsible media coverage that invokes the spectre of invading hordes coming to steal jobs and drain Western coffers.

2 Good governance programmes and security sector reform are, of course, inherently political—after all, what could be more political than donors telling a state how to organise its polity? However, and bizarrely, they tend to be represented as technocratic rather than political exercises.

3 This is less relevant when entities other than states (such as nongovernmental organisations or NGOs) are the ones doing the labelling. Nevertheless, it is worth noting that NGOs may also have interests in raising the spectre of state failure: warning about the prospect of imminent disaster may increase their fundraising potential.

4 Among other investments, the Chinese National Petroleum Company financed a 1,600 kilometre pipeline that takes oil from the south to Port Sudan on the Red Sea coast. Exports are now close to 500,000 barrels per day, with about 80% of that going directly to China (see Fisher, 2007).

References

Armstrong, A. & Rubin, B. R. (2005) The Great Lakes and south central Asia, in S. Chesterman, M. Ignatieff, & R. Thakur (eds) *Making States Work: State Failure and the Crisis of Governance* (Toyko: United Nations University Press).

Bakonyi, J. & Stuvøy, K. (2005) Violence and social order beyond the state: Somalia and Angola, *Review of African Political Economy*, 104(5), pp. 359–382.

Barnes Higgins, H. (2007) The road to Helmand, *Washington Post*, 4 February, http://www.washingtonpost.com/wp-dyn/content/article/2007 /02/02/ar20070 20201474_pf.html.

Brisard, J.-C. and Dasquie, G. (2002) *Bin Laden: The Forbidden Truth* (New York: Nation Books).

Bøås, M. (2001) Liberia and Sierra Leone – dead ringers? The logic of neopatrimonial rule, *Third World Quarterly*, 22(5), pp. 697–723.

Bøås, M. (2005) The Liberian civil war: new war/old war? *Global Society*, 19(1), pp. 73–88.

Bøås, M. (2007) Mellom fengsel og frihet i Musevenis Uganda, *Nordisk Tidsskrift for Menneskerettigheter*, 25(1), pp. 1–20.

Bøås, M. & Jennings, K. M. (2005) Insecurity and development: the rhetoric of the failed state, *European Journal of Development Research*, 17(3), pp. 385–395.

Bøås, M. & Dunn, K. C. (2007) African guerrilla politics: raging against the machine?, in M. Bøås & K. C. Dunn (eds) *African Guerrillas: Raging Against the Machine* (Boulder, CO: Lynne Rienner).

Chabal, P. & Daloz, J.-P. (1999) *Africa Works: Disorder as Political Instrument* (Oxford: James Currey).

Clapham, C. (2000) Failed states and non states in the international order, paper presented at the 'Conference on Failed States', Purdue University, Florence, 7–10 April.

Cordesman, A. H. (2006) *American Strategic and Tactical Failures in Iraq: An Update*, working draft paper (Washington, DC: Center for Strategic and International Studies).

Duffield, M. (2001) *Global Governance and the New Wars: the Merging of Development and Security* (London: Zed Books).

Einsiedel, S. Von (2005) Policy responses to state failure, in S. Chesterman, M. Ignatieff, & R. Thakur (eds) *Making States Work: State Failure and the Crisis of Governance* (Toyko: United Nations University Press).

Ellis, S. (1999) *The Mask of Anarchy: The Destruction of Liberia and the Religious Dimension of an African Civil War* (London: Hurst).

European Union (2003) *A Secure Europe in a Better World: European Security Strategy* (Brussels: European Union).

Fisher, J. (2007) Chinese leader boosts Sudan ties, *BBC News*, http://news.bbc.co.uk/2/hi/africa/6323017.stm.

Flint, J. & Waal, A. De (2005) *Darfur: A Short History of a Long War* (London: Zed Books).

Hassan, M. O. (2007) Fears stalk Somalia's capital once again, *BBC News*, http://news.bbc.co.uk/2/hi/africa/6252359.stm.

Herbst, J. (1996) Responding to state failure in Africa, *International Security*, 21(3), pp. 120–144.

Human Rights Watch (2007) *Chop Fine: The Human Rights Impact of Local Government Corruption and Mismanagement in Rivers State, Nigeria* (New York: Human Rights Watch).

Ignatieff, M. (2002) Intervention and state failure, *Dissent*, 49(1), pp. 114–123.

International Crisis Group (2002) *Somalia: Countering Terrorism in a Failed State*, Africa Report No. 45 (Brussels: International Crisis Group).

International Crisis Group (2003) *Tackling Liberia: The Eye of the Regional Storm*, Africa Report No. 62 (Brussels: International Crisis Group).

Jennings, K. M. (2007) *The War Zone as Social Space: Social Research in Conflict Zones* (Oslo: Fafo).

Johnson, D. H. (2003) *The Root Causes of Sudan's Civil Wars* (Oxford: James Currey).

Kapteijns, L. (2001) The disintegration of Somalia: a historiographical essay, *Bildhaaen – International Journal of Somali Studies*, 1(1), pp. 11–52.

Kessler, G. (2007) Bush approves plan to pressure Sudan, *Washington Post*, 7 February.

Krasner, S. (2005) The case for shared sovereignty, *Journal of Democracy*, 16(1), pp. 69–83.

Mkandawire, T. (1999) Crisis management and the making of choiceless democracies, in R. Joseph (ed.) *State, Conflict and Democracy in Africa* (Boulder, CO: Lynne Rienner).

Mayall, J. (2005) The legacy of colonialism, in S. Chesterman, M. Ignatieff, & R. Thakur (eds) *Making States Work: State Failure and the Crisis of Governance* (Toyko: United Nations University Press).

Omeje, K. (2006) *High Stakes and Stakeholders: Oil Conflict and Security in Nigeria* (Aldershot: Ashgate).

Paris, R. (2004) *At War's End: Building Peace After Civil Conflict* (Cambridge: Cambridge University Press).

Rashid, A. (2001) *Taliban: Militant Islam, Oil and Fundamentalism in Central Asia* (New Haven, CT: Yale University Press).

Reno, W. (1998) *Warlord Politics and African States* (Boulder, CO: Lynne Rienner).

Samatar, A. I. (2000) The Somali catastrophe: explanation and implications, in E. Braathen, M. Bøås, & G. Sæther (eds) *Ethnicity Kills? The Politics of War, Peace and Ethnicity in Sub-Saharan Africa* (Basingstoke: Macmillan).

Sørensen, G. (2006) Underlying structural factors shaping power and politics in weak states, *Forum for Development Studies*, 33(2), pp. 267–281.

Tisdall, S. (2007) The big Afghanistan push comes to shove, *The Guardian*, 30 January, http://www.guardian.co.uk/afghanistan/story/0,,2001621,00.html.

White House (2002) *The National Security Strategy of the United States of America* (Washington, DC: US Government).

USAID (2005) *Fragile States Strategy* (Washington, DC: USAID).

USIP (United States Institute for Peace) (2005) *Strategies for Peace in the Niger Delta* (Washington, DC: USIP).

From the Politics of Development to the Challenges of Globalization

JENNIFER BAIR

How did we get here? This is the question that contributors to this volume are grappling with, as we seek to understand and explain the dramatic transformation in development theory and praxis that occurred during the last quarter of the twentieth century. Many scholars have analyzed the International Monetary Fund and the World Bank as key institutions disseminating the current orthodoxy, but this essay focuses on what might be considered the forgotten Bretton Woods institution: the United Nations. While the United Nations has been effectively sidelined by its Washington-based brethren, I examine a period in which the UN was a vibrant site for the construction and contestation of development discourse, and one in which the countries of the global South, then aligned as the Group of 77 in their quest for a 'New International Economic Order' (NIEO), sought to shape the agenda.

My goal in revisiting the debates of the 1970s and 1980s is to historicize the market episteme (Da Costa and McMichael, 2007) structuring today's development field. Although the NIEO proved to be a brief and relatively inefficacious project, it merits attention because the G-77's challenge to the status quo, and its attempt to define and legitimate an alternative development discourse, illuminates the history of contestation that lies beneath the triumphal teleology of contemporary neoliberalism. I want to underscore two points about the meaning of development posited by the NIEO's proponents. First, these states saw development as a struggle for recognition, both of the sovereign equality of Southern and Northern states and of the latter's responsibility towards the G-77 for the structural damage caused by a global economy that benefited the rich nations at the developing world's expense. Second, accordingly, a demand was made for redistribution via reform of the existing order and the creation of a more equitable and just international economic regime.

In the first section, I describe the NIEO project and the broad agenda of reform that the G-77 sought to advance. The second section focuses on a particular plank of the NIEO platform, describing in some detail the effort to draft and implement the Code of Conduct on Transnational

Enterprises (hereafter Code), which was the most comprehensive and most controversial of the several code projects pursued during the NIEO. This analysis of the Code's protracted negotiations extends from the early 1970s, when the UN took up the issue of multinationals, to the 'quiet burial' (Tesner, 2000, p. 23) of the project in 1992. In the third and final section of the paper, I briefly describe the Global Compact, a partnership between UN agencies and global business launched in 1999. As Secretary-General Kofi Annan explained when introducing the project, the Global Compact reflects 'a fundamental shift . . . in recent years in the attitude of the U.N. towards the private sector' (Annan, 1999, para. 5). Indeed, while the Code of Conduct project proceeded from a wary skepticism about the obstacles multinationals might pose to the developmental objectives of states, the Compact posits a 'global public domain' (Ruggie, 2004, p.499) where corporations work alongside states as equal stakeholders in the search for solutions to the challenges of globalization.

I focus on the rehabilitation of the multinational corporation at the UN because the trajectory from Code to Compact is instructive for thinking about the broader transformation in development discourse that occurred during the last quarter of the twentieth century. Most accounts of this shift from 'developmentalism' to 'globalization' (Wallerstein, 2005) focus on structural changes in the international economy (e.g., the debt crisis of the 1980s) and the implications of these changes for the developing world, as the policy prescriptions of the new orthodoxy became institutionalized in post-crisis regimes and structural adjustment programs (Callinicos, 2001; Rodrik, 1994). While agreeing with the contours of this narrative as an accurate explanation of how we got here, I want to underscore the discursive dimension of the neoliberal turn by looking at the formation and dissemination of the ideas underlying the current consensus. What is the conceptualization of development that it offers, and how have alternative ways of thinking about the pursuit of economic growth and welfare been marginalized? Through what practices of articulation does this development paradigm achieve coherence as an ideational regime (Somers and Block, 2005), and how is it diffused?

Thus, rather than reading the trajectory from Code to Compact as simply an outcome of structural changes occurring in the global economy over this period, I approach these UN initiatives as moments in which we can use what Gramsci called 'the relative autonomy of the political sphere' to see the production of development discourse. At stake here is not merely the role of the multinational corporation in the development process, or the relative merits of a binding instrument versus a voluntary initiative as different means to the same end of responsible corporate behavior. Rather, what has been transformed in the journey from Code to Compact is the very meaning of development itself. In sum, while the NIEO moment sought to make visible and challenge the structural inequalities in power and wealth that the G-77 countries argued were at the root of the developing world's predicament, the Global Compact posits development as a collective challenge to be met by the combined efforts of diverse stakeholders, whose potentially conflicting interests are elided via the language of participatory pluralism.

In her critique of the Global Compact in this volume, Susanne Soederberg emphasizes that by serving as the institutional home of the initiative, the United Nations 'acts to legitimate ideologically the neoliberal norms of the world order' (2007, p. 507). However, not problematized in her account is the process by which these neoliberal norms achieve coherence as an ideational regime, and how the United Nations becomes complicit in their reproduction. In excavating the largely forgotten Code project, I analyze a period in which the hegemony of today's development orthodoxy was not a foregone conclusion. The G-77's demand for a new international economic order, embedded in the political-economic context of a bipolar international system and enabled by the dislocations of the 1970s oil crisis, was an attempt to transform the prevailing paradigm of developmentalism into a politics of global redistribution and supranational regulation. Only by examining this discursive moment can we fully comprehend the ideological transformation that underlies the present-day legitimation of the neoliberal development model at the United Nations to which Soederberg refers.

Redefining Developmentalism: The New International Economic Order

The NIEO signaled a development in the consolidation of Third World influence within the United Nations that began with the Asian-African Bandung conference in April 1955. Although the Non-Aligned Movement was initially focused on political issues related to decolonization, its agenda turned increasingly to economic concerns.

When representatives of African, Asian, and Latin American countries met in 1964 for the first United Nations Conference on Trade and Development (UNCTAD), they formed the Third World caucus known as the Group of 77. The G-77's first major success came later that year in the form of UN resolution 1995, which secured the institutionalization of UNCTAD as a permanent organ of the General Assembly. In laying out the rationale for UNCTAD's creation, the developing countries articulated several of the arguments for reform that would reappear a decade later in the NIEO platform. They sought to make explicit the link between political freedom and economic independence, arguing that the anti-colonial struggle would continue until the sovereignty of Third World states over their national economies was realized.

During its first decade of existence, UNCTAD scored a modest number of victories (most notably, agreement on the principle of a Generalized System of Preferences for developing-country exports) but also sustained bruising losses on critical fronts, such as commodity agreements and international monetary reform (Toye and Toye, 2004). While UNCTAD II in 1968 and UNCTAD III in 1972 produced little in the way of progress on the G-77 agenda, the developing countries nevertheless appeared to ratchet up their rhetoric in the early 1970s. In April 1972, Mexican President Luis Echeverría proposed that the UN undertake the drafting of a Charter on the Economic Rights and Duties of States, which would include, among other tenets, the right of states to the full exercise of national sovereignty over natural resources.

Events in the early 1970s, most importantly the vertiginous increase in the price of oil engineered by OPEC, created a perception on the part of several key G-77 members that the balance of international power had tilted in their favor. This newfound confidence was manifest in the call by President Boumedienne of Algeria (acting in his capacity as President of the Group of Non-Aligned States) for a special session of the United Nations 'with a view to establishing a new system of relations based on equality and common interests of all states' (Marshall, 1994). Although the industrialized countries wanted to confine the meeting's agenda to the issue of energy, they were anxious to bring the oil-exporting nations to the table, and realized that engagement over a broader range of development issues was the price to be paid (Gosovic and Ruggie, 1976, p. 321). Their agreement to the proposed session further emboldened the G-77, and the bloc's increasing radicalism culminated in the contentious Sixth Special Session of the General Assembly in spring 1974.

Appropriately enough, the Session opened with a two-hour address from President Boumedienne, who as an active player in OPEC aptly embodied the North's oil crisis-induced anxiety. In his speech, Boumedienne argued that 'a profound reorganization of economic relations between rich and poor countries' was necessary to overcome the continued dominance of 'colonialist and imperial powers' in the Third World. That this reorganization would feature some element of redistribution was strongly implied by his observation that the 'allocation of world resources' was the central issue to be addressed between developed and developing countries (Haight, 1975, p. 592).

As its *pièce de resistance*, the Sixth Special Session featured the adoption of UN resolution 3201, which declared the establishment of a new international economic order. This new order would be based on

> equity, sovereign equality, interdependence, common interest and cooperation among all states irrespective of their economic and social systems, which shall correct inequalities and redress existing injustices, making it possible to eliminate the widening gap between all the developed and the developing countries and ensure steadily accelerating economic and social development in peace and justice for present and future generations.

The NIEO platform contained 20 rather wide-ranging principles, including the inalienable right to 'permanent sovereignty of every State over its natural resources and all economic properties . . . including the right to nationalization or transfer of ownership to its nationals'. Resolution 3201 was adopted without a vote, despite considerable reservations on the part of some developed countries. It was followed by resolution 3202, Programme of Action on the Establishment of a New International Economic Order. This second resolution, also adopted in May 1974, outlined measures that should be taken to realize the NIEO, including reform of primary commodity trade and regulation and control of multinationals.

In December 1974, the General Assembly further registered its support for the NIEO agenda by passing the Charter on the Economic Rights and Duties of States that President Echeverria had proposed two years earlier. Affirming that freedom of action in domestic economic affairs is an element of meaningful sovereignty for developing countries, article 7 of the Charter declares that each state is reserved the 'rights and responsibilities to choose its means and goals of development, fully to mobilize resources, to implement progressive economic and social reforms and to ensure the full participation of its people in the process and benefits of development' (quoted in Brower and Tepe, 1975, p. 312). Unlike the NIEO resolution at the Sixth Special Session, which was adopted without a vote, the Charter was opposed by six developed countries (including the UK and the US), with 10 more OECD countries abstaining (Chatterjee, 1991, p. 672).

The themes of recognition and redistribution run throughout the text of the Charter. Article 17, for example, recognizes that: 'International cooperation for development is the shared goal and common duty of all States.' The implications of this formulation were underscored by Mexican ambassador Castañeda, the chair of the working group that had been appointed to draft the Charter. When presenting the document to the General Assembly, Castañeda emphasized that the rules, rights, and duties codified in the Charter were necessary for realizing the NIEO. Developed countries would also benefit from this new order, Castañeda argued, since the dividend of development—international peace and stability—was to be enjoyed by all nations. However, action was required to redress global inequality and confront 'the growing realization that the poverty of some created the wealth of others' (Haight, 1975, p. 596).

By the end of 1974, the United Nations had approved three resolutions outlining the G-77's challenge to the status quo: the Declaration on the Establishment of a New International Economic Order (resolution 3201), the Programme of Action on the Establishment of a New International Economic Order (resolution 3202), and the Charter of the Economic Rights and Duties of States (resolution 3281). These were followed by a fourth resolution, Development and International Cooperation (resolution 3362), passed in September 1975 during the

Seventh Special Session of the General Assembly. These four documents sketch out the position of the developing country coalition with regard to the NIEO agenda, enumerating seven primary areas on which progress was necessary. First was the issue of commodity price stabilization in the form of negotiated price floors. Second were preferential tariffs and increased access to Northern markets for developing country manufactures. Third, the G-77 countries sought 'an expansion and acceleration of foreign assistance, which, in their view, was transformed from being charity to being compensation, a rebate to the Third World for the years of declining commodity purchasing power' (Bello, 1998, p. 209). Fourth was alleviation of the debt burden. Reform of multilateral institutions (chiefly the World Bank and IMF) in order to increase the voice of the Third World was the fifth action item on the NIEO agenda. Sixth, various forms of developing country protectionism deemed necessary to promote autonomous industrialization through import substitution were to be legitimated, including increased control of multinational corporations in the Third World. The seventh and related point was an enhancement of technology transfer from the North to the South (Doyle, 1983).

The NIEO combined an emphasis on the prerogative of sovereign states to pursue the developmental strategies they freely chose with the conviction that far-reaching changes in the global political economy were necessary to level the playing field between the First and Third Worlds. The G-77 maintained that the United Nations should play a leadership role in implementing the necessary reforms, since its Charter enjoined that body to 'promote the economic advancement and social progress of all peoples'. This claim was combined with an argument about the rights and duties of sovereign states to aid in each other's economic development, buttressed by a normative appeal to the moral obligation of richer countries to their less-developed counterparts (Murphy, 1983; Rothstein, 1984).

While much of the G-77's rhetoric presented the NIEO agenda as a fundamental transformation of the existing regime, the developing countries also emphasized the continuities between the new order and the old. Rather than a departure from its mandate, the NIEO represented an opportunity for the United Nations to realize its objectives in a meaningful way. Furthermore, there was precedent for asserting the obligations of states towards other UN members in need. As the G-77 underscored in its arguments for the NIEO, such a claim had been advanced by the UN Relief and Rehabilitation Administration at the end of World War II with regard to the reconstruction of war-torn Europe.

Arguments for the NIEO thus evoked change and continuity simultaneously. This was made possible by the fact that in the period after 1945, North and South alike regarded developmentalism as the dominant paradigm for understanding the relationship between economic growth and social change. Its hegemony was such that by the time the United Nations 'declared that the 1970s would be the "decade of development," the term and the objective seemed virtually a piety' (Wallerstein, 2005, p. 124). However, the fragility of this consensus was revealed by the G-77's challenge to the status quo, which mobilized the language of developmentalism in criticizing the inequities that structured the international economy, and especially the extant trading regime. Thus, while the NIEO was carefully framed as an extension of post-war development discourse, it also revealed the limits of developmentalism because it cast into sharp relief a fundamental tension within it—a contradiction between the universal acceptance of development as a legitimate end to be pursued by states, and profound disagreement about the means necessary for achieving that goal.

Monitoring the activities of transnational or multinational corporations (MNCs) was a prominent issue on the G-77 agenda. Resolution 3201 declaring the NIEO called for the 'regulation and supervision of the activities of transnational corporations by taking measures in the interest of the national economies of the countries where such transnational corporations operate on the basis of the full sovereignty of those countries'. One group of Latin American countries had already taken decisive action with regard to MNCs by adopting an investment code known as Decision 24. This code, which was promulgated by the countries of the Andean Pact in December 1970, restricted foreign direct investment into the signatory countries in order to avoid competition between multinationals and foreign firms.[1] It also limited profit remittances and precluded companies with majority foreign ownership from the benefits of the Andean Common Market, which had been created one year earlier. The Andean Pact countries 'actively sought at the UN the means to internationalize this regional code' (Hamilton, 1984, p. 4), and in this endeavor they were joined by Brazil and Mexico as the two most significant host economies for MNC operations in Latin America. Their efforts were furthered by events in the early 1970s, which served to heighten concerns about the role of multinationals in developing countries and generate additional support for MNC regulation.

Putting the NIEO into Action: The Code of Conduct on Transnational Enterprises

The proximate origins of the UN Draft Code of Conduct on Transnational Enterprises can be found in complaints brought before the Economic and Social Council (ECOSOC) in the summer of 1972 by the Chilean representative to ECOSOC (Dell, 1990). In response to these concerns, the Secretary General appointed a Group of Eminent Persons to study and report on the role of MNCs (which were generally referred to as transnational corporations in UN nomenclature) in the world economy, focusing on their activities in the global South. In 1974, the Group submitted its report in the form of a UN publication entitled *The Impact of Multinational Corporations on Development and in International Relations*.

One of the Group's principal recommendations was fulfilled in December 1974 with the adoption of ECOSOC Resolution 1913, which created both a Commission on Transnational Corporations and a subsidiary body called the Information and Research Centre on Transnational Corporations, which was to be an independent body within the UN Secretariat.[2] The Centre was expected to 'develop a comprehensive information system on the activities of transnational corporations by gathering information made available by Governments and other sources, and by analyzing and disseminating such information to all Governments'. It was also charged 'to conduct research on various political, legal, economic and social aspects relating to transnational corporations, including work which might be useful for the elaboration of a code of conduct'.[3] The creation of such a code was another of the key recommendations issued by the Group of Eminent Persons. In measured language, the Report observed that

> the self-regulatory effect of multinational corporations should not be over-emphasized. Although multinational corporations are exceedingly effective initiators and organizers of economic activity and growth, they are also reactors to forces and institutions which define the political environment in which they operate. Multinational corporations, then, must be directed towards and constrained from certain types of activity, if they are to serve well the social purposes of development. (UN, 1974, p. 31)

In preparing its recommendations, the Group of Eminent Persons was able to draw on a growing body of academic research on multinational corporations. Some scholars argued that multinational corporations permitted the most effective allocation and use of resources (Caves, 1974; Kindleberger, 1969), while others underscored their growing power, and predicted a future in which global corporations would rival nation states (Ball, 1968; Vernon, 1971). A number of assessments were far from sanguine about the nature of MNCs and their impact on host countries. Multinationals were described in these various indictments as 'monopoly capital' (Baran and Sweezy, 1966) with 'global reach' (Barnet and Miller, 1974), many of which spanned sectors as 'transnational conglomerates' (Hymer, 1972). Collectively, this body of work addresses a question on the minds of diplomats, policymakers, and academics alike— the extent to which MNCs were better understood as engines of development or exploiters of Third World resources, both human and material.

Many observers agreed that the growth of multinationals warranted some kind of international guidelines to regulate their activity, and several argued that a carefully crafted instrument could benefit multinational corporations as much as the governments that hosted them (Davidow and Chiles, 1978; McCulloch, 1977). As early as 1970, two defenders of MNCs called for the creation of an 'agreement based on a limited set of universally accepted principles' (Goldberg and Kindleberger, 1970, p. 323). Writing later that same decade, another observed that 'MNCs are a good thing, but need to have their international conduct regulated by explicit codes and legal sanctions' (Bhagwati, 1977, p. 20).

Expressions of support for MNC regulation could even be found within the US government. The most prominent advocate of this view was George Ball, Under Secretary of State during the Johnson administration. Although Ball believed that the most vital objective of US foreign policy was the global expansion of capitalism, he also acknowledged that conflicts were likely to arise between MNCs and governments, and he assumed that resolution of such conflicts would require a regulatory framework. Specifically, he advocated that a supranational body be made responsible 'for chartering companies to operate in countries that are signatories of a negotiated multinational treaty consisting of established laws concerning international companies' (cited in Cohen et al., 1979, p. 9). The Nixon administration also voiced measured support for a code of conduct. In a statement read before the Seventh Special Session of the General Assembly in 1975 (at which the US representative reiterated his country's general opposition to the NIEO), US Secretary of State Henry Kissinger nevertheless identified a 'balanced code' (i.e., one applying to host country governments as well as MNCs) as one of the G-77's proposals that the United States was willing to entertain.[4]

As Kissinger's comments suggest, from the perspective of the developed countries the regulation of multinational corporations was among the more palatable planks of the NIEO platform. Writing in the *American Journal of International Law* in 1978, Davidow and Chiles expressed this view:

> In the past few years, developing countries have crystallized many of their demands in the form of comprehensive proposals to adjust global economic relationships into a 'new international economic order.' In principle, the current administration supports changes in the international economic order. Although the United States has been unable to agree to many of the specific demands made by the developing countries . . . certain of the proposals . . . have been viewed as acceptable. Among these is the formulation of a code or codes of conduct covering various aspects of international commerce, particularly the activities of transnational enterprises. (p. 248)

Supporters and detractors of the NIEO alike generally interpreted the creation of the Commission and Centre on Transnational Corporations as a development that advanced the G-77's broader agenda. According to Philippe de Seynes, Under Secretary General of the Department of Economic and Social Affairs, '[T]he decision of 1973 to create a focal point within the UN systems for transnational corporations, must be viewed as a landmark in the development of the institutions needed for a New International Economic Order' (1976, p. 15). Indeed, virtually every article that was written about the Code over the next 20 years includes a similar reference to the project's origins in the NIEO (e.g., Fatouros, 1980; Hamilton, 1984; Muchlinksi, 1995).

Typical in this respect is Nixson's (1983, p. 84) formulation that the Code initiative 'is best seen as part of, and as a consequence of, the demands of the L.D.C.s [less developed countries] for a so-called New International Economic Order'.

At its first meeting in March 1975, the Commission decided to make the formulation of a Code of Conduct the priority item on its agenda. Representatives to the Commission from the G-77 countries outlined 21 main areas of concern for the proposed instrument to address, while the industrialized countries countered by enumerating 23 concerns of their own, many dealing with issues of expropriation and compensation (Feld, 1980). At its second session in 1976, an Intergovernmental Working Group was appointed to prepare a draft Code, with work on the draft beginning in earnest in January 1977.

Although some initial appraisals were highly optimistic, predicting that the Code would be completed in a matter of months (Sauvant, 1977), disagreements between the members of the Working Group quickly emerged. The first disagreement arose from the fundamental question of to whom the Code would be addressed. Developed countries insisted that the Code should be a two-part instrument, with one section outlining the responsibilities of MNCs towards governments, and a second section prescribing guidelines for appropriate treatment of multi-nationals by host country governments. Developing countries objected, arguing that this would place MNCs and governments, symbolically or juridically, on the same level. This was unacceptable to the G-77, since the Southern countries understood the Code project, and indeed the entire NIEO agenda, as an opportunity to affirm the sovereignty of the nation-state as the ontological foundation of international relations, and to secure the integrity of those states as the unchallenged principals of the interstate system. However, some industrialized states were adamant that a two-part code was a *sine qua non* of their partici-pation in the exercise, and by 1980 the developing country representatives to the Commission had agreed to draft a two-part (or as the advocates of this position called it, a 'balanced') code.[5]

Between 1977 and 1982, 11 separate negotiating sessions of the Intergovernmental Working Group were held, resulting in a draft Code that was presented to the full Commis-sion. Well over half of the paragraphs in this annotated Code were bracketed, indicating that consensus was lacking within the Group and that additional negotiation in the Commission would be necessary. Given the work that remained to be done, the Commission decided to convene a special session in early 1983 that would be open to all states, with the express objective of completing the Code. This goal was not met, and although similar sessions were held annually for the next several years, progress on the outstanding issues remained elusive (Acquaah, 1980).

The provisions addressing expropriation and nationalization ultimately proved the most intractable. Ostensibly the disagreement centered on the following questions: Under what con-ditions might expropriation of foreign assets be appropriate, and in the event of such actions, what formula should be used to determine the amount of compensation paid to the affected parties? The developed countries wanted a reference to what they asserted was 'customary inter-national law', including specific language about the right of foreign investors to 'prompt, ade-quate, and effective compensation'. In contrast, many of the G-77 countries maintained that the laws of the host country must prevail in the event of a conflict.

From the perspective of the developing countries, this particular debate regarding expropria-tion and compensation was rooted in a more general disagreement about the relationship between domestic and international law. The G-77 framed the Northern position—that inter-national law was the ultimate recourse in the event of an investment dispute—as a threat to the sovereignty of Southern states, just as they had when the same disagreement arose during debate on the Charter of the Economic Rights and Duties of States. At the time of the General Assembly's vote on the Charter, the Mexican ambassador specifically rejected as 'intolerable' the proposition that 'extra-national' procedures or legal systems could trump domestic law and be made binding on host country governments in the event of a dispute with foreign investors. In the context of the Code negotiations, the Latin American countries were particularly intransigent on this point, and there was a shared sense within the G-77 that the Northern states had failed to recognize that the South had already made a major concession in agreeing to a two-part instrument—in other words, a Code *on* Transnationals as opposed to the Code *for* Transnationals that they had originally envisioned:

> They were not prepared to go so far as to allow governments and TNCs to be placed on an equal footing with one another in terms of mutual obligations. To them it seemed clear that TNCs must accept unconditionally the sovereignty of the countries in which they operate and there could not be, even in principle, any counterpart obligation of governments of equal weight or significance. (Dell, 1990, p. 83)

By 1980, members of the Economic and Social Council were expressing dissatisfaction with the pace of the Code-drafting effort, noting in an ECOSOC resolution (1980/60) that the 'progress made in the formulation of a code of conduct has not met the expectations of all'. The Commission continued to negotiate the Code throughout the 1980s, with ECOSOC offering periodic expressions of impatient support. However, over the course of that decade, assessments of the Code's prospects for success grew increasingly sober. As early as 1980, one close observer concluded that many of the developed countries 'under the leadership of the United States are forcefully resisting the efforts to give any real effectiveness to this (or any other) code of conduct' (Fatouros, 1980, p. 106). Several years later, another opined that it is 'fair to conclude that all negotiating groups are not hopeful that a code will materialize' (Hamilton, 1984). Although supporters of the Code project pointed out that full agreement had been reached on two-thirds of the Code's provisions by the mid-1980s, the distance separating the Northern and Southern positions on the remaining one-third, which dealt primarily with treatment of MNCs by host country governments, was substantial and did not diminish over time. Furthermore, the solidarity and strength of the G-77 had waned considerably by the end of the 1970s, and the developing country representatives at the Commission were characterized as 'unorganized and uncertain' (Fatouros, 1980, p. 124).

Work on the Code extended into yet another decade, with a new round of negotiations beginning in January 1990. By the end of May a new draft was finished, and a final vote on the Code was scheduled for that November. Around this time, the director of the Centre on Transnational Corporations characterized the negotiations as 'near completion', due in part to a new receptivity on the part of the developing countries to the OECD's suggested standards regarding the treatment of foreign investors (Hansen and Aranda, 1990). However, this rather optimistic assessment contrasted with the views of US officials, who expressed continued dissatisfaction with the Code. In Congressional hearings on the Code, US Deputy Assistant Secretary of State Jane Becker testified that the United States would not support the Code when it was brought to a vote at the United Nations. Characterizing the instrument as 'obsolete', she noted that it would provide 'only marginal benefit to the United States and American investors', and that it did not provide any protections which could not be secured through the more desirable options of bilateral investment treaties and the GATT (Bureau of National Affairs, 1990, pp. 1584–1585). The vote that was scheduled for November 1990 was postponed and rescheduled for 1991, but this deadline for finalizing the Code came and went as well. By this point, the Code was regarded by many as a relic of the NIEO period, increasingly incongruous in the new geopolitical landscape of the post-Cold War world, and so divorced from reality in recent times that the attention of most Government representatives and international business leaders has shifted elsewhere' (Kline, 1990, p. 2).

Negotiation of the Code was finally suspended in 1992. Announcing this decision, the president of the 46th General Assembly explained that 'delegations felt that the changed international economic environment and the importance attached to encouraging foreign investment required a fresh approach' (quoted in Tesner, 2000, p. 23). The Commission's counterpart in the Secretariat, the New York-based Centre on Transnational Corporations, was dispersed. Some of its staff were relocated to Geneva and folded into UNCTAD's Division on Investment and Technology, where they launched the annual *World Investment Report*, a new flagship publication for UNCTAD that reflected well this change in attitude.

From Code to Compact: Corporate Citizens Confront Globalization's Challenges

Only a few years after the Code project was abandoned, multinationals were once again on the agenda at the United Nations. The Global Compact (GC) initiative was announced by the Secretary General in January 1999 at the World Economic Forum, and officially launched in New York on 26 July of the following year. Recognizing that '[b]usiness, trade and investment are essential pillars for prosperity and peace,' the Global Compact is 'a framework for businesses that are committed to aligning their operations and strategies with 10 universally accepted principles in the areas of human rights, labour, the environment and anti-corruption. As the world's largest, global corporate citizenship initiative, the Global Compact is first and foremost concerned with exhibiting and building the social legitimacy of business and markets'.[6]

This goal is to be achieved through securing the commitment of participating businesses to observe the principles of the Compact in their own operations, thereby diffusing them throughout the world to all the locations where these companies have a presence. While the United Nations acts as the 'authoritative convener and facilitator' of the Global Compact, the Compact itself includes

> all the relevant social actors: governments, who defined the principles on which the initiative is based; companies, whose actions it seeks to influence; labour, in whose hands the concrete process of global production takes place; [and] civil society organizations, representing the wider community of stakeholders.)

In 2007, the GC website listed some 3,000 corporations from over 100 countries as members. A company chief can secure this status by sending a letter to the Secretary General of the United Nations, in which the chief executive officer expresses an intent to make the 'Compact and its principles . . . part of strategy, culture, and day-to-day operations'. Becoming a member does not entail any specific commitments or obligations, although participating companies are required to report periodically on the measures they are taking to promote the principles of the Compact. This reporting requirement is intended to introduce an element of accountability into the initiative, perhaps in response to denunciations of the GC as a toothless public relations operation allowing companies the costless benefit of association with the United Nations. In October 2006, 335 companies were delisted from the Global Compact after missing two consecutive deadlines for progress reporting (Kell et al., 2007).

Describing the GC as qualitatively different from other efforts to promote responsible corporate behavior past and present, its supporters underscore that the initiative 'is not and does not aspire to be a legally-binding code of conduct'. Emphasis of this point is important because some companies 'fear that even signing a letter of intent to comply with the ten principles could have legal repercussions. In response, the Global Compact has worked with the American Bar Association to develop a "litigation-proof" letter of commitment' (Kell et al., 2007, p. 4).[7] In other words, UN officials, keen to assuage fears regarding the possible legal exposure that might result from signing on to a UN initiative, assure corporations that the Global Compact does not commit signatories to any substantive commitments.

Advocates of the GC differentiate the voluntarist ethos of the project from 'previous attempts to clamp down on global commerce through "command and control" regulation' (Kell et al., 2007, p. 2). Yet what differentiates the Global Compact from earlier efforts is not simply its status as a voluntary initiative that companies are invited to join. Rather, as a 'case of non-state actors reaching agreement with an international organization' (Coleman, 2003, p. 354), it bypasses states altogether. The Global Compact, administered through the office of the Secretary General, exists independently of any inter-governmental body. Therefore, the opportunities of member states to participate in the initiative would appear to be limited, as would their ability to scrutinize the implementation or efficacy of the program.

In an interesting and largely approving review of the shift from Code to Compact, Coleman attempts to establish a line of continuity between these projects:

> A surprising outcome is that the TNC code of conduct, apparently dropped from the UN agenda by 1996, returned so shortly in the form of the Global Compact. With an end to attempts at constructing a policing code, UN considerations of TNC activity could have disappeared from its agenda indefinitely. Although the players and the process changed radically, the prescriptive code of conduct is doubtless the antecedent of the voluntary Global Compact. (2003, p. 350)

Indeed, but to understand the precise way in which the Code is an antecedent of the Compact, it is necessary to underscore the differences, not the similarities, between these two projects. The Code of Conduct, and the broader NIEO agenda of which it was part, was an effort by the G-77 to define development as the politics of recognition and redistribution. It rested ultimately, if tendentiously, on an ideology of Third World globalism, however fragile the coalition sustaining this solidarity proved to be. And the United Nations, as the institutional embodiment of the sovereign equality of states, was viewed as the appropriate vehicle for this agenda of structural reform. Rather than pursuing development, what the Global Compact seeks are solutions to the challenges of globalization. Multinationals, incarnated as corporate citizens, are conceived, alongside governments, as equal stakeholders in this collective effort.

Advocates of corporate social responsibility regard the Global Compact as a pragmatic attempt to harness the power of international business for progressive ends. This appears to be Coleman's (2003) view, and he emphasizes that, as a 'Secretariat-driven process in which the nation-states and its UN representatives play no part' (p. 350), the Global Compact is able to surmount the 'stultified inter-nation negotiations' (p. 354) that plagued the Code effort. However, it is worth revisiting those 'stultified negotiations' as part of the effort to understand how we got here, and it is critical to grasp how the Compact seeks to move development out of the realm of politics, and into a global public domain where the logic of mutually beneficial partnerships would seem to render anachronistic earlier and largely forgotten struggles by Southern states to advance claims for recognition and redistribution as necessary and constitutive elements of meaningful development.

Notes

1 Original signatories to the Cartagena Agreement which established the Andean Pact included Bolivia, Chile, Colombia, Ecuador, and Peru. Venezuela joined in 1973.
2 The Commission was composed of representatives from 48 countries.

3   Members of the Group of Eminent Persons from Germany, Sweden, and the US disagreed with some of the recommendations that they felt encouraged excessive government intervention (Dell, 1990). The Swiss member of the Group was particularly critical and voiced strong opposition to the proposed Code of Conduct (Baade, 1980). Upon release of the Report, the US government responded to the Group's recommendations by noting that it did not support any UN effort with regard to multinationals that was 'regulative in nature'. The fact that this pronouncement was issued even before drafting of the Code began led some analysts to question if the project might appear 'doomed from the very start' (Acquaah, 1980, pp. 159–160).

4   Kissinger (1975, p. 432) further noted that because in the developing world there is often 'no substitute for their [MNCs'] ability to marshal capital, management skills, technology and initiative', the controversy over their role and conduct was itself an obstacle to economic development.

5   This decision was confirmed in ECOSOC resolution 198-/60, 24 July, 1980.

6   See http://www.unglobalcompact.org. The Global Compact's 10 principles 'enjoy universal consensus' and are derived from three UN documents—the Universal Declaration of Human Rights, the ILO's Declaration on Fundamental Principles and Rights at Work, and the Rio Declaration on Environment and Development.

7   The authors note that this is a particularly important consideration for corporations 'based in the litigious American market' (Kell et al., 2007, p. 4). Currently companies headquartered in North America account for fewer than 4% of GC members.

References

Acquaah, K. (1980) *International Regulation of Transnational Corporations* (New York: Praeger).

Annan, K. (1999) Address to the US Chamber of Commerce, 8 June, Washington DC, http://global/policy/igc.org/socecon/tncs/annan1.htm.

Baade, H. (1980) Codes of conduct for multinational enterprises: an introductory survey, in N. Horn (ed.) *Legal Problems of Codes of Conduct for Multinational Enterprises* (Boston, MA: Kluwer).

Ball, G. (1968) Cosmocorp: the importance of being stateless, *Columbia Journal of World Business*, 2(6), pp. 25–30.

Baran, P. & Sweezy, P. (1966) *Monopoly Capital: An Essay on the American Economic and Social Order* (Harmondsworth: Penguin).

Barnet, R. & Miller, R. (1974) *Global Reach: The Power of the Multinational Corporations* (New York: Simon & Schuster).

Bello, W. (1998) Bretton Woods institutions and the demise of the UN development system, in A. Paolini & A. Parvis (eds) *Between Sovereignty and Global Governance: The United Nations, the State, and Civil Society* (New York: St. Martin's Press).

Bhagwati, J. (1977) Introduction, in J. N. Bhagwati (ed.) *The New International Economic Order: The North–South Debate* (Cambridge, MA: MIT Press).

Brower, C. N. & Tepe, J. B., Jr. (1975) The Charter of Economic Rights and Duties of States: a reflection or rejection of international law, *International Lawyer*, 9(2), pp. 295–318.

Bureau of National Affairs (1990) *International Trade Reporter*, 17 October, pp. 1584–1585.

Callinicos, A. (2001) *Against the Third Way* (Cambridge: Polity).

Caves, R. (1974) *International Trade, International Investment, and Imperfect Markets* (Princeton, NJ: Princeton University Press).

Chatterjee, S. K. (1991) The Charter of Economic Rights and Duties of States: an evaluation after 15 years, *International and Comparative Law Quarterly*, 40, pp. 669–684.

Cohen, R. B., Felton, N., Nkosi, M. & van Liere, J. (1977) *The Multinational Corporation, A Radical Approach: Papers by Stephen Herbert Hymer* (New York: Cambridge University Press).

Coleman, D. (2003) The United Nations and transnational corporations: from an inter-state to a "beyond-state" model of engagement, *Global Society*, 17(4), pp. 339–357.

Da Costa, D. & McMichael, P. (2007) The poverty of the global order, *Globalizations*, 4(4), pp. 588–602.

Davidow, J. & Chiles, L. (1978) The United States and the issue of the binding or voluntary nature of international codes of conduct regarding restrictive business practices, *American Journal of International Law*, 72, pp. 247–271.

Dell, S. (1990) *The United Nations and International Business* (Durham, NC: Duke University Press).

De Seynes, P. (1976) Transnational corporations in the framework of a new international economic order, *The CTC Reporter*, 1(1), p. 15.

Doyle, M. (1983) Stalemate in the North–South debate: strategies and the New International Economic Order, *World Politics*, 35(3), pp. 426–464.

Fatouros, A. (1980) The UN Code of Conduct on Transnational Corporations: a critical discussion of the first drafting phase, in N. Horn (ed.) *Legal Problems of Codes of Conduct for Multinational Enterprises* (Boston, MA: Kluwer).

Feld, W. J. (1980) *Multinational Corporations and U.N. Politics* (New York: Pergamon Press).

Goldberg, P. & Kindleberger, C. (1970) Toward a GATT for investment: a proposal for supervision of the international corporation, *Law and Policy in International Business*, 2, pp. 295–323.

Gosovic, B. & Ruggie, J. G. (1976) On the creation of a New International Economic Order: issue linkage and the Seventh Special Session of the UN General Assembly, *International Organization*, 30(2), pp. 309–345.

Haight, G. W. (1975) The New International Economic Order and the Charter of Economic Rights and Duties of States, *International Lawyer*, 9(4), pp. 591–604.

Hamilton, G. (1984) *The Control of Multinationals: What Future for International Codes of Conduct in the 1980s?* (Geneva: Institute for Research and Information on Multinationals).

Hansen, P. & Aranda, V. (1990) An emerging international framework for transnational corporations, *Fordham International Law Journal*, 14, pp. 881–891.

Hymer, S. (1972) The internationalization of capital, *Journal of Economic Issues*, 172, pp. 91–11.

Kell, G., Slaughter, A.-M. & Hale, T. (2007) Silent reform through the Global Compact, *UN Chronicle*, 1, pp. 1–5.

Kindleberger, C. (1969) *American Business Abroad* (New Haven, CT: Yale University Press).

Kissinger, H. (1975) Remarks to the Seventh Special Session of the General Assembly. *Department of State Bulletin*, no. 1891.

Kline, J. (1990) A new environment for the Code, *CTC Reporter*, 29(Spring), pp. 2–6.

Marshall, P. (1994) Whatever happened to the NIEO? *Round Table*, 331, pp. 331–340.

McCulloch, R. (1977) Economic policy in the United Nations: a new international economic order?, in K. Brunner & A. H. Meltzer (eds) *International Organizations, National Policies and Economic Development* (Amsterdam: North-Holland Publishing Company).

Muchlinksi, P. (1995) *Multinational Enterprises and the Law* (Cambridge. MA: Blackwell).

Murphy, C. (1983) What the Third World wants: an interpretation of the development and meaning of the New International Economic Order ideology, *International Studies Quarterly*, 27(1), pp. 55–76.

Nixson, F.I. (1983) Controlling the transnationals? Political economy and the UN Code of Conduct, *International Journal of the Sociology of Law*, 11(1), 83–103.

Rodrik, D. (1994) The rush to free trade in the developing world: why so late? Why now? Will it last?, in S. Haggard & S. Webb (eds) *Voting for Reform: Democracy, Political Liberalization, and Economic Adjustment* (New York: Oxford University Press).

Rothstein, R. (1984) Regime-creation by a coalition of the weak: lessons from the NIEO and the Integrated Programme for Commodities, *International Studies Quarterly*, 28(3), pp. 307–328.

Ruggie, J. (2004) Reconstituting the global public domain—issues, actors, and practices. *European Journal of International Relations*, 10(4), pp. 499–531.

Sauvant, K. P. (1977) Toward the New International Economic Order, in K. P. Sauvant & H. Hasenpflug (eds) *The New International Economic Order: Confrontation or Cooperation between North and South?* (Boulder, CO: Westview Press).

Soederberg, S. (2007) Taming corporations or buttressing market-led development? A critical assessment of the Global Compact, *Globalizations*, 4(4), pp. 500–513.

Somers, M. and Fred Block (2005) From poverty to peversity: ideas, markets and institutions over 200 years of welfare debate, *American Sociological Review*, 70(2), pp. 260–287.

Tesner, S. (2000) *The United Nations and Business: A Partnership Recovered* (London: Macmillan).

Toye, J. & Toye, R. (2004) *The U.N. and Global Political Economy: Trade, Finance, and Development* (Bloomington: Indiana University Press).

UN (1974) *The Impact of Multinational Corporations on Development and in International Relations*, doc. E/5500/Rev.1, 51/ESA/6. (New York: United Nations).

Vernon, R. (1971) *Sovereignty at Bay* (New York: Basic Books).

Wallerstein, I. (2005) After developmentalism and globalization, what? *Social Forces*, 83(3), pp. 1263–1278.

Taming Corporations or Buttressing Market-Led Development? A Critical Assessment of the Global Compact

SUSANNE SOEDERBERG

Introduction

The growing social and economic power of transnational corporations (TNCs), domiciled across the globe (cf. Sklair, 2002), has been marked by an underlying Polanyian tension, which assumes a more acute expression in Third World countries (Munck, 2006; Polanyi, 1957).

On the one hand, the past several decades of neoliberal governance, and its emphasis on the privatization of state-owned corporations and services, liberalization of trade and investment, and so forth, has led to greater dependence in Third World states and economies on private capital investment, especially in the form of foreign direct investment (FDI). Consider the fact that TNCs have come to replace official aid as the key source of development finance for Third World countries (World Bank, 2006). Through conditional lending practices, or structural adjustment policies (SAPs), the World Bank and the IMF have actively and aggressively encouraged Third World governments to create opportune investment climates for foreign capitalists. The latter have also been referred to as 'good governance' practices, including sound macroeconomic fundamentals, stable legal regimes, low levels of unionization and corporate taxation, lax environmental regulations, legal structures to protect private property, and so forth (Soederberg, 2004; UNCTAD, 2005; World Bank, 2005).

According to the neoliberal development paradigm, these market-friendly policies are believed to attract and retain FDI and financial flows (equity financing), which, with the 'correct' policy mix, will lead to economic growth. The latter is usually viewed as generating universal benefits, including social protection, which, in turn, will eradicate poverty. In this development paradigm, excess market regulation, especially in the form of constraining the profit-seeking activities of TNCs, is counter-productive, given that the market comprises rational actors who, largely through the means of competition and information-sharing, will create a robust and stable economy.

On the other side of the Polanyian equation lies deep-seated suspicion of the ability of the self-regulating market to ensure adequate levels of social protection. For a growing number of groups, individuals, and organizations, the increased power of TNCs in the global South has been accompanied by negative features that have served to threaten the social fabric of societies (Davis, 2006; Harvey, 2000; Saad-Filho and Johnston, 2005). The general discontent with mounting corporate power in the global South, and intensifying forms of commodification of basic services and natural resources, has led to various forms of resistance—all of which appear simultaneously at numerous spaces of political organization, such as local, national, and international These struggles of resistance to the neoliberal-led development model associate it with a litany of controversial and high-profile cases of corporate abuses against human rights, and environmental and labour standards (anti-union violence, child labour abuses, pollution, water depletion, and so forth). This has led to much suspicion of neoliberal-inspired forms of corporate-led development, and increased expressions of resistance and contestation in both the developed and developing worlds in the hopes of introducing policies aimed at ensuring social protection from market actors.

Until now, the official response to the Polanyian tension has not been to revise, and thus find fault in, the predominant neoliberal policies; instead, international policymakers and organizations have prescribed greater adherence to market-led solutions so as to encourage more, rather than less, foreign investment in Third World countries. Indeed, economic growth driven by the self-regulating market is stubbornly viewed as the necessary component in achieving 'development' and, in turn, winning the war against poverty (World Bank, 2005; cf. Escobar, 1995; McMichael, 2004). The fact that the dominance of the self-regulating market over legally mandated forms of social protection has continued to be called into question by numerous social forces—thereby potentially threatening to delegitimate the neoliberal hegemony of development—has not been lost on policymakers and the business community, however.

In a speech delivered at the World Economic Forum, whose members are the leading 1,000 corporations, in January 1999, the Secretary General of the United Nations, Kofi Annan, cautioned business leaders of an imminent backlash against globalization unless it was 'embedded in social values' and reflected the 'common objectives' of all segments of the world's population. Annan challenged the business community to join the UN in its aim to forge stronger social and environmental pillars to sustain the global economy in the form of a Global Compact (Compact or GC hereafter) (Ruggie, 2000). In an attempt to marry social values with common objectives, the United Nations operationalized its present CSR initiative in 2000, which, with 2,300 participating corporations, represents not only the world's largest, voluntary-based CSR strategy, but also the quintessence of mainstream conceptualizations of global governance. The Compact, for instance, is a 'coalition to make globalization work for all' involving corporations, leaders of labour and civic groups, and a consortium of NGOs from both industrialized and developing countries (Global Policy Forum, 2000).

According to its website, the Compact seeks to advance responsible corporate citizenship so that business can be part of the solution to the challenges of globalization. Within the parameters of the Compact, it is assumed that a more sustainable and inclusive global economy can be achieved if business enters into partnership with other social actors: states across the globe, who helped define the Compact's principles; companies, whose actions it seeks to influence; five UN agencies;[1] labour, in whose hands the concrete process of global production takes place; and not-for-profit, non-governmental organizations (NGOs), representing the wider community of stakeholders.[2]

In accordance with the dominant, free-market paradigm of neoliberalism, supporters of the GC believe that voluntary measures are more effective and viable in achieving socially accountable behaviour than regulatory means. Neither governments nor corporations are legally mandated to subscribe to regulations regarding the 10 principles that comprise the Compact, which fall under the headings of human rights, labour rights, the environment, and, more recently, anti-corruption (Ruggie, 2001).[3] Instead, the GC is to function as a 'learning network' that will encourage desirable behaviour in corporations through dialogue with different stakeholders and sharing of information (ibid.). It is hoped that through this non-regulatory, non-state-led arrangement, a 'progressive platform' can create a more inclusive institutional arena in which, and sites from which, a variety of social actors can graft their pursuit of broader social agendas onto the global reach and capacity of TNCs (Ruggie, 2004, p. 503).

To date, the GC, and its ability to bring about progressive change through dialogue around its 10 voluntary codes of conduct, has largely been, with a few exceptions (cf. Bair, 2007), analyzed within the mainstream frameworks of legal and business studies, and international relations theory, or, more specifically, liberal institutionalism, or, more generally, global governance theory (Hocking and Kelly, 2002; Ruggie, 2000, 2002, 2004; Thérien and Pouliot, 2006).[4] As I discuss below, the problem with these analyses of the Compact is that they tend to be firmly rooted in what Robert Cox (1993) refers to as problem-solving theory, as opposed to critical approaches, which would seek to explain social change by making sense of the underlying contradictions and struggles associated with the UN strategy of corporate citizenship.

To address this neglect, I transcend existing mainstream discussions about the GC by moving beyond some assumptions imbued in global governance theorizations. This will largely be accomplished by exploring more closely the Polanyian double-movement from which it emerged and forms of resistance and domination therein. More specifically, I argue that the origins of the GC must be understood first and foremost as a response to the underlying contradiction discussed above, particularly the push for social protection from corporate power and the associated threat to regulate the activities of TNCs in the Third World.[5] The Compact is a capitalist strategy, which has the effect of not only dividing struggle via exclusionary methods, but also co-opting struggle by attempting to depoliticize and exclude the ever-increasing expressions of discontent with corporate transgressions in the global South by relegating what David Harvey refers to as 'spaces of hope' (2000) to bourgeois forms of controlled institutionalized space—both in terms of the concrete space managed by the United Nations and abstract or cyber-space, such as the e-postings where the TNCs showcase their adherence to the guiding principles of the Compact.[6]

Seen from the above perspective, the GC represents what Antonio Gramsci refers to as a passive revolution, in that it is an attempt to freeze the contradictions linked to the growing power of TNCs over everyday life (Lefebvre, 2005) by depoliticizing struggles and paying lip-service to issues of inclusion and participation of a multiplicity of stakeholders in the woolly notion of global governance. The intended effect is not only to legitimize market-led, voluntary forms of CSR as the only viable alternative, thereby discrediting alternative forms of governing corporations primarily through regulatory standards, but also to promote the common-sense understanding that states and societies should seek to enter a compromise with TNCs—witnessed by Ruggie's (2004) insistence, discussed above, that social actors strive to graft their pursuit of broader social agendas onto the 'global reach and capacity' of corporations. The point that Ruggie, like many mainstream global governance theorists, tends to ignore is that the 'global reach and capacity' of corporations is not a natural occurrence driven by the unstoppable forces of globalization, but instead a social construct authored and legitimated by bourgeois states across the globe to serve particular class interests (see Soederberg, 2006).

I develop this argument in four sections. Section one identifies two general assumptions made by global governance theorists when discussing the Compact, and subsequent analytical limitations. The second section discusses resistance to corporate abuses in the developing world and the general anti-globalization backlash against the rising wave of corporate power. The third section demonstrates how the Compact legitimizes and recreates the social power of TNCs by normalizing voluntary codes of conduct and ensuring that radical voices are excluded from participating in the 'learning network', so as to preclude such alternatives as legally-binding rules enforced by states, independent verification teams, and so forth. The fourth section concludes by summarizing the argument and by highlighting some limitations and possibilities for social change *vis-à-vis* the GC.

The Limits to Mainstream Accounts of Global Governance

Since the mid-1990s, global governance has become the dominant framework for making sense of initiatives such as the Compact in the field of international relations, but also within international policy circles (Murphy, 2000). According to an influential policy document, Our Global Neighbourhood, global governance refers

> to the sum of the many ways individuals and institutions, public and private, manage their common affairs. It is a continuing process through which conflicting or diverse interests may be accommodated and co-operative action may be taken. It includes formal institutions and regimes empowered to enforce compliance, as well as informal arrangements that people and institutions either have agreed to or perceive to be in their interests. (Commission on Global Governance, 1995, p. 2)

The Report of the Commission on Global Governance (CGG) goes on to suggest that governance occurs not only at the national and global levels, but also at the local level. At each of these levels of analysis, there is said to be a multiplicity of actors ranging from local producers to TNCs, and from local and international NGOs to largely international organizations. According to the CGG, this understanding of global governance allows for more diversity and more lateral forms of decision-making than the traditional state-centric, top-down perspective that dominated much of the post-war period (CGG, 1995, p. 4). Given the private-public and multileveled nature of the Compact, it is easy to see why some scholars have tended to rely on the wider concept of global governance to make sense of this UN initiative.

Most of these global governance theorizations about the GC are what Robert Cox (1993) refers to as problem-solving as opposed to critical approaches. Problem-solving theories assume that the basic elements of the international system are not subject to fundamental transformation. 'While problem solving theory assumes functional coherence of existing phenomena, critical theory seeks out the sources of contradiction and conflict in these entities and evaluates their potential to change into different patterns' (Cox, 1996, pp. 5–6). Given the problem-solving focus of the mainstream debates about the Compact, they fail to acknowledge and interrogate several key assumptions that act to blur the capitalist nature of the initiative (Soederberg, 2006). In what follows, I identify several important assumptions imbued in global governance approaches and, by extension, the Compact. This exercise is useful, as it helps us to identify the limitations and possibilities for change with regard to the UN initiative.

The first common-sense assumption of global governance and the GC is that social actors are seen as existing on a smooth and even plane. That is to say, interactions involving various actors and institutions are understood as a neutral space devoid of power relations, which in turn allows for a highly optimistic view that anything is possible regardless of one's gender, race, material existence (social class), spatial location, and so forth. Robert Latham articulates this problem in the following manner:

> Governance, unlike *power* for instance, has not been a central term of contestation and analysis in political science or the social sciences more generally. Its meaning has basically been taken for granted. It is taken to be what decision-makers, administrators, or steering committees generate as they manage or administer the activities of their organizations or those of the people and things for which they assume responsibility. (1999, p. 25)

Seen through the above lens, a significant aspect of the Compact is its view of pluralist (frictionless) interactions between diverse actors in which inequality, exploitation, and class struggle are noticeably absent (Soederberg, 2006). Powerful TNCs, NGOs ranging from Oxfam to local organizations based in the Third World, the states of developing and industrialized countries— all are viewed as harmoniously co-existing on a smooth, level playing field, as opposed to the highly uneven and contradictory terrain of global capitalism. This assumption has led global governance renditions of the Compact to lump diverse actors into the seemingly innocuous concept of civil society. Ruggie, for instance, provides a scant definition in the form of a footnote as to what he means by the term 'civil society organizations', despite the fact that they are an integral feature of his concept of the global public domain. This vague term figures prominently in Ruggie's explanation of the Compact. His definition encompasses 'transnational social movements, coalitions, and activists campaigns as well as formal non-governmental organizations' (Ruggie, 2004, p. 522). The concept of civil society remains innocent and harmonious, as its pluralist treatment side-steps the diverse and highly exploitative social relationships within the ambit of the GC by refusing to nail down precisely where civil society begins and where it ends, especially with respect to the market. As Ellen Meiksins Wood observes, civil society

> has come to represent a separate sphere of human relations and activity, differentiated from the state but neither public nor private or perhaps both at once, embodying not only a whole range of social interactions apart from the private sphere of the household and the public sphere of the state, but more specifically a network of distinctly *economic* relations, the sphere of the market-place, the arena of production, distribution, and exchange. (1990, p. 61)

By contextualizing the GC within the wider contradictions and struggles associated with global capitalism, we are better placed to observe and explain why unequal and exploitative relations of power between TNCs and their global supply chains, NGOs, international organizations such as the World Trade Organization (WTO) and the IMF, and states, are not only unequal but also inherently exploitative in nature (Cox, 1993). Indeed, the very definition of CSR, which is imbued in the principles of the GC, is highly contested and is neither neutral nor static in content. According to Ronen Shamir, there are many definitions of CSR. The dominant meaning of this term is a product that is 'shaped through the interplay of popular pressures and the response of corporations to such pressures' (Shamir, 2004, p.4). This dialectical interplay does not occur on a smooth and level playing field of global governance, but instead is fought out on the highly uneven and exploitative terrain of global capital accumulation and the social relations of power therein.

A second limitation found in mainstream global governance accounts of the Compact is that they fail to evaluate critically not only the supremacy of the neoliberal agenda and its linkages with globalization, both within and across states, but also how global governance has been complicit with the dominance of neoliberalism (Murphy, 2000, p. 796). The reason for this is that, as they take a problem-solving approach, most global governance accounts of the Compact view neoliberalism not as a problem but rather as a neutral set of policies and processes that are a logical reaction to the external forces of globalization. The latter is viewed within the framework of global governance and the Compact as a natural and unstoppable occurrence, as opposed to a social construct rooted in the restructuring of global capitalism (Arrighi, 1996; Harvey, 2000). Neoliberalism is therefore seen as a suitable set of policies with which to react to and manage the overpowering effects of globalization, such as the growth of TNCs, global financial markets, and so forth. Neoliberal policies embodied in the so-called Washington Consensus have championed, *inter alia*, trade and financial liberalization, privatization, and deregulation schemes in order to afford a greater role to the market *vis-à-vis* the state in shaping economic and social policies, which in turn have greatly affected the power of trades unions and workers' rights, as well as those groups struggling for environmental protection.

From the 1980s to the present, the SAPs, with their emphasis on the privatization of state-owned industry and the liberalization of trade and finance, have helped to open markets for TNCs that were previously considered 'off limits', such as water, electricity, telecommunications, transportation networks, banking, and so forth. The launching of the Uruguay Round (1986–1994) of the Multilateral Trade Negotiations under GATT and the subsequent ministerial conferences from 1995 onwards under the auspices of the WTO is an example of how states, at the behest of powerful TNCs, actively sought to facilitate neoliberal strategies by reducing barriers to trade and investment flows. For instance, new projects included negotiating international agreements on trade-related intellectual property rights (TRIPs), which now fall under the authority of the WTO (Wilkinson, 2000). TRIPs facilitates deeper forms of neoliberalism by granting corporations increased capacity to privatize and patent life forms, including plant and other genetic resources of Third World countries.

As discussed above, many critics of neoliberal-led development argue that it has not made good on its promises to deliver a better standard of living. Indeed, for the majority of the world's population, life is getting increasingly worse. The explosive growth of informal labour markets and urban slums are just two of many manifestations of the widening gap between poor and rich countries over the past 20 years. In most countries, including in the global North, income inequality has increased or, at best, stabilized. Global inequality, as measured by World Bank economists, reached an incredible 0.67, based on the Gini coefficient scale, by the end of the twentieth century. This is mathematically equivalent to a situation where the poorest two-thirds of the world receive zero income, and the top third receive everything (Davis, 2006).[7]

Progressive struggles, or what David Harvey refers to as 'spaces of hope' (2000), that inevitably arise against, for example, corporate infringement on human and labour rights in the Third World, threaten the hegemonic position of free-market policies and institutions, which would affect not only the power of TNCs, but also, and more generally, the expanded reproduction of capital accumulation. It is from this perspective that the GC must be seen as a response, albeit itself highly contradictory, to the ongoing crisis of legitimacy of neoliberalism, or, more specifically, the growing power of TNCs over all aspects of social life. Before turning to this discussion, it is important to highlight briefly some important spaces of hope with regard to the global CSR movement.

Co-opting ('Corporatizing') Spaces of Hope

Largely due to the effective and active roles of shareholder organizations such as the Interfaith Centre on Corporate Social Responsibility, trades unions (AFL-CIO, IG Metall, and so on), and NGOs (e.g., Campaign for Labour Rights, Sweatshop Watch, Child Labour Coalition, Clean Clothes Campaign, and so forth), a litany of charges levied against TNCs by non-profit NGOs empowered by the Internet during the early 1990s continued to draw consumers' attention to horrific accounts of exploitation involving child and indentured labour, environmental degradation, and human rights abuses in the global South (Klein, 2000).

The pinnacle of anti-corporate resistance movements was the WTO Seattle protest in December 1999 (a few months after the GC was launched), which drew over 50,000 people from all over the world and all walks of life to show their disapproval of growing forms of corporate power. In response to the general backlash against corporate forms of neoliberal capitalist restructuring in the global South, TNCs have been taking measures to protect one of the central factors in determining company sales and value: reputation, or corporate image (Larkin, 2003; Paine, 2003; Pearson and Seyfang, 2001). According to the managing director of the high-profile, high-powered public relations company Burston-Marsteller in New York: 'Studies show that 40 percent to 45 percent of a company's stock price is a reflection of shareholder confidence in the CEO [Chief Executive Officer], his [or her] strategy and managing team' (Sparkes, 2002, p. 221). Millions of dollars are spent annually on spinning a good company image. TNCs take great pains to demonstrate that they are good corporate citizens. Many corporations, for example, have sought, with various degrees of transparency, to implement, on a voluntary basis, company codes of conduct which require contractors in the South to eradicate abusive working conditions.

To illustrate, the Fair Labour Association (FLA) was established to promote adherence to the International Labour Organization's Conventions[8] and improve working conditions worldwide. The FLA represents a multi-stakeholder coalition of companies, universities, and NGOs. There are 175 US colleges and universities and 12 leading brand-name companies participating in the FLA (e.g., Liz Claiborne, Adidas-Salomon, Nike, Patagonia, Puma, and Reebok). At the same time, TNCs were launching websites dedicated to CSR issues. This effort captures what I refer to as 'corporatizing' or co-opting spaces of hope *vis-à-vis* the CSR movement. Coca-Cola's website[9] features a section on citizenship, Royal Dutch Shell's website[10] has a section dedicated to the environment and society and a 'Shell Report' pertaining to issues of sustainable development, while the McDonald's website[11] includes an entire page dedicated to corporate social responsibility. There have also been international initiatives by business to forge linkages with environment and labour groups to address issues of monitoring and accountability. In 1997, for example, the Global Reporting Initiative (GRI)[12] was founded by the Coalition for Environmentally Responsible Economies. The GRI, which became independent in 2002, operates in co-operation with the Compact. There is also the Social Accountability SA8000 standard[13] for certifying firms. The Prince of Wales Business Leaders Forum,[14] which was formed in 1990, promotes more socially responsible business practices, and is working on indices and indicators to measure societal performance (Pearson and Seyfang, 2001).

These initiatives have, however, come under attack by many critics. Some reasons for this discontent are: (1) company codes are vaguely defined, thus leaving much room for interpretation; (2) the codes are incomplete in that they do not precisely specify the limits of their responsibility; (3) company codes are not implemented and monitored; (4) the codes are not independently verified, and instead are company-controlled or internally monitored, which is the principle upon which the GC is based (Scherer and Greven, 2001, pp. 87–88); and (5) the codes do not address the activities of powerful sourcing companies, which fall under the CSR radar and which can often dictate terms to weaker suppliers.

Global Compact: Institutionalizing Struggle in Bourgeois Spaces of Control

Given the Compact's scope and emphasis on forging new partnerships between both state and non-state actors, it has been heralded by many as global governance *par excellence*. Or, as one observer put it, Annan's 'most creative reinvention' yet of the United Nations (the *Christian Science Monitor*, quoted in Ruggie, 2001, p. 371). As noted in the introductory section of this essay, the main aim of the GC is to act as a 'learning network'. According to one of the key architects of the Compact, John Ruggie,[15] this learning network constitutes an attempt to reach—through dialogue—a broad consensus on good corporate practices. The definition of good practices,

> together with illustrative case studies, is then publicised in an on-line learning bank, which will become a standard reference source on corporate social responsibility. The hope and expectation is that good practices will help drive out bad ones through the power of dialogue, transparency, advocacy, and competition. (Ruggie, 2001, p. 373)

The GC is not without its critics, however. Many progressive NGOs, such as CorpWatch, NikeWatch, and Global Exchange, view the voluntary nature of the Compact as not going far enough in stomping out the raft of corporate crimes against human and animal rights, or transgressions against the environment (Transnational Resource and Action Centre, 2000). Moreover, these critics argue that the Compact's website offers companies a free forum to polish their images without their inputs being qualified by critical comment or even questions.[16] This has led to the charges that the Compact allows participating companies to 'bluewash' their image by wrapping themselves in the flag of the United Nations (Ruggie, 2001, p. 371).

Like other CSR initiatives, the Compact is not a regulatory arrangement with a legally binding code of conduct, but rather a voluntary corporate citizenship initiative. According to its website the GC has two objectives: to mainstream the 10 principles in business activities around the world, and to catalyze actions in support of UN goals. To achieve these goals, the Global Compact offers facilitation and engagement through several mechanisms (Rosenau, 1995): policy dialogues, learning, local structures, and projects (Ruggie, 2001, 2002). While the Compact's role of a learning network is praiseworthy, its attempts to integrate better, and on a voluntary basis, the social needs of those hardest hit by neoliberal-led restructuring strategies are limited by the contradictory policies pursued by the global trade architecture that is being constructed under the aegis of the WTO and the plethora of bilateral trade agreements. The latter's forms of trade liberalization are not only top-down and exclusive in nature, but also aim to serve corporate interests of profit maximization by making legal, and therefore legitimate, neoliberal restructuring strategies.

Another restriction of the GC lies in the fact that its creator, the UN, is neither a neutral nor a pluralist institution, but draws its power and contradictions from the relations of power found in global capitalism (Soederberg, 2006). Following Robert Cox (1993), the UN, like the WTO, is a product of the hegemonic world order. The Compact, as a creation of the UN, acts to legitimate ideologically the neoliberal norms of the world order, such as the self-regulation of powerful corporations, trade liberalization, and the superiority of market rationality over government intervention in the sphere of public goods like water, transportation, health, education, and welfare services.

The power relations in global capitalism do not involve merely the interstate system, but capitalists as well. It is therefore instructive to look more closely at the relationships between the Compact and its most powerful partner: the International Chamber of Commerce (ICC). With over 7,000 corporate members, the ICC represents one of the most powerful lobby groups in the world, counting some of the largest TNCs in its membership list, including General Motors, Novartis, Bayer, and Nestle. Given the sheer power of the ICC, it is interesting to emphasize two important points made by the Secretary-General of the ICC, Maria Livanos Cattaui, during an interview in 2001 with the *International Herald Tribune*. According to Cattaui, one of the main virtues of the GC is that it is about self-regulation, as opposed to heavy-handed government intervention as represented by the Compact's predecessor, the UN's Centre on Transnational Corporations (see Bair, 2007; Soederberg, 2006). Or, as Cattaui put it:

> The compact is – or should be – open-ended, free from 'command and control.' It can be a catalyst for good corporate citizenship and the spread of good business practices. It appeals to the competitive instincts of the market and will encourage companies always to raise their sights and go one better in upholding its principles. It mobilizes the virtues of private enterprise in fulfillment of the UN's goals. (Cattaui, 2001)

The avoidance of any monitoring or verification procedure suits the ICC in its attempts to use the Compact as a PR gimmick to legitimate the activities of its members. The ICC website, for instance, contains a collection of brief reports on environmental and human rights initiatives by BP-Amoco, Fiat, Unilever, and other corporations—some of which are not part of the Compact. As Raghavan notes, the website, combined with the UN's secrecy about who is and who is not a member of the GC, gives the impression that these highly controversial companies are part of the Compact. What is more, the ICC reports are presented as 'case studies' of 'how the private sector is fulfilling the Compact through corporate actions'.[17] The ICC invites companies to submit examples, but does not permit external comments from, for example, NGOs that are critical of the claims (Raghavan, 2001).

When asked about the ICC's position on civil society's participation in the GC, Cauttaui replied:

> The danger is that too many players will be brought in, and we have seen hints that that might happen in some of the rhetoric coming out of the UN. If labour unions and so-called civil society nongovernmental organizations are seen as full partners in the Global Compact, its nature will certainly be different from the concept that a group of CEOs – all of them ICC members – welcomed wholeheartedly when they pledged their support in July 1999. (Cattaui, 2001)

The ICC has lobbied the Compact to help discourage attacks by more radical NGOs on growing corporate abuse of power around the world. For instance, NGOs constantly draw attention to the ICC's long history of forceful lobbying to weaken international environmental treaties, such as the Kyoto Protocol, the Convention on Biodiversity, and the Basel Convention against trade in toxic waste. In the place of the GC's environmental principles, the ICC 'promotes a narrow corporate agenda, dominated by the commercial interests of some of the world's most environmentally irresponsible corporations – an agenda that often effectively undermines a precautionary approach and basic environmental responsibility' (Raghavan, 2001).

International organizations are not neutral bodies; rather, they play an important role in reproducing and legitimating the status quo in their ability to absorb counter-hegemonic ideas (Cox,

1987). The manner in which the GC seeks to invite major corporations to participate in grafting a human face onto the social and economic ills brought about through neoliberalism, including the constant increase in corporate power, represents a passive revolution. Antonio Gramsci developed this notion to explain how the ruling classes survive despite economic and political crises (Carnoy, 1984; Gramsci, 1971). Passive revolution refers to a top-down strategy aimed at preventing the development of a revolutionary adversary. The threat is not so much that those who oppose the constant increase of corporate power in the South cannot be silenced by coercion (economic or physical), but rather that the constant upheaval will have implications for bourgeois states in the global South who are seeking to create good business civilizations to attract and retain FDI (Gill and Law, 1993).

The Compact does accept certain demands from below, such as the need to enforce human rights, labour rights, and environmental protection through established state-sanctioned principles, such as the Universal Declaration of Human Rights, while concurrently encouraging counter-hegemonic movements to restrict their struggle to the electronic terrain of the learning network. This, in turn, prevents the dominance of neoliberalism from being challenged while TNCs are granted more and more freedoms to pursue neoliberal strategies in the developing world.

It is important to underscore that the above view complements mainstream theories of global governance, in that it promotes the perspective that there is no other alternative than to embrace the structural power of capital and work within the constraints posed by the 'realities' of globalization, by adopting the mode of governance that best promotes a healthy investment climate: neoliberalism. By denying the role of the state in the GC, and by moving away from regulatory mechanisms for TNCs operating in the Third World, the Compact's architects have not only depoliticized struggle (counter-hegemonic movements) around the activities of TNCs by attempting to delimit the site of struggle to cyber-space (the learning network), but also freed bourgeois states of any responsibilities for their decisions to implement business-friendly environments with human and ecological costs.

Conclusion

By transcending some of the common-sense assumptions underpinning the dominant, mainstream framework of global governance, I have argued that the GC is not a 'progressive platform' from which a broader social agenda may be grafted onto the activities of TNCs and their supply chains in the Third World, so as to achieve a more sustainable and inclusive global economy. Instead, I suggest that the Compact not only is an integral feature of neoliberal-led forms of global capital accumulation, but also has emerged from the contradictions therein. One such contradiction highlighted here is captured by a type of Polanyian double-movement. Seen from this perspective, the GC acts to legitimize and normalize the expropriation of labour, while seeking to neutralize and depoliticize struggle tied to the deepening and widening forms of economic exploitation in the global South by powerful TNCs and their global supply chains (see Taylor, 2007).

Aside from issues of exclusion, there are at least three significant and interlocking limitations to these top-down efforts aimed at forging a partnership between business and a variety of different social forces. First, there is an absence of hard-and-fast standards. As long as there are no common codes of conduct governing their reports, and no rigorous, independent, public audits, the information provided by these corporations is at best incomplete, or at worst misleading. Second, the creation of common standards is insufficient without some sort of formalized enforcement and penalty mechanism. The latter can only be achieved through active state involvement—something contrary to the current neoliberal times. Third, CSR initiatives need to be complemented by regulatory mechanisms in the ongoing strategies to liberalize trade and FDI flows under the aegis of multilateral trade and bilateral trade agreements.

Effective change can only take place beyond the parameters of the GC and its attempts to depoliticize contestation via exclusionary practices and relegating struggle to cyber-space. As Cox reminds us, the utility of critical theory lies in its ability to show us contradictions within the system and particular neoliberal strategies, such as the Compact. The Achilles' heel of the current neoliberal order and the fact that it is a social construct, as opposed to a necessary by-product of the inevitable and unstoppable tendency toward globalization, can be exposed and effectively challenged through formal and informal spaces of hope or counter-hegemonic struggles. By moving away from problem-solving approaches to explain strategies like the GC, we challenge versions of reality that claim that social actors must graft their CSR agenda onto the needs of TNCs by catering to the latter's need for market-based solutions, as opposed to developing state-led forms of regulation to ensure basic forms of social and environmental protection. Indeed, the inverse should be the dominant 'reality': TNCs should be made to accommodate, through state-led forms of re-regulation, the needs of workers, investors, the environment, and the communities from which corporations extract their wealth. Finally, any serious attempt to radicalize the Global Compact, and CSR initiatives more broadly, needs to question critically the separation of social and financial concerns which currently dominates the economic and business literature, as well as the nature of corporate power (Soederberg, forthcoming).

Notes

1 These five agencies are the Office of the High Commissioner for Human Rights, the United Nations Environment Programme, the International Labour Organization, the United Nations Development Programme, and the United Nations Industrial Development Organization.
2 See http://www.unglobalcompact.org.
3 See http://www.unglobalcompact.org/aboutthegc/thetenprinciples/index.html.
4 For a list of academic publications on the Compact, see http://www.unglobalcompact.org/newsandevents/academic_articles_and_books.html.
5 To grasp fully the capitalist nature of the Compact, it is imperative to contextualize it historically alongside the changing configuration of power regarding TNCs, North–South relations, states, and other international organizations. Given space limitations, I cannot enter into such a detailed analysis here; I do so, however, in my book *Global Governance in Question* (2006).
6 For more information, see http://www.unglobalcompact.org/communicatingprogress/index.html and http://www.unglobalcompact.org/networksaroundtheworld/gc_outreach_events.html.
7 The Gini coefficient measures income inequality. Its band ranges from zero to one. Zero means perfect equality in terms of income, whereas one means perfect inequality (i.e., one person possesses all the income, and everyone else has nothing).
8 For a listing of the ILO's Conventions, see http://www.ilo.org/public/english/standards/norm/whatare/fundam.
9 See http://www2.coca-cola.com/citizenship/index.html.
10 See http://www.shell.com/home/framework?siteid=home.
11 See http://www.mcdonalds.com/corp/values/socialrespons.html.
12 See http://www.globalreporting.org.
13 See http://www.cepaa.org/sa8000/sa8000.htm.
14 See http://www.princeofwales.gov.uk/trusts/bus_forum.html.
15 John Gerard Ruggie and George Kell were the key architects of the Compact.
16 See http://www.unglobalcompact.org.
17 See http://www.iccwbo.org/home/menu_global_compact.asp.

References

Annan, K. (1999) A Compact for a new century, UN Secretary-General's Address to the World Economic Forum in Davos, Switzerland, 31 January. Press release SG/SM/6881, http://www.un.org/news/press/docs/1999/19990201.sgsm6881.html.

Arrighi, G. (1996) *The Long Twentieth Century* (London: Verso).

Bair, J. (2007) From the politics of development to the challenges of globalization, *Globalizations*, 4(4), pp. 486–499.

Carnoy, M. (1984) *The State and Political Theory* (Princeton, NJ: Princeton University Press).

Cattaui, M. L. (2001) The Global Compact — Business and the UN, *International Herald Tribune*, 25 January, pp. 11–14.

Commission on Global Governance (1995) *Our Global Neighbourhood: The Report of the Commission on Global Governance* (New York: Oxford University Press).

Cox, R. (1987) *Production, Power, and World Order: Social Forces and the Making of History* (New York: Columbia University Press).

Cox, R. W. (1993) Structural issues of global governance: implications for Europe, in St. Gill (ed.) *Gramsci, Historical Materialism and International Relations* (Cambridge: Cambridge University Press).

Cox, R. W. & Sinclair, T. J. (1996) *Approaches to World Order* (Cambridge: Cambridge University Press).

Davis, M. (2006) *Planet of Slums* (London: Verso).

Escobar, A. (1995) *Encountering Development: The Making and Unmaking of the Third World* (Princeton, NJ: Princeton University Press).

Gill, S. & Law, D. (1993) Global hegemony and the structural power of capital, in S. Gill (ed.) *Gramsci, Historical Materialism, and International Relations* (Cambridge: Cambridge University Press).

Global Policy Forum (2000) The Global Compact, UN press briefing by Assistant Secretary-General and Special Adviser to Secretary-General John Ruggie, 20 July, http://www.globalpolicy.org/reform/ruggie.htm.

Gramsci, A. (1971) *Selections from Prison Notebooks* (New York: International Publishers).

Harvey, D. (2000) *Spaces of Hope* (Berkeley: University of California).

Hocking, B. & Kelly, D. (2002) Doing the business? The International Chamber of Commerce, the United Nations, and the Global Compact, in A. F. Cooper, J. English, & R. Thakur (eds) *Enhancing Global Governance: Towards a New Diplomacy?* (Tokyo: United Nations University Press).

Klein, N. (2000) *No Logo: Take Aim at the Brand Bullies* (Toronto: Vintage Canada).

Larkin, J. (2003) *Strategic Reputation Risk Management* (London: Palgrave).

Latham, R. (1999) Politics in a floating world: towards a critique of global governance, in M. Hewson & T. Sinclair (eds) *Approaches to Global Governance Theory* (New York: State University of New York Press).

Lefebvre, H. (2005) *Everyday Life in the Modern World* (New Brunswick, NJ: Transaction Publishers).

McMichael, P. (2004) *Development and Social Change: A Global Perspective* (Thousand Oaks, CA: Pine Forge Press).

Munck, R. (2006) Globalization and contestation: a Polanyian problematic, *Globalizations*, 3(2), pp. 175–186.

Murphy, C. N. (2000) Global governance: poorly done and poorly understood, *International Affairs*, 76(4), pp. 789–803.

Paine, L. S. (2003) *Value Shift: Why Companies Must Merge Social and Financial Imperatives to Achieve Superior Performance* (New York: McGraw-Hill).

Pearson, R. & Seyfang, G. (2001) New hope or false dawn? Voluntary codes of conduct, labour regulation and social policy in a globalizing world, *Global Social Policy*, 1(1), pp. 49–78.

Polanyi, K. (1957) *The Great Transformation: The Political and Economic Origins of our Times* (Boston, MA: Beacon Press).

Raghavan, C. (2001) Review Global Compact partnership with ICC, says study, *South-North Development Monitor (SUNS)* and Third World Network, http://www.twnside.org.sg/title/icc.htm.

Rosenau, J. N. (1995) Governance in the twenty-first century, *Global Governance*, 1(1), pp. 13–43.

Ruggie, J. G. (2000) Globalization, the Global Compact and corporate social responsibility, *Transnational Associations*, 52(6), pp. 54–69.

Ruggie, J. G. (2001) global_governance.net: the Global Compact as learning network, *Global Governance*, 7(4), pp. 371–378.

Ruggie, J. G. (2002) The theory and practice of learning networks: corporate social responsibility and the Global Compact, *Journal of Corporate Citizenship*, 5(Spring), pp. 27–36.

Ruggie, J. G. (2004) Reconstituting the global public domain: issues, actors, and practices, *European Journal of International Relations*, 10(4), pp. 499–531.

Saad-Filho, A. & Johnston, D. (2005) *Neoliberalism: A Critical Reader* (London: Pluto Press).

Scherer, C. & Greven, T. (2001) *Global Rules for Trade: Codes of Conduct, Social Labeling, Workers' Rights Clauses* (Muenster: Westfaelisches Dampfboot).

Shamir, R. (2004) The de-radicalization of corporate social responsibility, *Critical Sociology*, 30(3), pp. 669–689.

Sklair, L. (2002) Global capitalism and major corporations from the Third World, *Third World Quarterly*, 23(1), pp. 81–100.

Soederberg, S. (2004) *The Politics of the New International Financial Architecture: Reimposing Neoliberal Domination in the Global South* (London: Zed Books).

Soederberg, S. (2006) *Global Governance in Question: Empire, Class, and the New Common Sense in Managing Globalization* (London: Pluto Press).

Soederberg, S. (forthcoming) *Beyond Corporate Governance: Activism, Power, and Social Responsibility in the Era of Financialization.*

Sparkes, R. (2002) *Socially Responsible Investment: A Global Revolution* (Chichester: John Wiley & Sons).

Taylor, M. (2007) Rethinking the global production of uneven development, *Globalizations*, 4(4), pp. 529–542.

Thérien, J.-P. & Pouliot, V. (2006) The Global Compact: shifting the politics of international development? *Global Governance*, 12(1), pp. 34–49.

Transnational Resource and Action Center (2000) Tangled up in blue: corporate partnerships at the United Nations, http://www.corpwatch.org/trac/globalization/un/tangled.html.

UNCTAD (2005) *World Investment Report 2005: Transnational Corporations and the Internationalization of R&D* (New York: United Nations).

Wilkinson, R. (2000) *Multilateralism and the World Trade Organization: The Architecture and Extension of International Trade Regulation* (London: Routledge).

Wood, E. M. (1990) The uses and abuses of "civil society", in R. Miliband & L. Panitch (eds) *Socialist Register* (London: Merlin Press).

World Bank (2000) *World Development Report 2000/2001: Attacking Poverty* (New York: Oxford University Press).

World Bank (2005) *World Development Report 2005: A Better Investment Climate for Everyone* (New York: Oxford University Press).

World Bank (2006) *Global Development Finance 2006: The Development Potential of Surging Capital Flows* (Washington, DC: World Bank).

A Global Knowledge Bank? The World Bank and Bottom-Up Efforts to Reinforce Neoliberal Development Perspectives in the Post-Washington Consensus Era

DIETER PLEHWE

Reconsidering the 'Knowledge' Strategy

Over the course of the 1990s, in response to growing criticism from multiple sources—including occasional calls for its abolishment—the World Bank came up with the idea of reinvented itself as a *global knowledge bank* in an effort to improve its record after the apparent failure of 'one size fits all' prescriptions based on the so-called Washington Consensus. Although 'free market' ideas continue to play a central role in economic and development policy debates within and around the World Bank, the priorities of market-oriented restructuring (privatization, deregulation, financial liberalization, etc.) appear to be less taken for granted. Following on from an earlier emphasis on state planning (particularly import substitution industrialization), which gave way to private corporations (globalization, and an export orientation), the World Bank has now turned its attention to better knowledge management as the key to development.

In an effort to increase responsiveness to specific circumstances at the micro level, the World Bank officially adopted knowledge management concepts in 1996 (on their corporate/business school origins, see Evers et al., 2003; King, 2000). This led to the receipt of a prestigious award from the American Productivity and Quality Center (http://www.apqc.org) in recognition of its achievements. The new strategy aims to overcome the World Bank's 'disconnect' (Rich, 2002) from existing problems and conditions on the ground, and to address some if not many of the previous critiques in its revamped governance structure (cf. Kapur, 2002). While some NGOs are pleased about increasing consulting opportunities, neoliberal and conservative forces are pleased that the World Bank continues to emphasize private capital flows, albeit with a greater emphasis on social capital (see Fine, 1999, for a critique) and enabling institutions. Except for the North–South information divide recognized by the Bellanet Initiative,[1] structural conditions and imbalances at the macro-economic level and public sector lending in particular have remained low on the 'post-Washington' agenda that insists on knowledge as the key to economic growth and successful development. The World Bank Group now

> wants to be the source of best practices and cutting-edge economic development knowledge, an exemplar for internal and external development sharing, the home for a global network of development practitioners and the standard setter for a universal institutional approach to economic development. Knowledge management is the key to making this vision a reality. (Bukowitz and Williams, 2000, p. 269)

A number of internal institutional reforms have been implemented to advance the new agenda. Systematic knowledge sharing is supposed to overcome an internal culture of competition (between departments, projects, etc.), which came to be regarded as a factor limiting the internal co-operation of the 8,000 or so staff members, and limiting transparency in general. Intensified information flows are to be secured through communities of practice, or thematic groups comprising practitioners who work in different departments and countries on similar topics.[2] More than 9,000 'knowledge resources' have been developed (and are to some extent made available online), which can be considered to form the material basis of the World Bank's strategy of global development knowledge management (Evers et al., 2003, p. 53).

Internal institutional reforms with regard to the division and integration of labor were complemented by reforms designed to reap the benefits of technological advances in the field of information and communication technology, in terms of both the generation and the distribution of information and knowledge. To secure network advantages, the most important activities of the World Bank Group related to information and communication technologies have been merged into the Global Information and Communication Technologies Department. This department has been put in charge of a variety of initiatives designed to narrow the information/ knowledge gap between the North and the South; these initiatives include the Global Development Network (GDN, founded 1998), the Global Development Gateway (GDG), a Development Marketplace, the Global Knowledge Partnership (GKP, 1997), and the Information for Development Program (InfoDEV, 1995).

In addition, the World Bank has served as a catalyst for the development of specialized external knowledge networks, for which technological infrastructures and (partial funding) have been provided.[3] All these sprawling networks are supposed to aid the development of local and regional knowledge capacities, to synthesize structures and content, to safeguard further mobilization, and to integrate local problem-solving capacities at the global level (Evers et al., 2003, pp. 55–56).

World Bank efforts to decentralize knowledge management followed the example of major national development organizations. The new understanding of better knowledge (management) thus appears to be shared across many countries and global financial institutions. Since the World Bank remains majority-owned and controlled by the governments of the most developed nations, it remains unclear to what extent developing countries simply have to share the belief in the new strategy. While this is an important topic in its own right, I will refrain from state-centered issues in this paper, by and large, in order to concentrate on what has been a mostly neglected issue in studies critically examining the new pattern of knowledge (management): the upgraded (transnational) civil society dimension in the production and dissemination of *authoritative* development knowledge (see Goldman, 2005, for a notable exception).

'Knowledge' quite obviously had a key role to play in past development efforts. Both the post-1945 emphasis on state-guided modernization and development and the subsequent shift to the 'Washington Consensus' are examples of the social construction of particular kinds of knowledge, sets of assumptions, theoretical considerations, empirical validations, and policy prescriptions. In both cases they became authoritative and/or hegemonic for certain periods of time. At present, even if it is agreed that better knowledge and knowledge management are keys to greater development success, it remains to be asked: Which kinds of authoritative knowledge are now processed and managed better, and who is positioned to construct and distribute this knowledge? One of the early visionaries of the 'knowledge society' has already recognized some of the 'obsolete assumptions' about neutral knowledge accumulating in linear fashion, which have recently been refuted by St. Clair (2006, p. 78). Unlike many later voices, Daniel Bell (1973, p. 176) emphasized the important nexus of knowledge and power, which needs to be duly considered. For Bell, 'Knowledge is that which is objectively known, an intellectual property, attached to a name or a group of names and certified by copyright or some other form of social recognition (e.g. publication).'

Large numbers of think-tanks and individuals are involved in present-day development knowledge production. The World Bank-related Global Development Network currently counts more than 3,000 think-tanks and more than 6,000 individual researchers among its membership. It is thus difficult to assess the success of efforts to promote decentralized patterns of knowledge management, or ascertain the extent to which bureaucratic-technocratic circles retain influence or control in this process, let alone to assess the knowledge bank strategy at large.

Unsurprisingly, the hitherto available judgments are highly contradictory. In some instances they perceive a promising new pluralism within and around the World Bank, which is held to be likely to improve development projects due to greater opportunities for participation (Stone, 2000). Others see continuing or increasing ineffectiveness due to 'goal overload' (Pincus and Winters, 2002), while yet other observers emphasize that the changes in direction on the part of the World Bank facilitate the creation of new capacities to reinforce disciplinary neoliberalism (Cammack, 2002). These optimistic, skeptical, and negative assessments of the new knowledge strategy coincide roughly with incommensurable observations regarding neoliberal hegemony. The new pluralism advocates discount neoliberal hegemony—they detect either a 'post-Washington Consensus' or 'Washington Confusion'. Skeptics witness a certain atmospheric transformation of neoliberalism, which does not affect its structural foundations. And radical critics observe a deepening of neoliberal hegemony as a result of the new emphasis on *ex-ante* conditions for loans and aid and successful steps to accomplish neoliberal agendas, which were stalled due to the shortcomings of the 'Washington Consensus' (see Weber, 2006, on financial liberalization; Goldman, 2005, on 'greening' neoliberalism). Who is right? Can this puzzle be solved?

To examine the World Bank's knowledge strategy further, it is crucial to examine more closely and critically the transnational civil society networks involved in the social construction and validation of development knowledge, and the new patterns of knowledge management. While it is difficult to observe the new configuration empirically, St. Clair (2006) is right to insist on the nexus of knowledge and power.

The remainder of this paper is organized in the following way. First, I will look at the literature on the knowledge strategy and new emphasis on bottom-up civil society participation in World Bank governance. This literature review will explain why the concept of civil society fails to help explain the transnational civil society formation processes promoted by the World Bank and others. It is argued that a conflict-oriented neogramscian understanding of civil society is better suited to analyzing critically the new mix of public and private authority characteristic of the present transformation of global governance. I will present preliminary evidence gathered on the World Bank-related Global Development Network next, and on the global neoliberal network of think-tanks which has been coordinated by the US-based Atlas Economic Research Foundation since the 1980s (Plehwe and Walpen, 2006). In the light of the information available so far, I will draw preliminary conclusions. More research into the links between intellectual, corporate, and political interests is needed in order to understand better the contemporary transformation of the social construction of authoritative development knowledge.

Civil Society and Knowledge Production: Solution or Problem?

Johnson and Stone (2000, pp. 18–19) present the GDN as a 'consciously global network' (as opposed to other think-tank networks of allegedly more limited scope), but alert readers to concerns raised about the scope of pluralism within the GDN. Unnamed Scandinavians have apparently identified the core institutions around which the network is evolving to represent technical forms of neo-liberal analysis rather akin to the economic doctrines informing the Washington Consensus (Johnson and Stone, 2000, pp. 15–16; see also Stone, 2000, p. 248). Johnson and Stone reject such criticism, which they regard as 'inevitable ideological differences', although they proceed to emphasize that adequate governance mechanisms are considered necessary to uphold difference as the 'dominant reality' (Johnson and Stone, 2000, p. 16). Nustad and Sending (2000) also emphasize concerns over neoliberal influence if 'development is conceived in terms of economics' (Nustad and Sending, 2000, pp. 44–45). However, these authors contend that the problem is more fundamentally connected to a narrow (positivist) conception of knowledge as a technocratic instrument.

Knowledge Bank skeptics like Pincus and Winters cast further doubt on the extent of pluralism displayed within the ranks of the GDN. They challenge the widely perceived distance between Washington Consensus pundits and the GDN advocates:

> Stiglitz's critique centered not so much on the content of the policies themselves but rather on the prior need for institutional reform and an adequate regulatory framework in support of market-oriented reforms. The main problem of the Washington Consensus was, according to Stiglitz, a failure to understand the subtleties of the market economy, to understand that private property and 'getting the prizes right' (that is liberalization) are not sufficient to make a market economy work. (Pincus and Winters, 2002, p. 11)

Since much of the privatization and deregulation agenda has been completed, there may be simply more room (and need) now to consider how to cope with the results.

Others find that the World Bank did respond to the pressure exerted by the environmental movement, for example, but there is no agreement on the extent to which at least some of the demands have actually been met (Williams, 2000, p. 245). The increasing quantity of interaction between environmental NGOs and the World Bank should not lead to an assumption of increasing quality, because

> much of the policy dialogue between the Bank and NGOs is conducted informally … and Southern NGOs are therefore excluded from this process. Representation from the developing world is greater in respect of the more formal channels such as the World Bank-NGO Committee and consultations such as those on forest, water, and energy. (Williams, 2000, p. 248)

Williams observes a reverse pressure on civil society activists: 'In order to be heard, representatives of social movements of necessity must enter into a dialogue (and speak the language) of the holders of power' (Williams, 2000, p. 253). This may be one of the reasons why organizations involved in the global social protest movement against corporate globalization are notably absent from the ranks of the GDN.

Pincus and Winters (2002, p. 14) highlight the narrow political and ideological confines in which the World Bank's intellectual activities take place. Under these circumstances, they maintain, the knowledge bank vision is primarily appealing to US forces 'who significantly control the range of acceptable knowledge to be created, stored, and lent by the knowledge bank'. The rapid rise of think-tanks as prominent actors and decentralized knowledge production are both looked at with suspicion. In line with St. Clair (2006), they maintain that the decentralization of knowledge governance must be considered an effort to accomplish more control from the top. Guy Standing asked rhetorically: 'What kind or knowledge will an institution that conducts its own research without benefit of peer review, evaluates its own projects, and *sets up think tanks around the world that subscribe to its worldview* produce?' (quoted in Pincus and Winters, 2002, p. 22, emphasis added). Kapur (2002, p. 74) is more ambivalent about what he regards as a 'relative disempowerment of poor countries, although not necessarily of poor people' due to increasing attention to transparency and accountability in the new governance structure of the World Bank. However, he also points to a strengthening of power located in the US. Increasing NGO participation is held ultimately to reinforce Washington's dominant position due to the close proximity of a large number of US NGOs to the DC headquarters of the World Bank.

Theoretically, NGOs and think-tanks are officially presented as belonging to a third sector coexisting with the public (state) and private (business) spheres. Corporate foundations and business associations are also counted in such efforts to detail an emerging transnational civil society. The dominant conception of civil society emphasizes the positive contribution made by such actors towards securing public goods, which cannot be safeguarded by either the state or by the private business sector (in the fields of human, minority and women rights, and the environment in particular). They welcome charitable contributions to a wide range of causes, which are all considered philanthropic in character. However other, troubling, aspects have been discussed in recent scholarship on global civil society. For example, according to prevailing definitions of a not-for-profit third sector, organizations such as the racist KKK, fundamentalist religious forces, etc., are clearly civil society actors. And while normative concepts emphasize the contribution of all civil society actors, the conflicting political orientations of civil society organizations do not go unnoticed. Anheier et al. (2001, p. 10) distinguish between incommensurable positions held by civil society actors—globalization-supporting and globalization-rejecting, reformist and alternative.

It is unclear how much sense it makes to equate business associations with other not-for-profit civil society actors. Business associations represent for-profit organizations, and receive additional funding from the state (e.g., for development efforts), as is the case with regard to the US Chamber of Commerce. The role of both business and state forces in shaping competing (transnational) civil society forces can easily escape due attention if a three-sector model is adopted without further consideration.

It is in any case crucial to establish precisely which civil society groups succeed in playing a role (in knowledge production and management), and which are chosen if public functions are transferred to civil society. It makes a big difference if certain tasks are transferred to a trade union or a chamber of commerce, for example. It also makes a big difference which partners are promoted in the effort to obtain knowledge authority. Money plays a considerable role in the social construction of knowledge. Cash-rich neoliberal forces like corporate foundations compete with poor cousins who populate the intellectual field of the radical left, for example.

Neogramscian approaches to international political economy (first introduced by Robert Cox) and 'private authority' research critically examine corporate actors and business-related forces as key constituencies of civil society (Cutler et al., 1999; Gill, 1993; Higgott et al., 2000). This scholarship avoids the third-sector trap by concentrating on the overlap between the private, public, and civil society sectors. Substantial distinctions between public and private authority are rejected, since neither the state (the traditional notion of authority) nor the maintenance of order can be understood if confined to a narrowly conceived public sphere. Gramsci's theoretical perspective of an expanded state regards politics as the combination of political (the state in the narrow sense) and civil society (the political world in a wider sense). The latter sphere is considered critical for the exercise of hegemony rather than merely rule, for the organization of consent relies on means other than simple control. Since neoliberal knowledge and policy prescriptions appear to be no longer taken for granted after much of the Washington Consensus agenda has been achieved, we should expect to detect signs of a battle of social forces competing for cognitive and normative authority under the cover of the new knowledge strategy in a world that has been structurally transformed.

Strengthening and (selectively) co-operating with civil society organizations in the South is clearly a central goal in the overall effort to enhance problem-solving capacities in the age of (allegedly) diminishing state capacities. This is the quintessence of the normative desire to move from government to governance—if necessary, creating and enabling participants and increasing the legitimacy of para-state politics, since not all the previous responsibilities and tasks performed by state institutions and organizations are handled well by profit-seeking enterprise. Corresponding demands for a strengthening of bottom-up participation in new governance patterns did not entirely fall on deaf ears if we look at the GDN effort, for example. At the beginning of the new millennium, 2,000 institutes and 9,000 individual researchers from various disciplines had eagerly signed up for the World Bank-sponsored Global Development Network's online community (King, 2000, p. 36). By March 2004, the GDN website listed 2,500 institutes. By March 2007, the number had grown to 3,445 organizations.[4] Interestingly, the number of individual researchers has dropped to 6055.[5] Since many of the affiliated researchers are state officials, and many of the member organizations are public institutions (universities, for example), numbers alone do not suffice if one wants to know the ways in which the GDN has served to increase bottom-up participation and, possibly, to empower previously marginalized civil society actors.

Suspicions about the dominant role of the World Bank contributed to the reconstitution of the GDN as an international organization, and to the relocation of the GDN headquarters to New Delhi. Officially this was done in an effort to strengthen the global character and the Southern focus of the GDN, by way of securing a healthy distance from Washington-based (and other) centers of power. However, the current nine global partner organizations include Merck & Company, along with a range of public research institutes in developed and developing countries. Meanwhile, the former president of Mexico, Ernesto Zedillo (presently chair of Yale University's Centre for the Study of Globalization), heads the eminent GDN Board of Directors, which includes the director of the World Bank's Development Research Group, Alan Winters. The prominent roles granted to a leading global corporation, a high official of the World Bank, and a former leader of Mexico who presided over a crucial stage in that country's transition from import substitution to an export orientation, are not by themselves suggestive of promising pluralism. At the same time, it must be acknowledged that a great many think-tanks and research institutes of various political orientations play a role in the evolving GDN network in one way or another.

Revisiting the GDN

GDN Dual Structure: A Hub and Spoke System

While more than 3,000 organizations and 6,000 researchers are presently (2007) listed as GDN members and enjoy access to the online resources provided by the network, fewer organizations and individual members are part of the core of the network, which has been institutionalized at the world-regional level. Certain regional organizations serve as hubs for the larger number of local think-tanks (and national networks of think-tanks). Table 1 shows the various hubs, their founding dates, and the number of member think-tanks in each of the regional networks.

In terms of an institutionalized core to the GDN, then, there are just over 100 organizations in the South in addition to the 400-member Latin American and Caribbean Economic Association, which has been incorporated in the US. Presently (2007), 15 think-tanks are listed as members of the Sub-Saharan network up from the six in 2004, and the 27 universities comprising the African Economic Research Consortium are now also included. Certainly, efforts have been made to narrow the gap in the numbers of think-tanks illustrating the North–South information divide, but it appears that efforts were made basically to enlist all the existing organizations in the South to this end.

The 100-plus think-tanks in the developing world (including Eastern Europe) are coordinated by seven organizations, which each serve as a hub or a secretariat for regional members. Even 100 organizations are difficult to assess; this work is beyond the scope of this paper. I will confine the preliminary analysis to the six Sub-Saharan organizations which were members in 2004: the Economic and Social Research Foundation (ESRF; Tanzania), the Economic Policy Research Centre (EPRC; Uganda), the Centre for Policy Analysis (Ghana), the Trade and Industrial Policy Secretariat (TIPS; South Africa), the Macro Economic and Financial Management Institute (MEFMI; Zimbabwe), and the Centre de Recherche en Economie Applique (CREA; Senegal).[6]

Table 1. GDN regional hubs (2004)

1988–1999
- Sub-Saharan Africa: African Economic Research Consortium Nairobi, 1988, six think-tanks
- Latin America and Caribbean Economic Association, 1992, 400 members
- Middle East and North Africa: Economic Research Forum Cairo, 1993, 12 think-tanks
- Russia/CIS: Economic Education Research Consortium, Moscow, 1997, nine think-tanks
- Eastern European Network CERGE-EI, 1997, Charles University and Academy of Sciences
- South Asia: South Asian Network of Economic Institutes, Delhi, 1998, 48 think-tanks
- East Asian Development Network, Singapore, 1999, 32 think-tanks

2000–2004
- GDN-Japan: Japan Bank for International Cooperation (JBIC) Institute, Tokyo
- GDN-North America: Center for Global Development, US
- GDN Europe: European Development Research Network (EUDN): Center for Development Research (ZEF), Bonn, Germany, 46 individual members
- GDN Pacific, Australia, and New Zealand: University of the South Pacific, Fiji

Source: http://www.gdn.org.

Before discussing individual GDN-related think-tanks, it is necessary to turn to the funding structure of the GDN in Sub-Saharan Africa. Has the World Bank created organizations to her liking, rather than assuming a more detached role as the broker of knowledge generated by independent think-tanks? The straightforward answer has to be 'no', since the World Bank was but one player financing and helping to mobilize support for the think-tank network, which in fact appears to have gone far in setting up the African Economic Research Consortium of universities. However, the World Bank did not set up the (state) universities themselves. Table 2 shows the organizations listed as member and non-member funding institutions of the GDN.

The website does not provide figures on the amount contributed by each of the different funding institutions, unfortunately. But even if the World Bank contributed a large amount, it remains just one of 16 funding institutions, although it is also plays a role in some of the others (e.g., the African Capacity Building Foundation; see http://www.acbf-pact.org/). Still, it is unlikely that one could reasonably charge the World Bank with unilaterally controlling these organizations. The formation of a global 'civil society' of think-tanks to the liking of the World Bank—if it does exist—has more complex origins in fact.

With regard to the Sub-Saharan Africa GDN hub, we can go a step further and scrutinize and link information available from various sources. Funding member USAID, for example, closely cooperates with many partners: I will focus on a particularly important partner, one of the 'independent' civil society think-tanks in the United States, namely the Center for International Private Enterprise (CIPE).

CIPE can certainly not be considered independent of business interests. It was set up as a development policy tool by the US Chamber of Commerce in 1983

to promote private enterprise and market-oriented reform worldwide. As a principal participant in the National Endowment for Democracy, CIPE supports strategies and techniques that address

Table 2. Member and non-member funding institutions of the GDN

Member funders
- UK Department for International Development (DFID)
- International Development Research Centre of Canada (IDRC)
- The John D. and Catherine T. MacArthur Foundation
- Ministry of Foreign Affairs, Denmark
- Ministry of Foreign Affairs, France
- Ministry of Foreign Affairs, Netherlands
- Norwegian Agency for Development Cooperation (NORAD)
- The Rockefeller Foundation
- Swedish International Development Agency (SIDA)
- Swiss Agency for Development Cooperation (SDC)
- US Agency for International Development (USAID)
- The World Bank (IBRD)

Non-member funders
- African Capacity Building Foundation (ACBF)
- African Development Bank (AfDB)
- The European Commission
- Ford Foundation

Source: http://www.aercafrica.org/organization.asp.

market-based democratic development. CIPE receives support from the US Agency for International Development (USAID) in addition to funding from corporations and corporate foundations. Since its inception, CIPE has funded more than 700 projects in 80 countries and has conducted business association management training programs in Africa, Asia, Central and Eastern Europe, Eurasia, Latin America, and the Middle East. (http://www.cipe.org, 2004, emphasis added)

CIPE presently lists more than 150 think-tanks in all regions as members of its global reform network of think-tanks (http://www.cipe.org/programs/global/).

According to many definitions, CIPE and the US Chamber of Commerce belong to the civil society 'third sector'. The Chamber is also the largest and most comprehensive business association in the United States, which lobbies on behalf of its constituency. Its members include firms, local chambers of commerce, and other business organizations. The Chamber became an increasingly active political force in the 1970s, when it started to mobilize the business community in an effort to counter the mobilization efforts of trades unions and regulatory agencies in charge of social, consumer, and health issues. The membership of the US Chamber of Commerce grew from 50,000 in 1970 to 215,000 in 1983 (Edsall, 1984, p. 123).

CIPE lists one of the GDN hub think-tanks (Tanzania's Economic and Social Research Foundation) among its recommended research institutes in Sub-Saharan Africa and another one (the Economic Policy Research Center in Uganda) in its global partner success category, separately from the whole African Economic Research Consortium, which is listed as a recommended regional organization. CIPE describes the EPRC in Uganda in the following way:

Established in 1994 as an autonomous nonprofit organization, EPRC is Uganda's leading economic research institution engaged in the quantitative analysis of Uganda's economy. EPRC's principal missions are to enhance local capacity in conducting policy-relevant research and strengthen the national capacity for policy formulation, analysis, and decision-making. ... It is funded by the African Capacity Building Foundation (ACBF), the government of Uganda, the World Bank, and other donors. (http://www.cipe.org/programs/global/partners/disppartner.php?id=42, 2004)

'Independence' is stressed as regards the other CIPE-recommended organizations also, although CIPE makes no secret of the involvement of state and foreign public funding institutions in each case. In order to understand the character of the claimed 'independence' of the named organizations, further research is necessary. It appears to be not unrealistic, however, to assume that CIPE-recommended organizations have a certain affinity with the neoliberal outlook of their sponsoring partner from the US, which also sponsors a range of other allegedly 'independent' organizations in Sub-Saharan Africa.

While GDN members are usually described as professional and politically neutral, the CIPE description of think-tanks sponsored as part of the global reform network is explicit on the neoliberal cause, although they are also held to be 'independent'. In Sub-Saharan Africa, CIPE provides financing for the Inter Region Economic Network (IREN):

Inter Region Economic Network is based in Nairobi, Kenya. It was established to promote a pro-choice, pro-market approach to public policy issues, as a not-for-profit, non-partisan, and non-governmental organization. ... It specifically seeks to enhance accessibility to information on classical liberal economics. The policies put forth by IREN have been derived from academic research and will be completely independent of partisan politics.

    IREN's mission is to free the human mind, the mainspring of all development. IREN's vision is to help foster the creation of a free society, where markets inform people's choices and decisions, and people rely less on government solutions to problems they can solve on their own. (http://www.cipe.org/programs/publicpolicy/index.htm)

There is considerable overlap between CIPE-supported think-tanks like IREN (totaling 28 in Sub-Saharan Africa in 2007) and the members of the Economic Freedom of the World network led by one of the leading neoliberal partisan think-tanks, the Canadian Fraser Institute (Vancouver), for example. Both the Ghana Institute of Economic Affairs and the South African Free Market Foundation are CIPE-recommended research institutes and contribute to the yearly publication *Economic Freedom of the World Index*, which ranks countries according to their adherence to free market principles. The CIPE-supported South African Free Market Foundation is explicitly described as a business organization active in research and advocacy.

The Fraser-led effort constitutes one of the products of the more than 100 think-tanks directly related to members of the neoliberal Mont Pèlerin Society (MPS) founded in 1947 by Friedrich August von Hayek, Milton Friedman, and others (see Plehwe and Walpen, 2006), which have been coordinated by the US-based Atlas Economic Research Organization since the 1980s.[7] IREN's impact in Sub-Saharan Africa has been discussed in a *New York Times* feature entitled 'Preaching Free-Market Gospel to Skeptical Africa' (DeParle, 2006b). IREN founder James Shikwati originally received seed money and other support from Lawrence Reed's Mackinac Center for Public Policy in Midland, MI; Lawrence Reed is a think-tank entrepreneur dedicated to teach others how to set up and run free-market think-tanks both in the US and around the globe (DeParle, 2006a). 'By 2001, with Mr. Reed's help, Mr. Shikwati landed two grants ... one from Atlas and one from a related British Group, the International Policy Network. IREN now has a budget of $300,000 and seven full-time employees' (DeParle, 2006b).

CIPE, Atlas, and other neoliberal notions of 'independently created development knowledge' thus translate into support for a variety of more or less academic think-tanks, which may be 'non-partisan' in terms of official party political affiliation but nevertheless all share a partisan type of neoliberal knowledge production, which may be of a more technical or more obvious programmatic character. Interestingly, the CIPE-supported Sub-Saharan GDN partners mentioned in 2004 were not listed as members of this network in 2007. Each think-tank supported by CIPE is not necessarily hard-core neoliberal, but CIPE's support of GDN organizations should not be considered entirely independent of a larger neoliberal effort to influence the social construction of authoritative development knowledge. In this effort, CIPE has been joined by a wide range of likeminded forces.

In order to develop a better sense of the association by CIPE/MPS/ATLAS of GDN hub think-tanks, I provide some additional information on a 'go-between' between the CIPE and GDN worlds, Erik Johnson, and on World Bank-sponsored events dedicated to promoting civil society networks of think-tanks. Johnson co-authored the introduction of the Stone (2000) volume on the GDN. He moved from CIPE to take a role at the World Bank Institute in charge of developing the GDN. At CIPE, Johnson had been

> director of Policy Studies and Evaluation, responsible for developing and managing strategic partnerships with governmental and non/governmental development organizations to support indigenous nonprofit institutions involved in economic reform and democracy building ... which were jointly sponsored by the World Bank. (McGann and Weaver, 2000, pp. 591–592)

The edited volume by McGann and Weaver (to which Johnson contributed) was the output of a World Bank-sponsored conference held in Barcelona, Spain, which preceded the formation of the GDN. The conference bridged the academic and advocacy think-tank worlds, and prominently presented the perspective of hard-core neoliberals.[8] Johnson contributed two chapters (on Sub-Saharan Africa and on the Middle East).

Johnson (2000a) reports on a survey of think-tanks in Sub-Saharan Africa, which was complemented by a series of interviews with think-tank executives and key constituencies in six countries. According to his own account, they are not representative of the entire population, and limited due to a focus on economic policy. Only South African think-tanks are reported to have access to significant domestic financial support. Start-up money and subsequent financial support originates from the African Capacity Building Foundation and American, British, German, and Norwegian sources (Johnson, 2000a, p. 468). Strong dependence on key donors is regarded as 'perhaps the largest danger many African think tanks face' (p. 488). With the exception of the South Africa Institute of Race Relations, think-tank boards are found to display limited diversity. 'In most cases, the balance leans toward the private sector ... or academia' (p. 483). Think-tanks are reported to promote policy change frequently in partnership with other organizations/institutions: 75% work with local governments, mostly on an ad-hoc basis; 80% feature a staff member who also serves on a government advisory committee; and another 75% coordinate their efforts with other organizations. 'One prominent theme in this cooperation is partnerships between think tanks and business associations' (p. 476). Think-tanks are reported to have direct linkages with other organizations such as academic institutions or government agencies, which sometimes limits their independence, according to Johnson. Think-tanks are also reported to participate in a range of networks such as the Study and Research Group on Democracy, Economic and Social Development in Africa, the Global Coalition for Africa, the Africa Privatization Network, and the West African Enterprise Network. With regard to links to the United States, Johnson says that 'professional development relationships have also been established between African think tanks and foreign groups such as the Association of Public Policy Analysis and Management in the United States' (p. 471).

The information provided by Johnson is interesting with regard to both the information he provides and what he does not say. It is not difficult to understand that most of the examined think-tanks are rather closely related to both the state and the private business sector. Johnson presents think-tanks as brave fighters against big government and corrupt business if they are not tied up with or repressed by government. Notably absent from his report is an analysis of the relations fostered by the organization he worked for, CIPE. Why do Johnson (2000a) and Johnson and Stone (2000) not talk about the efforts by CIPE and other funding agencies to develop neoliberal partisan think-tanks further alongside (and within) the World Bank's GDN? Efforts to understand the GDN think-tank network better are clearly unpromising if no effort is made to situate the GDN organizations in the larger picture of cooperating and competing transnational networks of think-tanks. The notion of 'neutral' knowledge can only be upheld if competing efforts—including communitarian perspectives featured by the Soros Foundation, for example—to gain knowledge authority are neglected.

According to Johnson (2000b, p. 337), Middle Eastern think-tanks represent 'an opportunity to fundamentally change the nature of policy making'. Only some countries were found lacking with regard to policy think-tanks, partly due to 'tyrannical leaders ... as in Iraq or Libya' (p. 338). However, Johnson observes an accelerating movement of economic liberalization. The Mediterranean Policy Institute Network was originally established in 1995 by three think-tanks in Egypt, Lebanon, and Turkey 'similar to the Central East European *Privatization Network* based in Slovenia' (p. 359, emphasis added).

In Johnson and Stone's (2000) chapter, the histories of the regional forums are described as important stepping stones on the road to establishing the GDN. More research has to be conducted in order to establish the extent to which CIPE and likeminded partner organizations were crucial actors in setting up the original hubs of the GDN. Together with CIPE and the German Friedrich Naumann Foundation, Chesapeake Associates[9] started the neoliberal

Balkan and 3-E networks of economic think-tanks in Eastern Europe, for example. Ivan Krastev (2000, p. 285) credits the neoliberal think-tanks and the World Bank for maintaining the anti-collectivist paradigm against the mounting pressure of a 'new populism' in this region (cf. Bohle and Neunhöffer, 2006).

Johnson and Stone (2000, p. 10) also report on a 1999 meeting of 27 think-tank representatives with UN General Secretary Kofi Annan, in which high expectations for future collaborative efforts were expressed. Interestingly, the effort to increase the bottom-up participation of think-tanks in UN affairs was explicitly linked to top-down expectations. Think-tanks were considered potentially helpful to communicate and translate global values, to review international agreements, and to make national policy suggestions.

> Like many governments and other international organizations, the UN is confronted by the exploding numbers of non-governmental organizations (NGOs) and the avalanche of information. Research institutes represent useful intermediaries to shape, channel and coordinate UN relations with other non-state actors. (Johnson and Stone, 2000, p. 10)

Conclusion

The information presented here casts considerable doubt on overly optimistic assessments of the scope of pluralism and the participatory culture promoted within the GDN network of think-tanks. Dire warnings by Diane Stone (2000, p. 248) with regard to the capacity of certain (business-related, and neoliberal we may add) epistemic communities and advocacy coalitions are much easier to understand if the roles of neoliberal funding agencies and the formation of neoliberal policy research institutes around the globe are duly considered when subjecting the GDN to closer scrutiny. While other collective knowledge actors also pursue ideological agendas, we are currently unlikely to find other transnational civil society groups that are comparable to the neoliberal networks in terms of comprehensiveness and organizational capacities.

Quite a bit more research needs to be done on the GDN and other think-tank networks at the local level, however, before we can draw reasonable conclusions with regard to the GDN in Sub-Saharan African countries and elsewhere, since the relative influence of neoliberal forces is likely to differ from region to region, and from time to time. Recent changes in Latin America are likely to strengthen 'Bolivarian' think-tanks in some countries, for example, but they will have to cope with the intellectual fire-power of neoliberal partisan think-tanks, which has been patiently built up in the past. Chafuen (2006) calmed down worried neoliberal observers of recent political events in Latin America by pointing out that 35 free market think-tanks are presently listed in the Atlas Economic Research Foundation Database (Latin America), compared to just seven in 1975. Additionally, 40 universities across the region employ what he calls free market champions compared to just 10 universities 30 years ago. He counted 12 free market journals and magazines in Latin America compared to just five in 1975, and whereas there was no free market TV or radio station in 1975 there are seven on the air now.

We need to know much more about transnational networks of think-tanks, in addition to the World Bank-related GDN network, if we want to understand the recent bottom-up transformation of the 'global knowledge power structure' (Strange, 1988) with regard to development. In order to assess the present scope of pluralism within and around the World Bank strategy, we have to consider the new mode of governance in the frame of a larger picture of privatization of economic and political functions previously performed by the state (Goldman, 2005; Hartmann, 2004). The 'global knowledge bank' has a role, if not a leading role, in a new stage of this large-scale transformation of global development politics. It is most likely that the World Bank can rely safely on the GDN network of think-tanks to secure information required in this process and to develop new layers of transnational knowledge circuits.

Notes

1   The Bellanet Initiative was named after a seminar that took place at the Rockefeller Foundation-sponsored academy in Bellagio, Italy. Various development organizations met there to institutionalize an information exchange regarding experiences with knowledge management strategies.
2   There are 130 thematic groups (King, 2000, p. 3) sharing a general design, Each employee of the World Bank can only belong to one community at one time. Each community is coordinated by a steering person in one of the regional departments and anchored in a sector department. The sector resource person is in charge of securing the infrastructure for ongoing information exchange (systematic support for requests, production of reports on best practices and lessons learned, yellow pages on think tanks and experts, virtual libraries, and databases).
3   Parallel to the new initiatives and further documenting a changing self-conception (of broker rather than producer), the World Bank has significantly cut back its own scientific research capacities, retaining a small staff of eight, down from 37 (Guilhot, 2000; Kapur et al., 1997).
4   See http://www.gdnet.org.
5   See http://www.gdnet.org/middle.php?primary_link_id=4.
6   Presently (2007), the following nine think tanks are also listed as members: the Institute of Statistical, Social and Economic Research (ISSER; Ghana), the Nigerian Institute of Social and Economic Research (NISER), the National Centre for Economic Management and Administration (NCEMA; Nigeria), the Programme de Troisième Cycle Inter-Universitaire en Economie (PTCI; Burkina Faso), the Botswana Institute for Development Policy Analysis (BIDPA), the South African Trade and Research Network (SATRN; Botswana), the Namibian Economic Policy Research Unit (NEPRU), the Kenya Institute for Public Policy Research and Analysis (KIPPRA), and the Centre Ivoirien de Recherche Economique et Sociale (CIRES; Côte d' Ivoire).
7   The MPS includes a number of development economists among whom Peter Bauer was the leading advocate against state aid, a 'voice for the poor' and the 'Hayek of development' economics according to *The Economist* (2002; cf. Plehwe, 2006).
8   See the chapter on the Heritage Foundation by the former MPS president and secretary treasurer Ed Feulner (2000) for an example of the pluralism within neoliberal confines featured by MPS-related think-tanks.
9   Chesapeake Associates (http://www.chesapeakeassociates.org/) is another USAID-sponsored organization with historical ties to the CIA, according to Roelofs (2003).

References

Anheier, H., Glasius, M. & Kaldor, M. (2001) Introducing global civil society, in H. Anheier, M. Glasius, & M. Kaldor (eds) *Global Civil Society 2001* (Oxford: Oxford University Press).
Bell, D. (1973) *The Coming of the Post-Industrial Society* (New York: Basic Books).
Bohle, D. & Neunhöffer, G. (2006) Why is there no third way? The role of neoliberal ideology, networks and think tanks in combating market socialism and shaping transformation in Poland, in D. Plehwe, B. Walpen, & G Neunhöffer (eds) *Neoliberal Hegemony: A Global Critique* (London and New York: Routledge), pp. 89–104.
Bukowitz, W. & Williams, R. (2000) *The Knowledge Management Fieldbook* (London: Pearson Education Limited).
Cammack, P. (2002) The mother of all governments: the World Bank's matrix for global governance, in R. Wilkinson & S. Hughes (eds) *Global Governance: Critical Perspectives* (London and New York: Routledge), pp. 36–54.
Chafuen, A. A. (2006) Hope amid turmoil in Latin America? *Atlas Foundation Newsletter* (Spring)., http://www.atlasusa.org/V2/files/pdfs/2006-h-spring.pdf/
Cutler, A. C Haufer, V. & Porter, T. (eds) (1999) *Private Authority and International Affairs* (Albany: State University of New York Press).
Deparle, J. (2006a) The conservative reach: right-of-center guru goes wide with the gospel of small government, *The New York Times*, 17 November.

DeParle, J. (2006b) The conservative reach: preaching free market gospel to skeptical Africa, *The New York Times*, 18 November.

Edsall, T. B. (1984) *The New Politics of Inequality* (New York: Norton).

Evers, H.-D., Kaiser, M. & Müller, C. (2003) Entwicklung durch Wissen: eine globale Wissensarchitektur, *Soziale Welt*, 54(1), pp. 49–70.

Feulner, E. (2000) The Heritage Foundation, in J. G. McGann & R. K. Weaver (eds) *Think Tanks and Civil Society: Catalysts for Ideas and Action* (New Brunswick, NJ: Transaction Publishers).

Fine, B. (1999) The developmental state is dead: long live social capital? *Development and Change*, 30(1), pp. 1–19.

Gill, S. (ed.) (1993) *Gramsci, Historical Materialism and International Relations* (Cambridge: Cambridge University Press).

Goldman, M. (2005) *Imperial Nature: The World Bank and Struggles for Social Justice in the Age of Globalization* (New Haven, CT: Yale University Press).

Guihot, N. (2000) D'une vérité à l'autre, les politiques de la Banque mondiale, *Le Monde Diplomatique*, September.

Hartmann, E. (2004) Globalisierungskritische Netzwerke zwischen Systemstabilisierung und Gegenhegemonie, in N. Fröhler, S. Hürtgen, C. T. Schlüter & M. Thiedke (eds) *Wir Können Auch Anders: Perspektiven von Demokratie und Partizipation* (Münster: Westfälisches Dampfboot), pp. 97–109.

Higgott, R. (2000) Contested globalization: the changing context and normative challenges, *Review of International Studies*, 26, pp. 131–153.

Higgott, R. A., Underhill, G. & Bieler, A. (eds) (2000) *Non-State Actors and Authority in the Global System* (London and New York: Routledge).

Johnson, E. C. (2000a) Think tanks in Sub-Saharan Africa, in J. G. McGann & R. K. Weaver (eds) *Think Tanks and Civil Society: Catalysts for Ideas and Action* (New Brunswick, NJ: Transaction Publishers).

Johnson, E. C. (2000b) Policy making beyond the politics of conflict: civil society think tanks in the Middle East and North Africa, in J. G. McGann & R. K. Weaver (eds) *Think Tanks and Civil Society: Catalysts for Ideas and Action* (New Brunswick, NJ: Transaction Publishers).

Johnson, E. & Stone, D. (2000) The genesis of the GDN, in D. Stone (ed.) *Banking on Knowledge: The Genesis of the Global Development Network* (London: Routledge).

Kapur, D. (2002) The changing anatomy of governance of the World Bank, in J. R. Pincus & J. A. Winters (eds) *Reinventing the World Bank* (Ithaca: Cornell University Press), 54–75.

Kapur, D., Lewis, J. P. & Webb, R. (1997) *The World Bank: Its First Half Century, Vol. 1: History* (Washington, DC: Brookings Institution Press).

King, K. (2000) Towards knowledge-based aid: a new way of working or a new North–South divide? *Journal of International Cooperation in Education*, 3(2), pp. 23–48.

Krastev, I. (2000) The liberal estate: reflections on the role of think tanks in Central and Eastern Europe, in J. G. McGann & R. K. Weaver (eds) *Think Tanks and Civil Society: Catalysts for Ideas and Action* (New Brunswick, NJ: Transaction Publishers).

McGann, J. G. & Weaver, R. K. (eds) (2000) *Think Tanks and Civil Society: Catalysts for Ideas and Action* (New Brunswick, NJ: Transaction Publishers).

Nustad, K. G. & Sending, O. J. (2000) The instrumentalisation of development knowledge, in D. Stone (ed.) *Banking on Knowledge: The Genesis of the Global Development Network* (London: Routledge).

Pincus, J. & Winters, J. A. (eds) (2002) *Reinventing the World Bank* (Ithaca, NY: Cornell University Press).

Plehwe, D. (2006) Peter Bauer (1915–2002): Entwicklung allein durch die Kräfte des Marktes, *Entwicklungspolitik Nord–Süd*, 1–2(January), pp. 41–43.

Plehwe, D. & Walpen, B (2006) Between network and complex organization: the making of neoliberal knowledge and hegemony, in D. Plehwe, B, Walpen, & G. Neunhöffer (eds) *Neoliberal Hegemony: A Global Critique* (London: Routledge).

Rich, B. (2002) The World Bank under James Wolfensohn, in J. R. Pincus & J. A. Winters (eds) *Reinventing the World Bank* (Ithaca: Cornell University Press), pp. 26–53.

Roelofs, J. (2003) *Foundations and Public Policy: The Mask of Pluralism* (New York: State University of New York Press).

St. Clair, A. (2006) The World Bank as a transnational expertised institution, *Journal of Global Governance*, 12(1), pp. 77–95.

Stone, D. (ed.) (2000a) *Banking on Knowledge: The Genesis of the Global Development Network* (London: Routledge).

Strange, S. (1988) *States and Markets. An Introduction to International Political Economy* (London: Pinter Publishers).

The Economist (2002) A voice for the poor, 4 May.

Weber, H. (2006) A political analysis of the PRSP Initiative: social struggles and the organization of persistent relations of inequality, *Globalizations*, 3(2), pp. 187–206.

Williams, M. (2000) The World Bank, the World Trade Organization and the environmental social movement, in (Williams) in Higgott, R. A., Underhill, G. & Bieler, A. (eds) (2000) *Non-State Actors and Authority in the Global System* (London and New York: Routledge), pp. 241–255.

Rethinking the Global Production of Uneven Development

MARCUS TAYLOR

In the mid-1980s Nigel Harris provocatively argued that wide-scale changes to the structures of global production were transforming the essential characteristics of the global capitalist system. The dramatic ramifications of this shift, according to Harris, rendered obsolete the categories of 'First' and 'Third' Worlds and raised a new potentiality for development. As Harris (1986, pp. 200–201) put it:

> The conception of an interdependent, interacting, global manufacturing system cuts across the old view of a world consisting of nation-states as well as one of groups of countries, more or less developed and centrally planned – the First, the Third and the Second Worlds. Those notions bore some relationship to an older economy . . . but the new world that has superseded it is far more complex and does not lend itself to the simple identification of First and Third, haves and have-nots, rich and poor, industrialized and non-industrialized.... The process of dispersal of manufacturing capacity brings enormous hope to areas where poverty has hitherto appeared immovable.

Harris's text was indicative of a wave of Marxist and world systems theory-inspired work, spurred on by Folker Fröbel et al.'s (1977) provocative pronouncement of a 'new international division of labour', that sought to analyse critically how the internationalisation of productive capital would affect global development trends. However, despite this convergence of critical development theory on the theme of production in the early 1980s, such attention proved ephemeral. The 1982 debt crisis and the subsequent shockwaves of structural adjustment brought crashing down the existing intellectual architecture of development theory. This left academic traditions that had been geared to inform—or critique—the industrialisation policies of national-developmentalism peculiarly misplaced. Moreover, in the wake of the crisis of state socialism at the end of the decade, new critiques emerged that suggested liberal and neo-Marxist development theory, in both economic and sociological guises, could neither explain the heterogeneous nature of patterns of development and underdevelopment nor adequately inform policy (Booth, 1985; Escobar, 1995).

Development theory began to bifurcate. On the one hand, neoclassical economics rose to dominate official discourse, with its monolithic focus on trade and fiscal issues that were deemed key to market efficiency. On the other hand, a counter-current of post-structuralist-inspired work questioned the very notion of development, critiqued the older Marxist approaches for economic reductionism, and refocused emphasis on issues of civil society, social movements, and identity politics. Although the post-structuralist turn has illuminated many important conceptual issues, the relative neglect of production is problematic.[1] Comprehensive analysis of the process of production, including the production of both material items and of labouring bodies, is essential to understand the way in which global capitalism reproduces itself; it is therefore key to engage the questions concerning the (re)distribution of material and symbolic resources that motivate critical development studies. This has become increasingly clear as a range of issues facing scholars have arisen around the socio-economic and environmental effects of a rapidly changing international division of labour. Most vividly, the rapid expansion of industrial production in China compels critical development theorists to engage challenging questions concerning its effects upon workers and communities across the globe.

In the following sections this paper attempts to formulate a contribution towards rethinking development theory based on reconceptualising the global relations of production. The first section sets out the importance of production to development theory by highlighting and critiquing the foundational assumptions found in classical political economy, neoclassical economics, and institutional economics. The second section offers a critique of the contemporary sociological alternative, the 'global commodity chains' approach, which is perhaps the closest heir to the debates of the 1970s. This paper questions the invisibility of labour within the approach and argues that the contested relationships through which labour forces with particular attributes are socially produced, reproduced, and put to work in an organised process of production across different spatial locales are key determinants of the spatial distribution of productive processes. Finally, the third section extends the previous arguments to outline an alternative perspective based on the dialectical relationship between social embedding and social abstraction. From this perspective, it is argued, we can more precisely examine the social relations that underlie global productive structures and better conceptualise the causes and effects of uneven development for workers and communities on a global scale.

The Production–Development Nexus

The terms in which production is discussed in development theory tend to follow the agenda set by the classical political economists, who correlated the onset of capitalist modernity with dramatic increases in the productivity of human labour (cf. Cowen and Shenton, 1996). Adam Smith's foundational exposition, for example, tied the essence of modernity to an extended and ever-more specialised division of labour that was driven by and facilitated the growth of the market. This process was seen as a virtuous circle wherein specialisation induced greater productivity, higher national income, and, therein, the further enlargement of the market, with evident parallels to the current neoclassical orthodoxy. For Smith, the increasing productivity of labour constituted the material basis of what is now termed 'development' and he proclaimed that becoming part of an expanded division of labour allowed an 'industrious and frugal peasant' to accommodate his needs in a manner that exceeded 'many an African king, the absolute master of the lives and liberties of ten thousand naked savages' (Smith, 1990 [1776], p. 45]). Given that many industrious and frugal peasants across the global South are currently moving off the land at unprecedented rates to join productive processes within the urbanised industrial machine of global capitalism, one wonders whether the conditions of social marginalisation and the brutal nature of industrial relations facing such migrants, within, for example, the expanding industrial centres of coastal China, would lead them to concur with Smith's postulation? As in Smith's time, the expanding productivity of labour is matched by the expanding production of labourers, as proletarianisation accelerates apace through dispossession and primitive accumulation. The productive potentiality that appears innate to the social relations of capitalism therefore remains closely tied to uneven development, vast inequalities, and the poverty of an expanding global working class.

While this dark side of capitalism was discussed by the classical political economists, it was seen as a tangential and temporary evil that would be overcome by the productive revolution through which growing numbers of socially useful items (use-values) could be produced. Thus, capitalist development offered a potential solution to material scarcity. Beyond the satisfaction of material wants, moreover, severing humankind from an unending toil for subsistence theoretically provided the basis for personal and social development by increasing the amount of time available to augment human potentials. Material advancement could therefore be seen as paving the way for social, cultural, and political progress—a formulation that remains the implicit basis for liberal theories of development (Weisband, 1989). As a consequence, much development theory—both mainstream and critical—has focused on the conditions that may allow for 'modernisation' through the replication of this 'original transition' to capitalism and a subsequent 'catch-up' of productive prowess through technological transfer (Burkett and Hart-Landsberg, 2003; Roxborough, 1979).

In the contemporary era, neoclassical economics has maintained the essence of Smith's theory, yet without the caution Smith himself applied. On a theoretical level, neoclassical economics views production as an extension of the principles of exchange and therefore a simple extension of the market. Production is reduced to an offshoot of the barter between individuals who possess different yet necessary factors of production (capital, land, labour) in order to create final products with greater marginal utility. Subsumed under absurdly simplifying microfoundations, the basis of the neoclassical approach proclaims that, under proper macroeconomic management including trade liberalisation and fiscal responsibility, productive structures naturally take shape through rational and mutually beneficial market exchanges in a manner that reflects national comparative advantages, leading to long-run complementarities, income convergence, and global equilibrium (Dunkley, 2004; Weeks, 2001). From these theoretical grounds, the neoclassical stream follows Smith in presenting development as the result of a transhistorical spread and growing efficiency of markets innate to humankind's assumed need to 'truck, barter, and trade'.

On a political level, reducing history to a simple teleology of the market facilitated the construction of a one-size-fits-all remedy to open markets in the South that fitted comfortably into the political agenda of the United States and was avidly propagated by international financial institutions (cf. Berger, 2004). On an analytical level, through its focus on idealised models of exchange and market expansion, neoclassicism wilfully erases any appreciation of the important differences between the qualitatively distinct social relationships and processes that underscore production (cf. Clarke, 1991; Hodgson, 2002; Reinert, 2004). A backlash against this symbiosis of theoretical myopia and political expediency led many frustrated economists outside of the mainstream to decry the minimal attention given to production and the specific institutions that could encourage the establishment of increasing-returns industries. Alice Amsden's seminal article on 'bringing production back in', for example, lamented the 'infinitesimally small place' afforded to production within contemporary economics as compared to questions concerning fiscal prudence and international trade (Amsden, 1997).

Amsden's piece attempted to coerce fellow economists into taking seriously the state's role in promoting industrial development. Within institutional economics, which has most completely grappled with this task, the East Asian countries stand as exemplars of the complex relationship between state, production, and development that is lost within the neoclassical mainstream (Chang, 2002; Jomo and Chen, 1997; Reinert, 2004; Wade, 1990). For these authors, the role of the state in providing the correct institutional infrastructure for industrialisation—including infant industry protection, financial support, and technical support—was crucial to the development of prosperous industrial sectors, leading to the developmental results celebrated in notions of the 'East Asian miracle'. In critiquing market-essentialist accounts of East Asian industrialisation by emphasising state capacity in determining productive structures, institutionalists have been expressly important in shaping debates within critical development studies by propagating the need for other countries to learn from and potentially emulate the East Asian model.

Nonetheless, despite broadening the scope of analytical enquiry, institutionalist approaches tend to remain trapped in the fetishised categories of modern economics that see labour forces as simply one more factor of production, predisposed for a relationship with capital, rather than socially constructed and therefore imbued with specific social characteristics. As Martin Hart-Landsberg and Paul Burkett have persuasively argued, the institutionalists share with neoclassical economics a conceptualisation of workers and communities as 'passive inputs for an industrialisation process planned by (private or state) capitalists' (Burkett and Hart-Landsberg, 2003, p. 166). In so doing, they neglect to consider how productive structures are configured within the context of complex social relationships through which labour is reproduced, mobilised, and put to use. As a consequence, the celebration of state-led industrial policy in the guise of the East Asian model often comes at the expense of glossing over the complex and contradictory construction of production relations within these countries. Thus, little attention has been given to the repressive labour systems that undergirded the 'miracle' and how workers and communities pursued various forms of contestation that shaped these economic processes and outcomes (Burkett and Hart-Landsberg, 2000; Deyo, 1989).

Global Commodity Chains and the Invisibility of Labour

In sharp definition to the theoretical myopia of neoclassicism and the state-centric concerns of institutional economics, the 'global commodity chains' (GCC) approach offers a sociological alternative that professes to take seriously the social relations of global production on a transnational level. GCC analysis focuses upon the ways in which the diverse production processes necessary for the creation of a single commodity can be disintegrated, modularised, and distributed between a network of discrete production sites. Such networks—potentially linking together an assortment of formally independent lead firms, subsidiaries, and subcontractors on a transnational level—are considered in terms of their social embeddedness, which emphasises how they are 'situationally specific, socially constructed, and locally integrated' (Gereffi and Korzeniewicz, 1994, p. 2).

Two central concerns permeate GCC studies. First, the GCC approach analyses the construction of embedded inter-firm networks to shed critical light upon the interactions between firms within a commodity chain, with a specific concern with how hierarchical control can be exercised by lead firms without direct ownership of the entire chain. By integrating issues of trust, uneven technological capacity, and the need for joint problem solving activities that require mutual coordination, GCC analysis follows the 'new economic sociology' in emphasising how production chains rely on embedded relationships in order to achieve efficient economic outcomes in a manner quite distinct from the predictions of mainstream economic theory:

> Network actors in many instances control opportunism through the effects of repeat transactions, reputation, and social norms that are embedded in particular geographic locations or social groups ... trust, reputation, and mutual dependence dampen opportunistic behavior, and in so doing they make possible more complex inter-firm divisions of labor and interdependence than would be predicted by transaction costs theory. (Gereffi et al., 2005, p. 81)

GCC analysis interrogates the power relations that pervade such networks and that mediate the vertical and, to a lesser degree, horizontal linkages that compose commodity chains. While embedded relationships may be relationships of relative equality, longevity, mutual dependence, and trust, they can also reinforce hierarchy, power asymmetries, and the uneven appropriation of rents and, ultimately, profit. The latter situation is manifest in the governance structures of 'captive value chains', wherein lead firms use their financial and technological advantages to institutionalise dominant relationships with suppliers who are left dependent in terms of technology, information, and market access (Gereffi et al., 2005, p. 87). Within these relationships, the way in which information about market opportunities, quality standards, and production technologies is centralised, codified, and controlled across the network greatly shapes the exercise of power (Ponte and Gibbon, 2005). Access to such knowledge shapes the relative capacity of firms across the commodity chain to upgrade their technological capabilities and produce directly for markets, with asymmetrical outcomes that affect spatial distribution of productive activities and developmental horizons.

Second, in keeping with the concerns of the earlier 'new international division of labour' debates, GCC seeks to analyse the consequences for socio-economic development of the spatial distribution of nodes in the commodity chain and the power structures that mediate them. In particular, GCC authors are interested in the possibilities for firms in less-developed countries to upgrade their role in the production process by assuming more technologically advanced functions that allow for a greater value appropriation and further horizontal and vertical linkages with local firms (Bair and Gereffi, 2003; Gibbon, 2001). Technological upgrading is recognised to play a central, though not straightforward, role in socio-economic development. Whereas early research focused on the possibilities of and limits to industrial upgrading, recent studies have begun to question the presumed benefits of this form of 'catch-up' by considering wider questions about the concentration of wealth within 'total package' sectors in the developing world (Bair and Dussel Peters, 2006).

The insights of the GCC exploration of network dynamics and the power relations that traverse transnational supply chains are well taken, particularly the way the approach highlights how commodity chains are structured around significant power imbalances through which lead firms seek to control market access, shape the technical organisation of production, and influence the distribution of costs associated with production stages so as to maximise their control over the appropriation of value across the chain as a whole. The analysis, however, provides only a partial view of the social relations and institutional contexts that shape global production and mediate its developmental impacts. The theoretical foundations of the GCC approach lead it to prioritise conceptually the ways in which global production dynamics are moulded by the forms of network governance that structure commodity chains. The latter are seen to spring from a combination of technological imperatives—methods of modularisation, information coordination, relative technological capacity, the character of market access, and demand for a given commodity—that define the parameters within which networked firms attempt to shape the distribution of knowledge, resources, and profits. As a consequence, the approach tends towards a 'network essentialism', whereby the dynamics of global commodity chains are seen to flow from the functional characteristics of the governance network that constitutes them, thus ignoring the wider social and institutional context that shapes production. As a result, the complexity of the social relations that surround production is packaged into five ideal-type categories of network governance that represent the degree of embedding between firms along a spectrum—starting with un-embedded 'arms-length' market relations, moving through modular, relational, and captive value chains, and culminating in 'hierarchy', which relates to the complete vertical integration of production within a unitary transnational enterprise (Gereffi et al., 2005).

While the focus on networks allows the approach to gain useful analytical purchase on the distribution of accumulated value across supply chains, the approach remains curiously silent concerning the initial creation of value that precedes distribution among firms across the supply chain. Contributing to this myopia is the way that GCC analysis reduces the process of production to a technical issue of modularising and distributing tasks across a network of firms and sites that comprise an integrated division of labour. Production as left as an unopened 'black box', similarly to the neoclassical and institutional economics conceptualisations critiqued above, and the specific social relations through which local and national labour forces are produced, reproduced, and deployed to create value within the production process are marginalised. Labour is handled as a static factor of production, sidelining important questions about power and subjectivity both in the labour process and within the wider context of the creation and reproduction of labour forces.

GCC analysis is, of course, not entirely muted on labour issues. Nonetheless, studies within the genre tend to consider labour forces as an *a priori* factor in the spatial disbursement of productive processes within chains. This is often undertaken with the implicit assumption of the availability of cheap and/or disciplined labour-power without consideration of the social processes that socially construct and reproduce labour-power in the form of a commodity with particular attributes in specific locations. On this basis, GCC analysts often consider, albeit briefly, the effects of global commodity chain dynamics upon workforces in terms of their effects on wages and technological upgrading within the workplace (e.g., Bair and Dussel Peters, 2006; Bair and Gereffi, 2001; Czaban and Henderson, 2003). The latter are undoubtedly pertinent issues in need of elaboration and discussion. Nonetheless, labour is constructed as the passive object that is moulded through shifts within the overarching categories of networks and technological change central to GCC analysis. Often such studies are conducted within the paradigm of the effects of globalisation upon labour markets and workforces (Jenkins, 2004; Manda and Sen, 2004), whereby insufficient attention is placed upon the inverse—that is, what are the constitutive effects of constructed and contested workforces, labour markets, and production processes upon globalisation?

To answer this question, we would need to leave the top-down theoretical constructions of GCC analysis, in which the possibility of working people as subjects in the production of global development—involved in processes of conflict and accommodation both inside and outside the workplace that shape the global relations of production and social reproduction—is buried under the weight of technological and institutional determinism imputed from the networked structures of commodity chains and their particular modes of governance. Sympathetic critiques of the GCC approach suggest that, in order to overcome its limitations, it must consider a much fuller spectrum of institutions in which productive activities are embedded (Bair, 2005; Henderson et al., 2002). This is undoubtedly true, and below I empha-sise the necessity of making labour visible again by conceptualising global production dynamics within the context of the production, reproduction, and deployment of specific labour forces. However, on its own such an approach falls short because it continues to con-ceive of production as solely an embedded process. I argue that if we wish to take the concept of embeddedness seriously then we must not only engage a much fuller and richer spectrum of social relations in which global productive activities are embedded, but we must also con-sider the ways in which socially embedded economic activities undergo a repeated process of abstraction and re-embedding within the context of global capitalism. The latter is pivotal for a critical perspective on production because it permits us to see not only how the uneven effects of global economic integration impact upon workers and communities across the globe, but also how the struggles that surround embedded production have reciprocal effects upon the wider terrain of global accumulation.

Social Embedding Meets Social Abstraction

To elaborate the relationship between embedding and abstraction, it is useful to return to Marx's critique of political economy and his notion of the dual form of commodity-producing labour within capitalism. For Marx, labour within capitalist production has both concrete and abstract qualities.

On the one hand, labour is concrete and private because production involves a specific type of labour (e.g., stitching together jeans or assembling electronic parts) undertaken by waged labourers within the context of a private capitalist enterprise operating with distinct conditions of production in a specific locale. The concept of concrete labour thereby emphasises the embedded quality of production, whereby productive activities are embedded in specific social, cultural, and institutional contexts that include the relationships and institutions through which labour forces are reproduced and put to use. The unique social context in which every act of production takes place provides the basis for the qualitatively and quantitat-ively distinct economic activities upon which the uneven productive structures of global capit-alism are mapped out.

Alongside being embedded as concrete and private, however, labour within capitalism is sim-ultaneously social and abstract because every private and concrete process of production forms one moment of a social division of labour that is mediated through the exchange of commodities on a global level. Production creates no value unless the product itself can be socially validated through sale on the market and, as such, production must be understood not solely as a conjunc-ture of concrete, embedded relationships but as one moment in a circuit of capital spanning pro-duction and circulation. Through this social organisation of production, the relationships between producers are socially abstracted into relationships between commodities. As Simon Clarke (1991, p. 136) indicates:

> The commodity exists at the point of intersection of a series of social relationships between and within classes. Fluctuations in the prices of individual commodities are the means by which a range of social relations is regulated.

Through the circulation of commodities on the market, the specific social relations and labour-ing practices through which an individual act of production occurs are abstracted into the form of value, represented through the interplay of market prices. Value is not a pre-given quantity defined at the moment of production and embodied within the commodity. Rather, it is constituted socially and disclosed to producers *post-factum* in the market as a form of imposition. Producers that operate within embedded relations that do not meet the social ascription of value by producing a quality and quantity of product at a cheap enough price will lose ground against competitors and suffer from poor sales, decreasing profits, high costs to borrow capital, and potential collapse. Through the circuit of capital, therefore, each singular act of production enters into a disciplinary feedback loop with the social whole, through which it must be socially validated by way of the sale of commodities. As Massimo de Angelis (2005, p. 70) puts it:

> It is pursuing value within the confinement of market relations that individual 'actors' compare values of different products or compare among values of the same products produced with different methods and conditions of production and act upon this comparison. The effect of this acting enters into feedback relations with millions of others, it contributes to produce new average prices and profit and it produces effects that act as material forces for other actors making similar comparison and acting upon them. The ongoing process of this act of measurement of value and action upon it, is what gives rise to what we value socially [regardless of] our individual or collective aggregate ethical standpoint.

The market acts as an abstract disciplinary mechanism through which concrete productive activities are compared and value is socially ascribed in an abstract form—a process in which individual producers are either rewarded or punished in accordance with their ability to meet the quantitative and qualitative requirements of social reproduction.

The qualitative dimension represents the need to for producers to match the social validation of what constitutes a use-value—that is, a socially useful item. As Marx (1976 [1867], p. 48) put it: 'If the thing is useless, so is the labour contained within it; the labour does not count as labour, and therefore creates no value.' As Marx did not put it, however, the ascription of social utility to a commodity involves complex struggles over the social construction of consumption needs through such techniques as product differentiation and branding (Fine, 2002). This is extremely important because producers frequently attempt to mediate the social discipline imposed by the market by either creating new social needs—and thereby expanding the market—or by attempting to manipulate the symbolic capital associated with their particular product in an attempt to capture market share and displace the competition. The ability to do so, however, is generally temporary as other producers mimic those techniques, thereby reconstituting the social average around a new definition and re-launching the process of differentiation anew.

Simultaneously, the quantitative dimension of value is imposed through the constant struggle of capitals to cut costs and increase the productivity of labour for the production of a given commodity. This is reflected in the notion of 'socially necessary labour time', which was used by Marx to indicate how the value of any generic commodity is established by

> the labour-time socially necessary to produce an article under the normal conditions of production, and with the average degree of skill and intensity prevalent at the time. . . . Each individual commodity, in this connexion, is to be considered as an average sample of its class. (Marx, 1976, p. 47)

The imposition of value upon commodities in terms of socially necessary labour time forces firms to conform their embedded conditions of production towards the social norm of productivity, on pain of extinction. Firms whose production relations allow them to produce below the socially necessary labour time will capture a greater market share, forcing competitors to attempt to catch up to the new social average by changing the embedded conditions in which their production occurs. This process, in turn, will be refracted back coercively upon localities through a change in the social average, and compel the further restructuring of locally embedded social organisation in a continuous process to maintain profitability and the accumulation of capital. The embedding–abstraction relationship thereby illuminates what Marx meant by production being indivisibly material and social. Every act of production not only produces a material item but also produces social relations by contributing to the re-creation of a social average for production that establishes the abstract context in which all other production takes place.

Objectified in the form of global economic forces such as shifting market prices and fickle investment flows, the pressures of social abstraction compel a process of ongoing social restructuring through revolutions in the social, technical, and frequently spatial organisation of production. When the socially embedded relations of production for a specific firm no longer meet the social ascription of value, production must be dis-embedded from its existing social context, and those social relations must be restructured before production can be profitably re-embedded. A focus on social abstraction, therefore, helps us put social embedding in motion. The latter, however, is an uneven and conflict-ridden process that forces capitals and state bodies—concerned with a potential drop in regional or national competitiveness—to attempt to restructure a wide range of social relations spanning multiple social institutions. Within the process of production itself, Marx's work highlighted the ways in which capital repeatedly attempts to restructure its foundational class relationship in attempts to impose extensive (longer, harder work) and/or intensive (productivity increase through mechanisation) methods of increasing the surplus extracted from labour (cf. Fine, 2004). To halt the analysis there, however, would be to take too narrow a view of social embedding.

In its analysis of the vertical disintegration of production, global commodity chains analysis has provided part of the wider picture, as some seek to shelter themselves from the pressures of abstraction by institutionalising themselves as the lead player in a network of outsourced firms. Nike, for example, has attempted to separate itself from the labour-intensive aspects of production by outsourcing the latter to firms such as Yue-Yuen, a large Taiwanese conglomerate that makes approximately 17% of the world's athletic shoes (Merk, 2008). Nike's aim is to shed the pressures of productive reorganisation onto its suppliers and use its market position to displace any incurred costs onto the latter, as typically described in the GCC literature. However, these dynamics cannot be adequately understood outside of the context of the ongoing wide-scale restructuring of labour forces in the global South (particularly China, in this case) within which such production processes are embedded (cf. Cantin and Taylor, 2008).

The fetish of labour as simply a factor of production—a ready-made commodity to be added to the ingredients of production—must be shed. As both Marx and Karl Polanyi emphasised, labour in commodity form is a fictitious commodity. Its existence not only has to be socially constituted through the separation of workers from alternative means of subsistence; also, specific labour forces have to be socially constructed as resources that can be profitably employed within particular processes of production. This involves a complex conjuncture of contested material, social, and cultural processes. As a consequence, productive activities are not merely embedded in the networked relationships between interrelated firms that compose a commodity chain, they are also embedded in the social fabric of the fragmented relationships between capital and labour within the process of production and in the social reproduction of waged labour in its commodity form, mediated by the household, labour market, and state.

The embedding–abstraction relation is therefore constituted by and constitutive of the contested and evolving relations of what Fred Deyo has termed 'labour systems'. The latter comprise the mechanisms through which labour is 'socially reproduced, mobilised for economic ends, utilised in production and controlled and motivated in support of economic goals'

(Deyo, 2001, p. 259). The role of the state in fashioning the social context in which labour forces are created and deployed is pivotal. While some authors have suggested that a 'new era' of capitalism under globalisation has rendered it necessary to think in terms of transnational classes and transnational states (Robinson, 2002), this perspective tends to ignore the centrality of the national state in creating the conditions within which productive activities are embedded, and thereby its role in socially differentiating productive activities across space. At a very minimum, the state fashions the institutional basis for the contracting of labour and the legal basis on which industrial relations occur, and has a function in the reproduction of differentiated labouring bodies through various forms of social policy (cf. Edwards and Elger, 1999). The institutional forms of the state are intrinsic to the embedding–abstraction relationship and, as a result, stand as the constant target of struggles that aim to redefine the social context of production (Taylor, 2006).

Of course, notwithstanding its importance, the state is far from being the sole social institution that configures the social context in which labour forces are constructed and put to work. The complex interplay between the social embedding of production and the social reproduction of labour forces is shaped by struggles across a range of social institutions including: (1) the institutional environment established by national and regional state bodies through social, labour, and industrial policies; (2) the hiring and labour control strategies of employers in their attempt to forge a cohesive, efficient, and disciplined workforce; (3) practices of exclusion or inclusion that structure workforces based on social origin, age, gender, or ethnicity; and (4) social relationships within the family unit that constrict which family members can enter paid labour and under what conditions.

Intrinsic to these relationships are important issues of power and conflict associated with class and patriarchy, which are often left out of GCC and institutionalist approaches despite being pivotal factors that shape the dynamics and spatial distribution of productive processes. They permeate the forms assumed by production relations, such as the development of modes of labour control within the factory and their integration with the technologies of production. Class struggles centred around the production process and the functioning of labour markets have been shaped by the establishment of new centres of industrial production and ongoing conflicts over 'labour flexibilisation' through which capital seeks to improve its flexibility to hire, fire, and utilise workers within production (Taylor, 2006). The outcomes tend to be both path-dependent and profoundly uneven, forging major qualitative and quantitative differences between workforces across social space. Anita Chan and Hong-zen Wang, for example, have illustrated the starkly different forms of labour control employed by Taiwanese firms producing the same labour-intensive goods in China and Vietnam respectively (Chan and Wang, 2004). While a brutally militaristic form of worker discipline was employed in the Chinese factories under study—including extensive working hours, widespread rights abuses, and habitually unpaid wages—the factories studied around Hanoi and Ho Chi Minh City in Vietnam were characterised by a 'softer' form of labour management where the above abuses were notably less present. The authors relate such differences—which belie the notion of a homogenous global 'cheap labour army'—to the distinct institutional contexts for production established by the interaction between firms, state, and workers, as reflected in vastly different levels of worker rights awareness and divergent strategies of contestation pursued by workers at the level of the factory and at the national level through unions.

Concurrently, as highlighted by feminist studies of work and labour markets, the distinct ways in which gender is socially constructed in different locations is also pivotal to this creation of socially specific labour forces. For example, Leslie Salzinger has closely elaborated how the ongoing creation and contestation of gender identities within Mexico's maquiladora zones has been a crucial process in the attempt of capital and the state to reproduce a profitable assembly sector. Reproducing the trope of a female maquila worker in Ciudad Juárez—cheap, docile, and productive owing to her femininity—created a battlefield over the construction of gender that stretched from the household to the factory and the labour market, and into the mechanisms of cultural production including the local and international media:

> In this context, gender certainly shapes the export-processing labor market, but not through transnationals' capacity to leverage the ineluctable productivity of young, third-world women. Rather, gender intervenes because it is the terrain upon which the question of who looks like a maquila worker, and who doesn't, is decided, thus establishing the context within which hiring takes place and production is initiated. (Salzinger, 2003, pp. 35–36)

The process of production is therefore inseparable from the production of labouring bodies and, as such, the restructuring of labour—specifically the dramatic effects of the incorporation of Chinese labour forces within the international division of labour—is therefore every bit as important as the restructuring of capital for the distribution of productive activities on a global level. Set within the context of the embedding–abstraction dialectic, the creation and utilisation of labouring bodies involves complex social struggles that interlock production and social reproduction through which actors—ranging from firms and state organisations (national and international) to individual and collective bodies of workers, families, and communities—attempt to redefine the institutional structures and processes in which production, including the production of waged labourers, is embedded. This does not simply pit workers against capital, but repeatedly involves conflicts between different groups of workers stratified by sector and skill level, and divided between different spatial locales, that compete to retain investment and jobs. The uneven development of capital on a global level therefore raises a greater need for international labour solidarity at the same time as it constructs significant barriers to it (cf. Arrighi and Silver, 2000; Munck, 2007).

Conclusion

This paper has argued that we need to move beyond existing approaches to production within development theory in order to grasp the contradictory dynamics that bind together production and social reproduction on local, national, and global levels. It has been argued that conceptualising production in terms of a dialectical relationship between social embedding and social abstraction is a useful way to achieve this. When approaching the question of social embedding, it is essential to consider the processes through which labour forces with particular attributes are socially produced, reproduced, and put to work in an organised process of production across different spatial locales. Production is not solely an embedded process, however, because it also involves the production of abstract social relations that refract back coercively across the international division of labour in the form of value. The latter process reconfigures the terrain of global accumulation, compelling the constant restructuring of production and the social relations in which it is embedded. The outcome of the embedding–abstraction dialectic is therefore constant upheaval and conflict. On the one hand, the process indeed drives the incredible productive drive of capitalism that underscores the association made between capitalism and development in liberal theory. On the other, it produces the vast and growing socio-economic disparities between and within different national social formations and the labour forces located within them.

Note

1 An important exception is the study of production within feminist political economy, which I draw upon in this paper.

References

Amsden, A. (1997) Bringing production back in: understanding government's economic role in late industrialization, *World Development*, 25(4), pp. 469–480.

Arrighi, G. & Silver, B. (2000) Workers north and south, in L. Panitch & C. Leys (eds) *Socialist Register 2001: Working Classes, Global Realities* (London: Merlin Press).

Bair, J. (2005) Global capitalism and commodity chains: looking back, going forward, *Competition and Change*, 9(2), pp. 153–180.

Bair, J. & Dussel Peters, E. (2006) Global commodity chains and endogenous growth: export dynamism and development in Mexico and Honduras, *World Development*, 34(2), pp. 203–221.

Bair, J. & Gereffi, G. (2001) Local clusters in global chains: the causes and consequences of export dynamism in Torreon's blue jeans industry, *World Development*, 29(11), pp. 1885–1903.

Bair, J. and Gereffi, G. (2003) Upgrading, uneven development, and jobs in the North American apparel industry, *Global Networks*, 3(2), pp. 143–169.

Berger, M. (2004) *The Battle for Asia: From Decolonization to Globalization* (London: Routledge).

Booth, D. (1985) Marxism and development sociology: beyond the impasse, *World Development*, 13(7), pp. 761–787.

Burkett, P. & Hart-Landsberg, M. (2000) *Development, Crisis and Class Struggle: Learning from Japan and East Asia* (New York: St. Martin's Press).

Burkett, P. & Hart-Landsberg, M. (2003) A critique of "catch-up" theories of development, *Journal of Contemporary Asia*, 33(2), pp. 147–171.

Cantin, É. & Taylor, M. (2008) Making the 'workshop of the world': China and the transformation of the international division of labour, in M. Taylor (ed.) *Global Economy Contested: Power and Conflict Across the International Division of Labour* (London: Routledge).

Chan, A. & Wang, H.-Z. (2004) The impact of the state on workers' conditions: comparing Taiwanese factories in China and Vietnam, *Pacific Affairs*, 77(4), pp. 629–646.

Chang, H.-J. (2002) *Kicking Away the Ladder: Development Strategy in Historical Perspective* (London: Anthem).

Clarke, S. (1991) *Marx, Marginalism and Modern Sociology* (London: MacMillan).

Cowen, M. & Shenton, R. (1996) *Doctrines of development* (London: Routledge).

Czaban, L. & Henderson, J. (2003) Commodity chains, foreign investment and labour issues in Eastern Europe, *Global Networks*, 3(1), pp. 171–196.

Deyo, F. (1989) *Beneath the Miracle: Labor Subordination in the New Asian Industrialism* (Berkeley: University of California Press).

De Angelis, M. (2005) Values, measures and disciplinary markets, *The Commoner*, 10, pp. 66–86.

Deyo, F. (2001) The social construction of developmental labour systems: South-East Asian industrial restructuring, in G. Rodan, K. Hewison & R. Robinson (eds) *The Political Economy of South-East Asia: Conflicts, Crises and Change* (Oxford: Oxford University Press).

Dunkley, G. (2004) *Free Trade: Myth, Reality and Alternatives* (London: Zed Books).

Edwards, P. & Elger, T. (eds) (1999) *The Global Economy, National States and the Regulation of Labour* (London: Mansell).

Escobar, A. (1995) *Encountering Development: The Making and Unmaking of the Third World* (Princeton, NJ: Princeton University Press).

Fine, B. (2002) *The World of Consumption: The Material and Cultural Revisited* (London: Routledge).

Fine, B. (2004) Value theory and the study of contemporary capitalism, in by R. Westra & A. Zuege (eds) *Value and the World Economy Today: Production, Finance and Globalization* (London: Palgrave).

Fröbel, F., Heinrichs, J. & Kreye, O. (1977) The tendency towards a new international division of labour, *Review*, 1(1), pp. 73–88.

Gereffi, G., Humphrey, J. & Sturgeon, T. (2005) The governance of global value chains, *Review of International Political Economy*, 12(1), pp. 78–104.

Gereffi, G. & Korzeniewicz, M. (1994) *Commodity Chains and Global Capitalism* (Westport, CT: Greenwood Press).

Gibbon, P. (2001) Upgrading primary production: a global commodity chain approach, *World Development*, 29(2), pp. 345–363.

Harris, N. (1986) *The End of the Third World: Newly Industrializing Countries and the End of an Ideology* (London: Penguin Books).

Henderson, J., Dicken, P., Hess, M., Coe, N. & Yeung, H. W.-C. (2002) Global production networks and the analysis of economic development, *Review of International Political Economy*, 9(3), pp. 436–464.

Hodgson, G. (2002) *How Economics Forgot History: The Problem of Historical Specificity in Social Science* (London: Routledge).

Jenkins, R. (2004) Vietnam in the global economy: trade, employment and poverty, *Journal of International Development*, 16(1), pp. 13–28.

Jomo, K. S. & Chen, Y.-C. (1997) *Southeast Asia's Misunderstood Miracle: Industrial Policy and Economic Development in Thailand, Malaysia and Indonesia* (Boulder, CO: Westview Press).

Manda, D. & Sen, K. (2004) The labour market effects of globalization in Kenya, *Journal of International Development*, 16(1), pp. 1629–43.

Marx, K. (1976[1867]) *Capital, Vol. 1* (London: Penguin Books).

Merk, J. (2008) Nike's mirror image: Yue Yuen and the implementation of labour standards, in M. Taylor (ed.) *Global Economy Contested: Power and Conflict Across the International Division of Labour* (London: Routledge).

Munck, R. (2008) Globalization and contestation: a transformationalist labour perspective, in M. Taylor (ed.) *Global Economy Contested: Power and Conflict Across the International Division of Labour* (London: Routledge).

Ponte, S. & Gibbon, P. (2005) Quality standards, conventions and the governance of global value chains, *Economy and Society*, 34(1), pp. 1–31.

Reinert, E. (2004) *Globalization, Economic Development and Inequality: An Alternative Perspective* (Cheltenham: Edward Elgar).

Robinson, W. (2002) Remapping development in light of globalization: from a territorial to a social cartography, *Third World Quarterly*, 23(6), pp. 1047–1071.

Roxborough, I. (1979) *Theories of Underdevelopment* (London: Macmillan Press).

Salzinger, L. (2003) *Genders in Production: Marking Workers in Mexico's Global Factories* (Berkeley: University of California Press).

Smith, A. (1990 [1776]) *An Inquiry into the Nature and Causes of the Wealth of Nations* (Chicago: Encyclopædia Britannica, Inc.).

Taylor, M. (2006) *From Pinochet to the Third Way: Neoliberalism and Social Transformation in Chile* (London: Pluto Press).

Wade, R. (1990[1776]) *Governing the Market: Economic Theory and the Role of Government in East Asian Industrialization* (Princeton, NJ: Princeton University Press).

Weeks, J. (2001) The expansion of capital and uneven development on a world scale, *Capital and Class*, 74, pp. 9–31.

Weisband, E. (1989) *Poverty Amidst Plenty: World Political Economy and Distributive Justice* (Boulder, CO: Westview Press).

Re-Envisioning Global Development:
Conceptual and Methodological Issues

SANDRA HALPERIN

Among the most pervasive and durable beliefs of the past half-century is that economic growth in the countries of the 'Third World' will bring about the conditions of life that exist in the advanced industrial countries of 'the West'. There was scant progress towards this goal during the 1970s and 1980s, precipitating a 'crisis' in the field of development studies; however, by the end of the 1980s, levels of industrialisation between the developing and developed worlds appeared to be converging, leading many scholars and practitioners to proclaim the imminent end of the 'Third World' as a political, economic, and ideological entity. It soon became apparent however that, despite converging levels of industrialisation between the 'First' and 'Third' Worlds, a concomitant convergence of incomes had failed to materialise and that, in fact, the divide in income and wealth was widening.

The dilemma of industrialisation without development, and the inability of theorists to formulate a coherent response to it, might be seen as indicative not of a new or continuing crisis in development theory, but of its utter exhaustion. This, it will be argued here, is due in large part to three features common to all perspectives on development: (1) the analysis of whole nations or countries; (2) the use of a profoundly erroneous account of modern European history as a starting point and comparative focus for analysing contemporary 'Third World' development; and (3) the acceptance of core–periphery and other binary schemas that have relevance, and very superficially if at all, for only the post-World War II decades.

The first section of this paper traces these features of development theory, from their origins in liberal 'modernisation and development' theories produced in the United States from the 1950s, through their reproduction in a wide array of neo-Marxist and newer critical approaches, including post-colonial theory and subaltern studies. While neo-Marxist and newer critical perspectives challenge many aspects of the liberal perspective, they fail to break decisively with the ontology and history on which liberal theories are based and, so, fail to escape their own critique. Consequently, in the second section, the discussion turns to the task of elaborating a different ontology and history of global development. It is argued that capitalist expansion has been, everywhere and from the start, essentially trans-national in nature and global in scope, involving not whole societies but sectors, regions, and groups in Europe, the Americas, Asia, and Africa—characterised not by processes centred on empires and nation-states, but by trans-local/cross-regional interactions and connections.

The Development Project: Variations on the Themes of National Development and Western Modernity

Theories and expectations of development over the past half-century have been crucially shaped by a policy initiative and scholastic programme which emerged in the United States after World War II and which, following a number of scholars, shall here be referred to as the 'development project' (see, e.g., McMichael, 1996, pp. 13–76; So, 1990, chapter 1). This project enlisted social scientists to study and devise ways of promoting capitalist economic development and political stability in newly independent and 'developing' states throughout the world. The product of this effort was modernisation theory: a body of research and writing concerned with how to shape the economies of developing countries along capitalist lines.[1] During these decades, the study of development, and of many other areas of inquiry as well, markedly converged around a common set of analytic conventions and general themes. One of these conventions, the division of the social world into nationally-bounded societies, had a particularly decisive impact on the social sciences and on our understanding of development.

National Development

From the start, the development project conceived of development as national growth. This conception was the basis of modernisation theory and its narrative of how the already developed countries had moved from backwardness to modernity.

Many aspects of this narrative were challenged by the dependency perspective that emerged in the late 1960s. The dependency perspective, as first articulated by Andre Gunder Frank (1967, 1969) and elaborated by Immanuel Wallerstein (1974) and world systems theorists, advanced a conception of capitalist development as a world-wide process that produces structurally different developmental outcomes in the core and periphery of the system.

According to the dependency perspective, a key developmental outcome in peripheral societies is dualism—the presence of a modern economic sector that fails to transform the rest of society (e.g., Amin, 1976; Cardoso and Faletto, 1973; Dos Santos, 1970; Frank, 1972; Sunkel, 1973). Dependency theorists argue that while industrialising countries in the West had leading sectors that were essentially indigenous and closely interwoven with other sectors of the economy (e.g., cotton textiles in the British take-off, railroads in France), the leading sectors found in contemporary developing countries are imposed by external agents acting on behalf of the reproductive requirements of advanced capitalist economies. These sectors remain largely alien to the other sectors, and the sectorally uneven capitalist development that results restricts the growth of the domestic economy. Thus, the economy as a whole is characterised by a lack of internal structural integration, and by dependency on outside capital, labour, and markets; an advanced or modern sector coexists with a backward or traditional sector, and concomitantly pre-capitalist and capitalist relations of production coexist.

While dependency theory provides a descriptively accurate model of how many Third World countries are developing, it has failed to provide a coherent explanation of this trajectory.

This failure is due in part to its acceptance of the profoundly erroneous account developed by modernisation theorists of how Western countries moved from backwardness to modernity.[2] What this narrative obscures is that dualism and all the features of dependent development are not idiosyncratic to the contemporary Third World, but were also characteristic of the development of today's advanced industrial countries.[3] Until the world wars, European development was dualistic: sectorally and geographically limited; largely carried out by atomised, low-wage, and low-skilled labour forces; based on production, not for local mass consumption, but for export to governments, elites, and ruling groups in other states and territories; and characterised by restricted and weakly integrated domestic markets. Many European countries were unable to diversify their exports or trading partners until well into the twentieth century; most adopted from abroad an already developed technology while retaining their 'traditional' social structure; all were dependent on foreign capital to finance growth.[4] Nowhere in Europe was there a strong, independent industrial capitalist bourgeoisie: in most of the region, the bourgeoisie was either a foreign class or politically and economically weak, regionally confined, and dependent on the state or the landholding aristocracy. Development was financed not by an independent indigenous capitalist bourgeoisie but by the state, by banks, and by foreign investment. Alliances between business and landed interests were forged, as in the Third World—for similar purposes, and with similar consequences for class structure and for national development. These alliances were so successful in preserving and reinforcing pre-industrial civil society that, on the eve of World War I, Europe was still largely 'agrarian, nobilitarian, and monarchic' (Mayer, 1981, p. 129).

European Historical Development

One of the most significant achievements of the development project was its success in producing and gaining wide acceptance of a profoundly erroneous account of Western historical development. Walter Rostow's *Stages of Economic Growth* (1960), which provided the blueprint for modernisation theory, asserted that Europe's 'past formula for development, up to and including capitalism, was the only workable formula for non-Europe's future development' (Blaut, 1993, p. 53). But modernisation theory neither drew on nor related itself to 'the existing body of theory about development that had been prompted by the original advent of capitalism itself' (Leys, 1996, p. 5). Instead, it constructed a highly idealised account of the path that had been traversed by today's advanced countries, and then claimed that developing countries could follow it. Dependency and world systems theories accepted this account and, using it as an analytic starting point and basis of comparison, defined and sought to explain differences between contemporary Third World and European historical development that do not exist.

Let us consider again, briefly, dualism—one of the features of contemporary developing countries highlighted by dependency theorists as distinctly non-Western. Some theorists conceptualise dualism as emerging from the 'internationalisation of the domestic market'. This happens because dependent development prevents the indigenous bourgeoisie from acquiring either political or economic hegemony. Consequently, within Third World countries there forms an 'internationalised bourgeoisie' dominated by a 'transnational kernel' (Sunkel, 1973, p. 146)—'a complex of activities, social groups and regions in different countries ... closely linked transnationally through many concrete interests as well as by similar styles, ways and levels of living and cultural affinities' (Cardoso and Faletto, 1973, p. 135). This provides as good a description of Europe's nineteenth-century and early twentieth-century industrial expansion as it does of the contemporary Third World.

Many scholars claim that, in Britain, industrial development was 'promoted and led by an independent capitalist middle class which fought against the old aristocracy as well as against the restrictive power of the state' (Chirot, 1977, p. 223), and that in the nineteenth century this class, with minimum help from the state, was able to 'convert a large part of the globe into [its] trading area' (Moore, 1966, p. 32). However, the aristocracy remained the dominant faction of the bourgeoisie in Europe until the world wars, and it was this faction that led Europe's development and formed the basis of its 'capitalist class'. Contrary to the claims of a large and influential body of writing concerning the end of absolutism and the 'new' liberal age, it is not the case that the creation of the bourgeois state and bourgeois law brought about the separation of economic (class) power from political (state) power: rather, it brought about a fusion of both, for the extraction of surplus, locally and abroad, by extra-economic compulsion.

Below (Table 1) are listed (1) indices of landowning elite that is (a) 'commercialised and bourgeoisified' and (b) 'pre-bourgeois'; (1) and a list of features depicting structures of class and state power and patterns of industrial development that overlap and are associated with a complete and incomplete 'bourgeois revolution'. The following sections of this chapter will argue that the characteristics that are in boldface are those which predominated in Britain throughout the nineteenth century.

Table 1. Britain's nineteenth-century industrial expansion: two models compared[a]

The 'European model'	The Dependency Model[b]
1. The Landowning Class	
a. Commercialised, bourgeoisified	*b. Pre-bourgeois*
• willingness to sell land for money	• **concentration of land ownership**
• peasants transformed into a rural proletariat based on wage labour	• **incomplete proletarianisation of peasants; wages in kind; highly repressive labour conditions**
• use of mechanised harvesting	• **limited mechanisation of agriculture**
• **diversification of assets: speculation in non-landed assets (stocks and bonds)**	• landowner assets remain in landed property
• commercialised distribution of crops	• **high-cost, single-crop, staple agriculture; lack of flexibility in switching crops[c]**
• commodification of agriculture: large-scale marketing of crops on a regional and global scale	• **production for local consumption**
2. The Structure of Class and State Power	
• strong, independent, industrial, capitalist bourgeoisie	• **alliance of capitalist bourgeoisie, the state, and the landholding aristocracy (and MNCs)**
• separation of economic (class) power from political (state) power; creation of bourgeois state and bourgeois law	• **the fusion of economic power and political (state) power for extraction of surplus[d]**
3. The Mode of Production	
a. Capitalist	*b. Pre-capitalist[e]*
• **labour is**	• **labour is**
(1) 'free' of feudal obligations	(1) **bound by feudal obligations**
(2) **dispossessed (separated from the means of production)**	(2) in possession of means of production
• surplus is extracted from the dispossessed producer by economic 'coercion'	• **surplus is extracted from the dispossessed producer by extra-economic compulsion**

(Table continued)

Table 1.   *Continued*

The 'European model'	The Dependency Model[b]
• generalised commodity production (production primarily for sale; labour power itself a commodity)[f]	• **self-sufficient localised economy supplemented by simple circulation of commodities**
• extended reproduction of capital and rise of organic composition of capital[f]	• **simple reproduction where surplus is largely consumed**

4 The Industrial Sphere

The 'European model'	The Dependency Model[b]
• liberal, competitive, bourgeois ethos	• **aristocratic values**
• industrial competition	• **monopolisation of industry**
• development of a domestic market for the products of national industry	• **limited, weakly integrated domestic economy; strong linkages between its sectors and foreign economies (dualism)**
• diversified industrial structure with numerous linkages, including economically strategic capital goods industries	• **dependence on a narrow range of export goods and a few trading partners**
• diversification of the export structure, trade partners, and sources of capital and technology	• **dependence on foreign supply of important factors of production (technology, capital)**
• diffusion and more egalitarian distribution of purchasing power and assets	• **inequality of income and land structures; growing gap between elites and masses**
• **'national' control over the investment of capital and the accumulation process**	• limited developmental choices

Source: based on Halperin (2004, chapter 3).
Boldface indicates characteristics which predominated throughout the century.
[a]As Britain represents the 'hard case' for these arguments, it is the focus of much of what follows.
[b]For a complete list of elements comprising dependent development and a discussion of each, see Halperin (1997, chapter 5).
[c]This was true of wheat production, for example, which comprised half of Britain's grain output in 1870 (Mathias, 1983, p. 316).
[d]Locally, state-controlled systems of paramilitary and police forces, and concentrations of regular troops on permanent garrison duty in working class areas of industrial towns; elsewhere, the opening up and control of territories for exploitation by armed aggression.
[e]Based on the feudal mode of production, in which heavy extraction of surplus from small producers is applied through extra-economic coercion and economic growth is primarily extensive—through the expansion of the area under cultivation.
[f]Found only in industrial sectors producing for export.

The West and the Rest

This brings us to a third weakness of development theory: schemas that place Western Europe and the contemporary 'third world' on different sides of a global divide that has relevance only for the immediate post-World War II decades. The division of the world into the advanced industrial world and the Third World is the basis of modernisation theory and has been reproduced by most other perspectives. Most perspectives also accept the related 'diffusionist' assumptions of modernisation theory: that the modern world began with the 'rise of Europe', that this rise was the result of factors and conditions internal to Europe, and that a Western or European core shaped development outcomes everywhere else in the world.

Beginning in the 1970s, these assumptions became the target of a critique by post-colonial theory. The key concern of post-colonial theory was to focus attention on the relationship between Eurocentric and nationalist historiography and the exercise of Western power. It focused in particular on the legacy of nineteenth-century British and French colonial rule, especially the difficulties faced by former colonial peoples in developing national identity, the ways knowledge of colonized people has served the interests of colonizers, and how the colonial relationship itself represses, excludes, marginalises, and objectifies the 'other'.

Within this general perspective, a project emerged that became known as 'subaltern studies'.[5] Subaltern studies rejects elite-centred colonialist (liberal), nationalist, and Marxist narratives as European teleologies—meta-narratives of the advance of capitalism and the triumph of the nation-state that seek either to endorse or to universalise Europe's historical experience, and that obscure the history, agency, and autonomy of the masses in the Third World (e.g., Chakrabarty, 2000, 1992; Gupta, 1998; Prakash, 1996). Its concern is to recover history 'from the bottom up'.

Despite these concerns, the subaltern studies literature tends to treat whole, internally undifferentiated, societies as objects of European oppression, and of independence, decolonisation, and post-colonialism. One of the most characteristic features of subaltern studies is its insistence on the overriding influence and unitary experience of external domination, and the primacy of race, rather than class, as relevant to understanding Third World masses. Consequently, one of its foremost targets is the 'Cambridge School' which sees nationalism as emerging from the involvement of local and regional elites in colonial institutions, and as a means to secure their power and advance their interests. This perspective is rejected as an elitist-based analysis that turns 'the common people into dupes of their superiors' (Prakash, 1994, p. 1477; see also Gallagher et al., 1973).

Another target is Marxist analysis and Marxist teleology, which 'empties subaltern movements of their specific types of consciousness and experience' (O'Hanlon, 1988, p. 191). The subaltern studies perspective insists that class is inapplicable to 'backward capitalism', and that racial, religious, ethnic, tribal, and other identities are the relevant focus for illuminating the subject positions of colonised people and, more generally, understanding developmental outcomes. It argues that while workers might have multiple oppressors, imperial oppression is the dominant condition.

However, it is difficult to see why or how the impact of European imperialism would render the experience of miners, railwaymen, weavers, and artisans in Anatolia, Damascus, and Egypt fundamentally different from those in Europe. Why should it be assumed that the conditions of their lives were shaped more by European imperialism than by the relations of power that shaped working-class experience elsewhere?

The opposition that subalternist critiques of Marxism set up between class and race tends to obscure how class overlaps, is embedded in, or intersects with all the categories that are placed in opposition to it.[6] Class is a relationship of inequality and exploitation that gives rise to conflicts over the distribution of wealth, income, and power. In all societies where the production of a surplus beyond the bare necessities of life is appropriated by a small minority, class 'provides a means of collectively expressing the fact of this exploitation and the way in which it is embodied in a social structure' (de Ste. Croix, 1981). This relationship may overlap with a variety of communities and identities and be defined in a diversity of ways. Classes are embedded in ethnic, national, and other communities and identities; consequently, the 'banners' raised in struggles are often those of communal identification rather than those specifically of class identification.[7]

The rejection of a class-based approach fosters illusions of the absence of class and of exploitation within Third World societies; in fact, post-colonial theory and subaltern studies downplay the role of Third World elites in exploiting other classes and in controlling, inhibiting, or preventing development.[8] Their central concern is with the monopolisation of productive assets by foreign elites, and the growing income gap between developed and less developed countries that is thought to result from this. But local elites also monopolise resources, and the historical record suggests that the monopolisation of productive assets by these elites is as detrimental to development as the monopolisation of assets by foreign groups. Whatever the role of foreign states and groups, it is local elites that are decisive in bringing about external reliance, in translating it into structural distortions, and in determining how the benefits of collaboration with foreign capital are distributed and used. States that are fully independent and able to capture a large share of global product do not necessarily distribute their gains more equitably or use them more productively internally. It is local dominant classes that dictate the form, substance, timing, and pace of change, and determine if and how economic development and its benefits spread across sectors and regions.[9]

Colonialism did not victimise whole societies. It helped to create or further enrich privileged classes who exploited or contributed to the exploitation of others. Third World societies were divided by class before, during, and after European imperialism and colonialism. The ability of colonialism to re-shape societies so profoundly attests to the extent to which societies were fragmented and riven by class and other divisions.

A second way in which these critical approaches fail to escape their own critique is by promoting a racialised divide between 'the West' and 'the rest', and in this way reproducing the binary schema—West/rest, core/periphery, coloniser/colonised, modern/traditional—intrinsic to modernisation theory.

Large areas of the Third World were never formally colonised by Europeans, some were colonised for only a short time, and some were victimised by non-European colonialism and imperialism—in some cases to a greater degree and for a longer time than by European colonisers. European colonialism was not the only colonialism imposed on Third World populations, and it was not necessarily the colonialism that had the most widespread and enduring impact. Moreover, the victims of colonialism are themselves colonists and descendants of colonists. Third World states are among the internationally recognised settler states throughout the world that impose sovereignty over thousands of indigenous nations.

Moreover, colonialism is not unique to the Third World: it was also a central part of the recent experience of countries and populations in Europe. Europe experienced forms of colonial exploitation similar to those found in the countries of the contemporary Third World and, during the nineteenth and early twentieth centuries, several states experienced direct colonial control.[10] However, the colonial discourse denies the colonial history and dependent development of European states, and promotes an ethno-centric notion of subalternity as referring exclusively to the victims of Europe's colonialism overseas.

In sum, critical approaches have failed to rethink 'the West' itself—its account of its own history. In common with modernisation theory, they promote an account of European development as devoid of subalternity, racism, exploitation, and imperial domination. But Europeans replicated abroad what they were doing at home. Large populations, in both western and eastern Europe, were subjected to various forms, and suffered similar consequences, of colonial and imperial domination in the nineteenth century.

Global Development: A Horizontal Perspective

Most perspectives on development take as their analytic starting point a conception of the 'social' as (already) divided into a multiplicity of bounded national societies. 'Society' refers, more often than not, to bounded national societies. However, territorial states of various sorts, and modern national societies, were built up within a pre-existing trans-local social field. This system of social institutions, relationships, and norms was not displaced or destroyed by the rise and fall of states and state systems:[11] trans-local sources of power and stability continued, and continue today, to transect the boundaries of states and to shape relations and developmental outcomes across and within them.

Throughout the rise and fall of states and state systems, technological advance and the development of productive forces was driven and shaped, not by nations, but by local and trans-local classes engaged in the exchange of technology, institutions, cultural ideas, values, and other symbolic products. Values, consumption practices, and innovations spread, not across broad fronts but along routes of contacts, and these shaped the direction of social change across large areas in broadly similar ways.

The forging of ties of solidarity, identity, and unity, and the integration and expansion of markets—all are predominantly trans-national (horizontal) rather than national (vertical) phenomena. Elites move in a horizontally differentiated system; their concern is not with vertical inequality (exploitation) but with inclusion in or exclusion from the overall system.

Groups of elites along networks of exchange are not separate-but-similar classes: they form a single supra-local elite, and their broadly similar interests, capabilities, and policies are constituted and reproduced through interaction and interdependence. While the properties of dominant groups in different parts of the world have varied, the connections and interactions among them are rich and concrete and, within the constraints and opportunities present in different contexts, produced a set of common solutions to the problems of organising production along new lines.

The reorganisation of relations of production as a result of the industrial revolution brought different groups across states and regions into closer relations of interdependence. As a result, the structure and behaviour of the network increasingly reflected broadly similar local relations.

One salient outcome of this was the broadly similar nationalist policies and rhetoric which emerged across different regions. As Charles Tilly observes, state-led processes 'created visible, prestigious, transferable models for exploitation and opportunity hoarding'. As a result, 'Throughout the world, administrative structures, constitutions, and declared commitments of regimes to development, stability, and democracy came to resemble each other far more than did the diversity of their material conditions and actual accomplishments' (1999, p. 180).

The enclosure of territory within legally sovereign governates of various sorts organised around permanent military establishments was part of a system constructed by elites to preserve their power and monopolise access to the human and material resources of bounded territorial domains. National institutions tie the mass of the local population to a bounded political and cultural realm, but this realm remains transected by trans-local classes.[12] The whole apparatus of national culture and national-state ideology tends to render invisible the existence of a trans-continental mercantile capitalist elite (and, today, masks an increasingly global finance capitalism) and the interdependence of sites of production.

As many scholars have noted, Europe's elite was more closely tied by culture and concrete interests to a pan-regional international class than to the classes below them. The elite, while bearing something like a family resemblance to one another, were often physically distinct from peasants within their own countries; often they were of a different nationality or religion, or spoke a different language. Even where they had the same nationality and religion, their mode of life had in all respects more in common with elites elsewhere in Europe than with the lower classes within their own countries.[13]

Distinctions of class, rank, and race are more important within than between political units. Thus, to reinforce their claim of representing the people/nation, leaders assert that the whole nation is locked into a vertical/exploitative relationship with other nations.

What accounts, then, for the unevenness of development that we observe across national societies? The short answer is that not all capitalists or ruling classes seek to industrialise their economies: industrialisation entails the growth of new classes, and, as shall be discussed in the next section, there are less dangerous ways to accumulate wealth and maintain power. One might also ask: What accounts for the geopolitical rivalry and conflict that characterise international relations? A short answer, again, can be offered: the supra-local elite, sometimes cooperatively, but often competitively and conflictually, divides up the territory and population of regions and sometimes whole continents among its members. It is often torn by civil war, within local cadres as well as between and across them. The fact of international war does not invalidate the notion of a supra-local elite, any more than the occurrence of internal wars makes the notion of domestic society invalid. Throughout the history of the modern states system, the domestic relations of states have been characterised by violent and protracted struggles, continual rebellions, and waves of revolutions—yet we continue to speak of the local rather than the international domain as a society.

Global Development from the Eighteenth Century

On the eve of Europe's 'rise', a world system stretched from western and southern Europe through the Middle East to China. This system was characterised not only by a prosperous and far-flung trading network, but also by an active and important network of intercultural exchange linking a great many political societies and encompassing many different fields of thought.[14] This was a cosmopolitan order, Janet Abu-Lughod (1989) has argued, a relatively peaceful one governed by unwritten laws and rules of reciprocity.

Europe's military expansion did not displace or destroy this system of economic and cultural interconnection and exchange. Thus, after the 'lights went on in Europe', the actual pattern of economic expansion throughout the world continued to resemble, to borrow the image James Blaut used to describe the network of medieval mercantile port cities, 'a string of electric lights' strung across Asia, the Middle East, Africa, Latin America, and Europe. These lights illuminated small islands of urbanised industrial society and export sectors in Asia, Latin America, Europe, and elsewhere, each surrounded by traditional communities and institutions and underdeveloped, weakly integrated local economies. It was not a Europe-centred world system, but a network of exchange linking the advanced sectors of dualistic economies in various parts of the world.

A key chapter in the worldwide expansion of industrial capitalism was the half-century of war and revolutionary ferment that included two world wars (the Seven Years War of 1756–1763, which was simultaneously fought in North America, Europe, India, and the Caribbean, and the Napoleonic Wars), and a series of revolutions, including the French and industrial revolutions.[15]

The Great War, and the revolutionary currents that had unleashed and been released by it, revealed the dangers of a trained and compact mass army: many analogies were drawn between the mass army of soldiers created in the Great War and the mass industrial army of workers needed for industrial capitalist production. This was the context in which elites throughout the world undertook to mobilise labour for industrial production.

Maintaining the subordination of labour is always a key concern for elites, as evidenced by their great fear throughout history of slave revolts and peasant uprisings. The temptation to reorganise production along the lines of industrial capitalism presented elites with a somewhat different dilemma: how to mobilise, train, and educate labour for industrial production while, at the same time, maintaining its subordination to capital. The dominant 'solution' everywhere was very slowly and selectively to introduce mechanisation while predominantly using methods of production that deskilled workers and kept labour, as a whole, fragmented and poorly paid. However, this solution raised an addition problem: if the standard of consumption of the mass of the local population remained the same or was reduced, where would consumers be found for the products of expanded production? The overall solution, therefore, was to create the dualistic expansion that came to characterise industrial capitalism: an expansion based not on the growth and integration of local markets, but on production principally for export to foreign ruling groups or areas of 'new' settlement abroad;[16] an expansion based not on the development of mass purchasing power at home, but on its development among foreign groups and ruling bodies through loans and investment in infrastructure, railroads, and armaments. Consequently, there developed a circuit of production and exchange of raw materials and manufactured goods into which elites of different countries were integrated with the help of British financiers and firms. In sum: to expand industrial production and, at the same time, maintain the subordination of labour to capital required the development of purchasing power and markets *outside the political unit*. This dualistic development became the model for industrial expansion throughout the world.

Beginning in the eighteenth century, goods and services were produced principally for an expanding network of elites, ruling groups, and governments in other countries. The creation and linking of export sectors in Europe and other regions underpinned a global economic expansion that enriched elites around the world, while leaving traditional social structures largely intact.

Britain expanded its shipbuilding, boiler making, gun, and ammunition industries, and built foreign railways, canals, and other public works including banks, telegraphs, and other public services owned or dependent upon governments. Its exports of capital provided purchasing power among foreign governments and elites for these goods and services, and funded the development and transport of food and raw material exports to Europe, thus creating additional foreign purchasing power and demand for British goods. At the centre of this circuit was the City of London, which like the advanced sector of a dependent Third World economy worked to build strong linkages between British export industries and foreign economies, rather than to integrate various parts of the domestic economy.

Throughout the world, this circuit of production and exchange produced railroads, shipping companies, ports, electric power companies, tramways, telegraphs, and urban water supply companies. These activities—in Europe and in other regions—created modern sectors producing sometimes as much as half of the income of the local economy, and affecting only small segments of the indigenous population.

Every dominant group seeking to increase profits by expanding production confronted the problem of how to realise the value of a rising mountain of goods without a corresponding democratisation of consumption at home. How this problem was resolved varied across different societies, according to the type of goods it produced for sale and the relative power of capital and labour. However, similar capabilities, as well as a common system-wide context, tended to shape the interaction with labour in similar ways. It is generally the case that elites are interested in adopting the most up-to-date methods of multiplying their revenue, wealth, and power. The success of the British elite in this regard would have been expected to inspire elites elsewhere to emulate British economic, social, administrative, and intellectual trends. Elites (whether in colonies, former colonies, or states that had never been colonies) extended, consolidated, and maintained their power and become wealthy, by importing capital and goods, developing mines and raw material exports, and building railways and ports. They were generally cohesive, had much to gain, controlled immense resources, and were free to deploy them in a sustained pursuit of their aims.

The World Wars and After

In Europe, as elsewhere, dualistic economic expansion made it possible for elites to increase production and profits without extensive redistribution and reform. However, as more countries began to pursue dualistic, externally-oriented economic expansion, opportunities to expand overseas quickly diminished, and the expansionist aims of European powers began increasingly to focus on Europe itself. When the European balance of power and imperialist regimes collapsed, a multi-lateral imperialist war in Europe forced governments and ruling elites to do precisely what a century of overseas imperialist expansion had enabled them to avoid: mobilise the masses.

In the eighteenth century, governments had relied on the social elite to pay for mercenary troops and to provide military leaders to fight professional wars. Consequently, these wars tended to heighten existing social inequalities. However, the wars fought by Napoleon's mass 'citizen' army and the mass armies mobilised to fight against it enhanced the power of labour and strengthened its market position.[17] Thus, after the end of the Napoleonic Wars, there was a return in Europe to old-style armies of paid professionals, mercenaries, and 'gentlemen' (Silver and Slater, 1999, p. 190). However, in 1914, aggressive imperialist threats on their frontiers forced European states to use again what had remained the most powerful weapon of mass destruction: the *lévee en masse*.

Many contemporary observers assumed that working-class participation in the war represented a victory of nationalism over socialist solidarity, but labour struggles continued throughout the war and, in many places, increased both in number and intensity. In fact, the war proved to be a watershed in the development of socialism and of organised labour in Europe. At its end, left-wing parties and movements emerged throughout Europe, and trade union membership skyrocketed as unskilled and agricultural labour and women joined the ranks of organised labour for the first time.

By the end of World War I, labour's wartime mobilisation and participation had increased its relative power within European societies. Throughout Europe, the mobilisation of urban working classes and peasant masses to fight the war had produced stronger, larger, more united, better organised urban and rural labour movements. By 1920, Europe had 34 million trade unionists (Ogg, 1930, p. 759). Skilled and unskilled workers, workers of different occupations, anarchists and socialists, social democrats and communists, revolutionaries and reformists—all closed ranks.[18] Policies designed to block the rising 'red tide', by among other things actively aiding and abetting the re-armament and expansion of Germany as a bulwark against Bolshevism (see Halperin, 2004, chapter 7), led directly to World War II. It was the demand for labour and the need for its cooperation in a second European war that compelled a political accommodation of working-class movements.[19]

After World War II, post-war development policies were designed to expand domestic markets through increased production, to raise the level of earnings and the welfare of the working class, and to increase and regulate domestic investment. The achievement of a relatively more balanced and internally-oriented development led, for a time, to unprecedented growth and relative peace and stability.

The world wars provided an opportunity for elites in other regions of the world to better their position as regards European ruling groups. As had been the case in similar intra-elite struggles in Europe, nationalism was used by these contending elites to articulate their demands, win the support of the lower classes, and gain state power. And as had been the case in nineteenth-century Europe, in the newly 'independent' states established after World War II these nationalist movements became fused with a programme of capitalist expansion that consolidated dualism.

Thus, decolonisation and nationalism did not mark the end of the pattern of development that had emerged over the previous century, but was rather a modernised, more efficient form of it. Nationalist elites who won 'independence' were able to police local labour more effectively and consolidate different systems for transnational and local interests and actors. In fact, their identification of nationalism with national development was part of a broad vision that they shared with retreating colonial administrators and a transnational elite.

Eventually, after Britain and America had become the world's two largest weapons exporters, their expanding military-industrial complexes began to draw industrial capital from the mass-consumption goods sector and to free it from the need to maintain mass purchasing power. As a result, wage levels and work conditions began to erode, along with other gains which labour had made in those and other Western countries as a result of the post-war social settlements.

The adoption of social democratic policies after World War II effectively ended the dualism that had once characterised European economies and enabled them to expand in ways that became associated with First World and Second World development. However, once socialism had been destroyed in both the Third World and the Second World, Western states began a campaign to reverse their own post-World War II social settlements. The emerging trend, therefore, might be seen as one of re-integration, of the Second World and eventually the First World, into a system of local and trans-local relations similar to the one that, in those areas of the world, pre-dated the crisis of the world wars and the great depression.

Conclusions

Economic growth is usually experienced not by whole countries, but by sectors and geographic areas within them. Consequently, while many Third World countries have achieved a level of industrialisation comparable to that found in the First World, for the majority of their people, who are rural and poor, the conditions of life are not significantly different from when the industrial age began more than 200 years ago. This sort of dualistic development is found, with variations and in varying degrees, throughout the Third World; it was also characteristic of the development of today's advanced industrial countries. Consequently, this paper has argued that two base assumptions of most approaches to understanding contemporary development —that development takes place within and through national entities, and that the nature and pattern of contemporary Third World development differs significantly from that which characterised European development—are factually wrong and analytically unproductive. It has offered an alternative perspective and, in its defense, has endeavoured to explain why trans-local/cross-regional circuits of production and exchange developed in the eighteenth century, and how and in what ways they shaped synchronous and interdependent socio-economic and political developments throughout the world. By bringing into focus a horizontal set of connections, relations, and processes, our focus on whole nations or regions dissolves, and much of what national historiography and social science tends to obscure becomes more visible: the anatomy of trans-local social power; its relationship to different developmental outcomes; how it has evolved over time locally, trans-nationally, and cross-regionally; and the factors and conditions that, historically, have proved necessary for its reproduction and transformation.

Notes

1   As Colin Leys observes, 'It was implicit that the development under discussion was not socialist,' but its capitalist character went unacknowledged: capitalist development was simply 'development' (1996, p. 11). This is made

explicit in the subtitle of what became the basic blueprint for modernization theory: Walter Rostow's 1960 book *The Stages of Economic Growth: A Non-Communist Manifesto*.

2 Moreover, despite its elaboration of dualistic development, it is national growth that is dualistic, and national societies that are locked into relations of dependency with other national societies. Even in the influential analysis of Henrique Cardoso and Enzo Faletto (1979), the primary focus is on the nation state. Immanuel Wallerstein's (1974) analysis also focuses on whole nations or regions.

3 An economy is dependent when the accumulation and expansion of capital cannot find its essential dynamic component inside the system.

4 As Phyllis Deane has pointed out, a 'distinctive and significant dimension' of British industrial growth was 'the extent to which it was dependent on the international economy both for material inputs and for final demand' (1979, p. 294). The crucial input in Britain's cotton industry (its leading sector) was imported, so linkages were with foreign rather than domestic industries.

5 The term 'subaltern' is taken from the writings of Antonio Gramsci. It refers to 'subordination in terms of class, caste, gender, race, language, and culture and was used to signify the centrality of dominant/dominated relationships in history' (Prakash, 1994, p. 1477).

6 Dipesh Chakrabarty finds that working-class organisation and politics in Bengal were animated by Indian traditions of caste and religion, a finding that supposedly poses a problem for Marxist historiography (see Chakrabarty 2007).

7 On the intimate relationship between nationalism and class, see Hobsbawm (1990), Gellner (1983), and Wallerstein (1983).

8 Often they characterise them as somehow only tangentially related to their own societies, as primarily intermediaries or representatives of foreign interests, or 'compradores'.

9 Robert Packenham asks: '[W]hat were the powerful egalitarian elements in the Brazilian tradition that were being smothered by foreign pressures?' Elitism, tolerance for massive socioeconomic disparities, capitalism, and authoritarianism 'are powerful and authentic national traditions' (1992, p. 147).

10 These states were Norway, Finland, various Hapsburg territories, Italy, Hungary, Poland, Ireland, Greece, the Baltic states, Romania, Bulgaria, and Albania.

11 The term 'state' includes a variety of forms, including city-states, empires, theocracies, and other forms. States have been around for more than 5,000 years, as have state systems, including the Greek city-state system and state systems in the ancient Middle East, China, Indonesia, West Africa, South America, and the Indian subcontinent.

12 Nation-states are a form of state for controlling the more mobile and productive labour force needed for the expansion of trade and industry. The national arena is, first and foremost, a system of labour control. Filling these legal entities with meaning has been the primary work of intellectuals for the past two centuries.

13 The French nobility, for instance, considered itself to be a separate nation, one tied to an international aristocracy rather than to the French classes below (Arendt, 1958, p. 162).

14 The Islamic Caliphate internationalised learning by undertaking a massive and systematic translation into Arabic of ancient Greek scientific and philosophical texts. Muslim scholars translated Greek, Indian, and Persian works on medicine, astronomy, mathematics, and philosophy. They studied science, alchemy, history, theology, geography, cosmology, and botany, and set up universities, libraries, translation bureaus, observatories, and medical schools (Menocal, 2002, p. 205).

15 The latter was not so much a 'revolution' as a reorganisation of production relationships and a sharp acceleration of the globalisation of capital.

16 Between 1830 and 1914 about 50 million Europeans, 30% of Europe's population in 1830, emigrated to the Americas. The Americas provided a habitat for European consumers overseas, rather than locally, thus enabling Europeans to expand production without dangerously impacting social relations at home.

17 Among other things, governments had to ensure their loyalty by extending to them various rights. Serfdom was abolished in Prussia concurrently with Stein's military reforms, as it was in Russia when Alexander II transformed the army from a professional into a conscript force. In Austria, the adoption of universal military service coincided with reforms that established a constitutional monarchy (Andreski, 1968, p. 69).

18 James Cronin observes that before the war, the distinction within the working class 'between the skilled and organized and the unskilled and unorganized' had been 'very real to contemporaries and was reflected in many aspects of politics and collective action'. Following the war, however, the working class was, 'if not more internally homogeneous, a least less sharply divided within itself, and also more culturally distinct from middle and upper class society' (1982, pp. 139, 121).

19   Fascism and the sacrifices entailed in defeating it effectively discredited the old right throughout Europe. Thus, even where workers were not mobilised for the war effort—as, for instance, in France—the balance of political power after the war shifted in their favour.

References

Abu-Lughod, J. (1989) *Before European Hegemony: The World System A. D. 1250–1350* (New York: Oxford University Press).

Amin, S. (1976) *Accumulation on a World Scale*, vol. 2 (London: Monthly Review Press).

Andreski, S. (1968) *Military Organization and Society* (Berkeley: University of California Press).

Arendt, H. (1958) *The Origins of Totalitarianism* (New York: Meridian).

Blaut, J. (1993) *The Colonizer's Model of the World* (London: Guilford Press).

Cardoso, F. H., & Faletto, E. (1973) *Dependencia e Desenvolvimento no America Latina: Ensaio de Interpretacao Sociologia* (Rio de Janeiro: Editora Zahar).

Cardoso, F. H., & Faletto, E. (1979) *Dependency and Development in Latin America* (Berkeley: University of California Press).

Chakrabarty, D. (1992) Postcoloniality and the artifice of history: who speaks for "Indian" pasts? *Representations*, 37 (Winter), pp. 1–26.

Chakrabarty, D. (2000) *Provincializing Europe: Postcolonial Thought and Historical Difference* (Princeton, NJ: Princeton University Press).

Chakrabarty, D. (2007) "In the name of politics": sovereignty, democracy, and the multitude in India, in P. Wagner & N. Karagiannis (eds) *Varieties of World-Making* (London: Liverpool University Press).

Chirot, D. (1977) *Social Change in the Twentieth Century* (New York: Harcourt, Brace Jovanovich).

Cronin, J. (1982) Labor insurgency and class formation: comparative perspectives on the crisis of 1917–1920 in Europe, in J. Cronin & C. Sirianni (eds) *Work, Community and Power: The Experience of Labor in Europe and America, 1900–1925* (Philadelphia: Temple University Press).

Deane, P. (1979) *The First Industrial Revolution*, 2nd ed. (New York: Cambridge University Press).

de Ste. Croix, G. E. M. (1981) *The Class Struggle in the Ancient Greek World* (Ithaca: Cornell University Press).

Dos Santos (1970) The structure of dependence, *American Economic Review*, 60, pp. 235–246.

Frank, A. (1967) *Capitalism and Underdevelopment in Latin America* (New York: Monthly Review Press).

Frank, A. (1969) *Latin America: Underdevelopment or Revolution* (New York: Monthly Review Press).

Frank, A. (1972) The development of underdevelopment, in J. Cockcroft, A. Frank & D. Johnson (eds) *Dependence and Underdevelopment: Latin America's Political Economy* (New York: Anchor Books).

Gallagher, J., Johnson, G. & Seal, A. (eds) (1973) *Locality, Province, and Nation: Essays on Indian Politics, 1870–1940* (Cambridge: Cambridge University Press).

Gellner, E. (1983) *Nations and Nationalism* (Ithaca, NY: Cornell University Press).

Gupta, A. (1998) *Postcolonial Developments: Agriculture in the Making of Modern India* (Durham, NC: Duke University Press).

Halperin, S. (1997) *In the Mirror of the Third World: Industrial Capitalist Development in Modern Europe* (Ithaca, NY: Cornell University Press).

Halperin, S. (2004) *War and Social Change in Modern Europe: The Great Transformation Revisited* (Cambridge: Cambridge University Press).

Hobsbawm, E. (1990) *Nations and Nationalism since 1780* (Cambridge: Cambridge University Press).

Leys, C. (1996) *The Rise and Fall of Development Theory* (Bloomington: Indiana University Press).

Mathias, P. (1983) *The First Industrial Nation*, 2nd ed. (New York: Methuen).

Mayer, A. (1981) *The Persistence of the Ancien Regime* (New York: Pantheon Books).

McMichael, P. (1996) *Development and Social Change: A Global Perspective* (Thousand Oaks, CA: Pine Forge Press).

Menocal, M. (2002) *The Ornament of the World: How Muslims, Jews and Christians Created a Culture of Tolerance in Medieval Spain* (Boston, MA: Little, Brown).

Moore, B., Jr. (1966) *Social Origins of Democracy and Dictatorship* (Boston, MA: Beacon).

Ogg, F. A. (1930) *Economic Development of Modern Europe* (New York: Macmillan).

O'Hanlon, R. (1988) Recovering the subject: subaltern studies and histories of resistance in colonial South Asia, *Modern Asian Studies*, 22(1), pp. 189–224.

Packenham, R. (1992) *The Dependency Movement: Scholarship and Politics in Development Studies* (Cambridge, MA: Harvard University Press).

Prakash, G. (1994) Subaltern studies as postcolonial criticism, *American Historical Review*, 99(December), pp. 1475–1490.

Prakash, G. (1996) *After Colonialism: Imperial Histories and Postcolonial Displacements* (Princeton, NJ: Princeton University Press).

Rostow, W. W. (1960) *The Stages of Economic Growth* (Cambridge, MA: Cambridge University Press).

Silver, B. J. & Slater, E. (1999) The social origins of world hegemonies, in G. Arrighi & B. J. Silver (eds) *Chaos and Governance in the Modern World System* (Minnesota: University of Minnesota Press).

So, A.Y. (1990) *Social Change and Development* (Newbury Park, CA: Sage).

Sunkel, O. (1973) Transnational capitalism and national disintegration in Latin America, *Social and Economic Studies*, 22, pp. 132–176.

Tilly, C. (1999) *Durable Inequality* (Berkeley: University of California Press).

Wallerstein, I. (1974) *The Modern World System I* (New York: Academic Press).

Wallerstein, I. (1983) *Historical Capitalism*, 2nd ed. (London: Verso).

A Political Analysis of the Formal Comparative Method: Historicizing the Globalization and Development Debate

Introduction

Not long ago, R. J. B. Walker argued:

> [The] modern division of scholarly labor is used to solving the contradictions of modern politics by constituting theoretical discourses on either side of a distinction – politics and international relations, the international and the colonial/modernizing – but these discourses *necessarily* run into trouble when novelty implies less a new variation on an established theme than a challenge to the distinctions that enable the established principles of political life. (Walker, 2002, p. 11, emphasis added)

What Walker refers to in terms of the established principles of political life include the practices of inclusion and exclusion that are defined by the imaginary of the formal boundary of the political as represented by the cartography of the state. Central to these practices of inclusion and exclusion have been the spatial-cum-temporal demarcations of political community with all their attenuated corollaries. The latter have entailed temporalized notions of progress defined by reference to spatial categories, such as North–South or West–East, which always implied 'developed' and 'underdeveloped' respectively. These representations have conveyed an imaginary of progress to be realized in temporal terms—one only has to think of the various development plans that continue to be associated with the 'developing' countries—and progress in turn was (and continues to be) associated with modernization.

The inequalities that such categories define are ostensibly also premised on notions of equality (Walker, 2002). That is, spatial and temporal demarcations of inclusion and exclusion are precisely conceived as necessary to realize the principles of equality and justice: However, as Walker observed in this context:

> The problem of inequality is already deeply inscribed in our modern accounts of the international, and thus of modern politics, even before any consideration of the dynamics associated with modern

capitalism as a specific form of economic life that thrives on the production of inequality as a condition of its own dynamism. (pp. 21–22)

The relevance of such insights for development are obvious: Development theory and analyses implicitly and explicitly work with these categories and assumptions, and in so doing they naturalize a representation of political structure that is itself deeply implicated in the reproduction of social and political power, and thus inequality. The consequences are summed up in Walker's astute observation:

> Theories of international relations are thereby enabled to treat the international as synonymous with the world as such, to read all forms of inclusion and exclusion as a relation between friends and enemies, and either to leave the temporal process of modernization, of bringing the unmodern into modernity, to some other discourse, or to use all the half-buried tropes of civilizational difference as a way of building up a statist logic of friends and enemies into a battle between the civilized and the damned, those who are capable of becoming equal because they are unequal and those who seem incapable of becoming equal because they are unequal. (p. 23)

Implicit to this insight is how the relationship between acts of (mis)recognition and ideas about (re)distributive justice has come to frame modern social and political life through a particular form of representation (see also Balakrishnan, 2003; Bleiker, 2001; Dalby, 2005; Hobson, 2007). This modern framing—and the projection of its 'naturalness'—means of course to render invisible and irrelevant alternative accounts of social and political life, while privileging a social and political order conducive to the reproduction of inequality and violence (cf. Hindess, 2006).

Therefore, to discuss inequality and poverty meaningfully it is necessary to examine the foundational premises of development themselves—its frame of reference. To do this, I explore some initial thoughts on methodological and epistemological issues relating to development theory and analyses in historical and contemporary contexts.[1] An objective of the argument is to expose the way in which orthodox development discourse has been implicated in the reproduction of substantive experiences of inequality and poverty in world politics; thus, rethinking development entails dispensing with some foundational methodological and epistemological premises. I argue that a more appropriate approach would be one premised upon more inclusive concepts of the political and of politics (cf. Balakrishnan, 2003; Bleiker, 2001; Dalby, 2005; Hobson, 2007; Walker, 2002).

I develop my argument by explicitly engaging the formal comparative method and its political implications. I do so because it is premised upon core assumptions which—even if inadvertently—reproduce the dominant framework of inclusion and exclusion, and thus also the practices they engender. At the same time, it has the consequence of rendering invisible social struggles which have been constitutive of social and political life.

To put the argument into perspective more clearly, the problem of development—or the challenges of development—have, since the universalization of the nation-state system, been confined primarily to that generalized category, the 'Third World'. The Third World in turn, has been primarily conceptualized by reference to the former post-colonial states. Within this constellation, the state was conceived of as both the agent and the unit of development. Related to this spatial dimension has been a temporal logic: the division of the world (spatially) was coterminous with an identification of such 'spaces' in terms of stages of growth, which in turn has been conceptualized primarily in terms of economic indicators. From this perspective development occurs in a temporal sequence premised upon modernization with reference to a linearly defined temporal and developmental logic (Rostow, 1960).

Underlying this is a theory of development that enables the articulation of such a logic precisely because of its epistemological premises—the reduction of development and the developmental subject to *Homo oeconomicus*, thus abstracting the individual from complex social and political power relations (cf. Da Costa & McMichael, 2007; Rojas, 2007; Taylor, 2007; M. Weber, 2007) and reducing such complexity to an abstract economic category. Such an epistemological approach renders both invisible and inexplicable those aspects of social relations that resist and proactively struggle for more humane alternatives to the orthodoxy.

The argument is developed as follows. The first section begins with a brief discussion of attempts to theorize the development implications of what appears as an ostensibly new dynamic: globalization. In the second section, I work backwards by exploring the context of decolonization and particular conjunctures that gave rise to the idea of the national development project. In this context, the problematic conflation of formal sovereign independence with a politics of identity as concomitantly reflecting the possibility of self-determination through national development is examined. The third section engages key reinterpretations of colonial history and the organization of the world political economy. The latter lays the foundations for rendering the formal comparative method problematic. In the final section I briefly discuss the contemporary poverty reduction agenda to substantiate further the overall argument as well as the specific point about incorporating social struggle as an analytic category into the method of 'incorporating comparison' within a world historical perspective (McMichael, 1990). This latter intervention is intended to foreground the contested nature of development in historical and contemporary contexts. Being able to render visible such struggles as the substantive political dynamics of world historical development relates to the significance of understanding politics and the political in more inclusive terms.

Development and Globalization: The Need for a New Analytical Framework?

The making of what has been described as the 'First Development Project' (McMichael, 2004a) was related to struggles for decolonization and the universalization of the nation-state system. In this context the formal comparative method gained prominence as the plausible and acceptable method of development analysis. The unit of analysis—the territorial state—became, to borrow a line from Julian Saurin, the 'point of departure and the point of return' in most if not all developmental analysis (1995). As a consequence, causal explanations of poverty and social formations were (generally) theorized by reference to, and in terms of, that unit of analysis— the state.

Development theory was revised, partly as a consequence of the unfulfilled promises of modernization theory through dependency theory (and its variants). The latter, while explicating structural features of exploitation immanent in the organization of world politics, nevertheless by defending the ideology of 'national development' inadvertently committed to the inside/ outside imaginary, even if methodologically speaking, their analysis of the organization of development was contrary to that of modernization theorists.

More recently, however, in accounts of globalization there have been calls to re-think development theory. While there have been several studies in this vein, I focus on examples in which authors integrate questions of development with reference to the international, and thus implicitly problematize the core premises of the formal comparative method. William I. Robinson (2002), for instance, in an article entitled 'From a Territorial to a Social Cartography of Development', has made one such contribution to the debate, based on what he identifies as a 'new' conjunctural phase wherein social relations and forms of solidarity that define relations of inclusion and exclusion are seen to transcend increasingly the boundary of the nation-state. Although it might be correct to identify intensified forms and mechanisms of governance which are global in scope and reach under current conjunctures, Robinson's approach is nevertheless ahistorical in that he presumes the underlying assumptions of the formal comparative method to be problematic only as a consequence of more recent globalizing dynamics.[2] A study by Neil Brenner (1999), 'Beyond State Centrism', offers a critical engagement of globalization theorists, and the work of Jan Aart Scholte in particular. While Brenner accepts the need to dispense with methodological nationalism and adopt a more globally conceived approach to social change, such as methodological cosmopolitanism, he adds an important qualifier to this debate by cautioning that such approaches might, if only inadvertently, succumb to reifying a global space as an analytic category. Brenner's more circumspect intervention in globalization debates thus cautions against reifying space, and instead calls for a focus on (global) social relations and the quality of those relations. However, in a similar vein to Robinson, Brenner—although to a lesser degree than Robinson—takes as his point of departure an understanding of a distinctively different phase in history.[3] This observation notwithstanding, their insights problematize the premises and implications of the formal comparative method. Out of the works of Robinson and Brenner, then arises at least a more comprehensively relational analysis, even if, in their works, this is not carried through to issues of identity and identity formation.

While identity and identity politics are perceived as important today, they have also been an important constitutive element of struggles over development (cf., Hobson, 2007; Said, 1978); in other words, material inequality and difference (identity) are not independent of development struggles properly conceived. At the very least, this recognition requires a methodological cosmopolitan frame of reference as a precondition for adequately understanding the substantively contested, and related, conceptions and experiences of development among social actors across the 'global' in ways that overcome formally established spatial delineations (Hobson, 2007). Such an approach would also require an alternative account of the subjects of development (in terms of the conception of agency and agents). The current approach, of utilizing a methodological individualist premise at a meta-theoretical level for explaining and theorizing micro-political relations, is at one and the same time non-relational (not inter-subjective in the sense of minimally situating individuals within social contexts) and an abstraction in terms of the knowledge it produces of, for instance, individuals merely as utility-maximizing agents (cf. Brohman, 1995; Fine, 2001). Since the 1980s, a rethinking of some of the conventional assumptions of development theory has been taking place within different academic disciplines. However, in most cases they have tended not to engage with the conventional macro-political unit of development—the nation-state—which they generally take for granted, although many have questioned the episteme of mainstream development, with particular reference to the identity given to the subject of development (cf. Brohman, 1995; Fine, 2001).

Having briefly discussed some attempts to rethink development through globalization, I now turn to engage two important studies in order to elucidate the formation of ideas and practices that synchronized around the nation-state, and by implication served as the basis upon which the formal comparative method is premised. They illustrate the way in which the concept of the international associated with the concept of sovereignty (as defining equality in the formal political sense) played out in ways that altered power structures generally, but also came to represent an imagination that detracted from the context of global social relations.

Decolonization and Struggles for International Development: Nationalism, Methodological Nationalism, and the Comparative Method

Anti-colonial struggles and the subsequent processes of decolonization, which resulted in the universalization of the nation-state system, set in motion a specific and targeted development project (McMichael, 2004a). Anti-colonial struggles were motivated not least by socio-psychological and identity-related issues arising from the colonial encounter. These struggles were thus as much over the politics of representation in world politics more generally. In this context, decolonization and the gaining of formal sovereign independence was a crucial psychological marker. However, it was also more than this. The new legal recognition received through formalized universal rights (such as self-determination) also changed the political dynamics and power structures prevalent in the colonial era (cf. Bair, 2007; Berger, 2007). The promise of self-determination, and to be recognized as equals, gave impetus to the anti-colonial struggles and ideas about subsequently achieving the promises of development through the project of national development.

The construction of a national imaginary was important to anti-colonial struggles but, as Frederick Cooper (2005, esp. pp. 204–230) has so eloquently reminded us, this was not the only struggle around, and neither were such struggles confined to—or realized merely by reference to—the political imagination of social relations as defined by the nation-state; rather, they entailed complex relational dimensions as a consequence of encounters with Others (cf. Hobson, 2007). Global relations included, among others, the abolitionist movement and labour movements, yet an imagination of a homogenous nation was crucial in fostering a sense of national unity in struggles for decolonization. This sociological and psychological aspect, which privileged national identity and national liberation, broadly prevailed in many contexts, which also worked to define and represent a form of collective memory over individual experiences. Cooper's example of Guinea under the guidance of Sekou Toure is instructive here (2005, p. 229): the politics of identity as represented through nationalism(s) appeared crucial for consolidating the social basis for self-determination. Sovereignty in this context was a crucial enabling concept for emancipation of one kind: decolonization and the formation of an imagination of equality among the new states. The nation-state system provided a normative basis for emancipation of a kind, and still holds out such a promise for some.[4] However, sovereignty did not necessarily mean liberation for all, or indeed the anticipated degree of autonomy from ('outside') others.

The idea of sovereignty as non-intervention (in the post 1945 era) was problematized by Caroline Thomas (1985) in her work *New States, Sovereignty and Intervention*. In the wider social and political context of this time, self-determination was formally established and conceptualized in relation to the norm of sovereignty, and the corresponding norm of non-intervention that it ostensibly implied. From the perspective of the formal conception of sovereign nation-states (at one level always implying a degree of the right to autonomy), the possibility of explaining social and political relations across borders in terms other than 'intervention' was problematic. The state as the unit of analysis was given ontological primacy.[5] However, in many ways important criticisms about development and inequality were already framed at this point in terms that violated the norm of non-intervention, which mirrored and complemented dependency theory. They complemented the dependency approaches in the sense that such arguments were grounded in discourses about the structural organization of inequality. However, most critical arguments about intervention were really only deployed to redress the unequal international division of labour of that time. Sovereignty would be compromised under conditions that were conducive to strategies and policies that were more in sync with the identified needs of the new states (cf. Bair, 2007).

Thus, nationalism provided a unifying imaginary for decolonization and the organization of the national development project, and precisely how development was conceptualized and to be achieved politically was always contested 'within' (Cooper, 2005, pp. 230, 231–242). The fallacy of the assumption of a unified conception of political development underpinning the idea of national development was embedded within an analytical framework of nation-states (as ontologically prior), which prevented substantive inquiry into the relationship between development and inequality organized in a global space.

Sovereignty in Question?

An important contribution to the issue of the problem of sovereignty (and assumptions of anarchy) in international relations was Justin Rosenberg's *Empire of Civil Society* (1994), which problematized the idea of autonomous national development. Rosenberg's argument in this study is premised on two interrelated conceptual moves at the level of ontology. In keeping with structuralist premises, he conceives in the first move of global capitalism as a pervasive system of functional imperatives. The second move renders these systemic imperatives through the spatial imaginary of the international system, in effect making both these moves prior to the analysis of inequality and struggle. Additionally, Rosenberg's historical materialist work does not account for the complexity and multiple implications of sovereignty in world historical development, including for instance the degree to which the extension of sovereignty in the context of anti-colonial struggles to the former colonial entities reconfigured power relations and the dynamics of international politics more generally (cf. Bair, 2007; Cooper, 2005). More recently, Rosenberg (2006) has developed a more explicit argument about global development in a socially relational way.[6]

To sum up, Rosenberg is circumspect in his disaggregation of the formal from the substantive, but in his earlier work does not sufficiently address the normative thrust of sovereignty in the context of decolonization. This is not to suggest that sovereignty resolved the contradictions of development. On the contrary, Rosenberg's (1994) and Thomas's (1985, 1986) work brings out these contradictions. As Cooper has argued, historical narratives that tend toward mono-causal (or dominant) explanations foreclose the possibility of also making sense of concrete social struggles and developing insights about the 'paths that were not taken' (2005, p. 18).

Historicizing Global Development: Reinterpretations of the Colonial Encounter and the Making of the Post-Colonial World Economy

As stated above, the conventional narratives of development have been very much premised on the cornerstone myths of world historical development, such as development as a progressive process for all (a process without contradictions). This image is often associated with an idealized notion of the experiences of the peoples of the developed West. This is not to say that there have not been exceptions to the historical narrative (cf. Berger & Borer, 2007; Cooper, 2005; Halperin, 1997; McMichael, 2004b [1984]). Here, I engage two of these for the purposes of explicating problems with the formal comparative method: the work of Sandra Halperin, and in particular her book *In the Mirror of the Third World: Capitalist Development in Modern Europe* (1997), and the work of Philip McMichael and his book *Settlers and the Agrarian*

Question: Capitalism in Colonial Australia (2004b [1984]), and his later work on the method of 'incorporating comparison' (1990).

Halperin does not set out to question explicitly the problem of the formal comparative method, and she does not engage the relationship between identity and social and political power, but she does demonstrate that there was a relationship between European development processes and colonialism. Halperin's analysis implicitly problematizes limitations of the comparative method in that she demonstrates the way in which certain groups or social classes organized across a global space, and also how specific classes and groups benefited more than others from the modern development project (cf. Halperin, 2007). In this sense, Halperin pursues an explicitly critical, qualitative analysis of world historical development. These social classes were 'transnational' and, in her words, the development project was neither driven by the state as such, nor was the state the primary beneficiary; rather, it has been a process driven 'by classes and class struggles within social formations' (Halperin, 1997, p. 198). Halperin's focus on class struggles has continued in a more recent reminder of the relevance of struggles for social and political change (2004).

McMichael's work, while similar to Halperin's in the sense that it also maps and exposes the relationships between social, political, and economic formations in different spatial domains within a global space, is, however, significantly different in that he develops an alternative analytical framework. McMichael adopts a non-state-centred analysis, and his approach is not grounded within a structuralist analytical framework. Rather, his approach gives content to concepts (such as the world economy) by focusing on substantive processes constitutive of the formation of the world political economy. It explicitly parts with the formal comparative method because 'comparison becomes the substance of the inquiry rather than the framework' (McMichael, 1990, p. 386). From such a perspective, both spatial and temporal dynamics are incorporated into the analysis through a non-state-centred lens. While such an approach does not foreground the dynamics of social and political trends and transformations as an analytic category *per se*, it does allow for the possibility of incorporating the dimension of social struggles into the method of analysis of global social formations.

The other global approach to the study of the world economy is the world systems approach. While this takes a global space as its point of reference, the structure of the world economy is nevertheless ontologically prior to substantive social and political dynamics. By giving primacy to the structure in ontological terms, as McMichael has argued, the world economy in the world systems approach is posited as an entity extraneous to substantive social and political relations. An attempt to give substantive content to the world political economy, McMichael's method of 'incorporated comparison' was, in this context, perhaps the most significant contribution to development analysis. The method of 'incorporating comparison' neither posits ontological primacy to structure, nor does it take the fixed unit of the nation state as the point of departure for analysis. In this sense, substantive inquiry is necessarily prior to the formal method. As he argues:

> The logic of the comparative inquiry requires independent or independent uniform 'case' and formal quasi-experimental designs for comparative generalization. Global conceptions of social change violate formal comparative requirements, necessitating an alternative form of 'incorporated comparison,' that takes both multiple/diachronic and singular/synchronic forms. Incorporated comparison is used to conceptualize variation across time and space when time and space dimensions are neither separate nor uniform. (1990, p. 385)

This is an alternative, sophisticated version of a methodological cosmopolitan approach to the study of global social change. McMichael's approach focuses on the substantive aspects of social and political relations, but it does not in and of itself foreground a reading of such relations in a normative sense. While this may have merit, it would be enriched if analyses of such relations were approached from the perspective of social struggles—the objective of this being not merely to expose struggles *per se*, but to be able to recognize and engage the moral grammar of such struggles as reflective of contending visions of (in)justice and, thus, of struggles for recognition.[7]

While the inquiry has so far worked to problematize the formal comparative method, in so doing I have also worked to explicate what it renders invisible: not just social relations constitutive of the formations of world political dynamics but, importantly, the struggles constitutive of such dynamics. Such struggles, however, cannot be accounted for in terms of the circumscribed identity assigned to the 'subject of development' by mainstream theoretical perspectives embedded within a reductionist discourse of rational, profit-maximizing agents. It is this problem that I turn to next. In this context, I briefly address two contemporary development initiatives to illustrate the critical argument developed so far, and the specific point about the political implications of the ostensibly neutral identity of the developmental subject.

Global Politics of International Development: Theory and Policy

Development in an age of globalization has received global attention, from international institutions to NGOs and governmental representatives. We can recall here the declaration of and commitments to the Millennium Development Goals (MDGs) initiative to the comprehensive framing of the World Trade Organization (WTO) in terms of poverty reduction and development (for a critique, see Higgott and Weber, 2005). This development agenda—and the meaning of development it projects—is presented by its advocates as if it were accepted globally, rather than contested. Development strategies central to this project are thus globally organized, in terms of macro-political (re)structuring which is increasingly coordinated with micro-political poverty interventions, yet the development problem is still represented in national terms and corroborated by the formal comparative method.

At the macro-political level we have, for example, overarching legal frameworks for development, such as the Poverty Reduction Strategy Paper (PRSP) initiative. The PRSP initiative and its wider development context have been presented as a revised institutional response to concerns about poverty and under-development. However, careful scrutiny of the policy process and policy content it engenders has revealed that the PRSP initiative is a comprehensive extension of the neoliberal development policies that emerged in the 1980s. Moreover, the micro-political policies incorporated within PRSPs, such as microcredit schemes, emerged as strategic responses in the context of social struggles (primarily in the context of SAPs) in the 1980s (Weber, 2004a). These micro-political strategies were soon to be replicated in other contexts implementing neo-liberal-oriented development strategies. As a neo-liberal approach to development, such a micro-political strategy is organized and functions within a global context, rather than merely within national contexts. Microcredit schemes are embedded within the global re-organization of credit and finance specifically, and within the global process of neo-liberal restructuring more generally. It is premised on a methodological individualist approach to development which constructs the subjects of development, epistemologically, in terms of *Homo oeconomicus* (see Soederberg, 2007; Taylor, 2007; Weber, 2002, 2004a, 2006).

The example of microfinance schemes as an approach to poverty reduction illustrates well the continued inscription of development and poverty reduction efforts through the national imagination, although in substantive terms such schemes function within a set of global relations. First, microcredit schemes are advanced globally, and are constituted within a globally organized regulatory system. Second, a careful analysis of the context in which microcredit schemes came to prominence as a poverty reduction strategy reveals social struggles to be a constitutive dynamic immanent to the (re)-ordering of macro–micro social and political relations on a global scale.[7] Social struggles, so conceived, cannot be understood merely in relation to specific state strategies; rather, they are constitutive of global politics. It is clear, as McMichael has argued, that the formal comparative method is premised upon a form of abstraction from substantive social and political relations of global scale.

I have drawn on the examples of contemporary development policy not to suggest that for the first time we are confronted with a global strategy for global development, but rather to demonstrate the degree to which the ideology of the national development project continues to frame theory and practice, thus reproducing the form of representation which engenders the problems identified in the beginning.

Beyond International Development: Recognition and Redistribution

As stated above, a more appropriate approach to the study of development can found in the method of 'incorporating comparison' advanced by McMichael. Such an approach would be more in tune with praxis, although not premised upon an empiricist epistemology. It would entail, among other things, moving beyond the rationalist assumptions which underpin mainstream development theory so as to enable an articulation of actually existing social struggles—struggles which can viewed as expressions of diverse and alternative epistemes—which can neither be rendered visible nor given recognition from the perspective of the abstract premises of liberal political economy (cf. Da Costa and McMichael, 2007). Orthodox approaches naturalize social relations in accordance with rationalist assumptions, and render invisible the struggles for alternative conceptions of recognition. What is at stake here is, ultimately, both a normative issue and one that is integral to the question of the social mediation of political relations. As Axel Honneth argued in his debate with Nancy Fraser (2003), rationalist assumptions obscure the way in which social and political power mediates what appears through a rationalist lens as a neutral process of social reproduction.

> Even on the problematic assumption that economic imperatives possess a pure, culturally unmediated form, we must still admit the influence of normative constraints that stem from achieved legal guarantees: the expectations individuals can articulate are continually undermined by supposedly anonymous, norm-free market processes because their claims to social recognition are already somehow institutionalized in legal regulations or payment schemes. Analyzing the development of the labor market without taking such recognition expectations based on law or achievement into account seems to me a typical product of the economists' fiction of the *homo oeconomicus*. (pp. 252–253)

To capture meaningfully the dynamics of social and political relations in development, we need to render visible struggles constitutive of such dynamics (see also McMichael, 2006, esp. p. 490). This would require and engagement with perspectives and imaginations that are concealed from mainstream development theory and analyses. It would entail, among other things, the retrieval of alternative epistemes that posit the self in relation to others not in terms of individual profit-maximizing agents, but rather in terms of socially constituted beings situated within complex contexts within a constellation of complex identities. To elucidate this dynamic would require a move beyond the deployment of both proprietary individualism and methodological individualism in development analysis (cf. M Weber, 2007). Through such an approach, we can reach a more inclusive conception of politics. Engaging the social basis of relations of recognition in development would, however, be incomplete if confined to formal political boundaries. One of the consequences, as indicated above, would be rendering invisible the global dimensions of social and political struggles in development.

Politics of the 'Invisible'/'Visible'

The continued deployment of the formal comparative method as the analytical and conceptual framework of development analysis is premised upon a misapprehension of politics and the political. From this perspective, the spatial domain of the political remains tied to the territorial limits defined by the state. It would, however, be equally erroneous to suggest that the national imagination and the particular practices it has enabled (and constrained) within particular historical periods have little or no relevance to the political formations and political identities that have ensued. But this would require more careful analysis integrating events, moments, and conjunctures diachronically and synchronically (Berger and Borer, 2007; Cooper, 2005; Dalby, 2005; McMichael, 2006).

In order to render visible the 'sociology of the absences' (de Sousa Santos, 2001, p. 191) we need to address—in order to overcome—the socialization and naturalization of a social and political order in which the division of labour has for so long fostered an imagination of scarcity and growth, for which the fiction of *Homo oeconomicus* has been a justification (Fine, 2001; Sahlins, 1974). This has had an effect tantamount to what Alex Honneth and Avishai Margalit (2001) outlined in their engagement of the protagonist's experiences of being invisible in Ralph Ellison's novel *The Invisible Man*. As Honneth and Margalit recount this scenario:

> In regard to the question of how he came to be invisible, the narrator answers that it must be due to the 'construction' of the 'inner eye' of those who look through him unrelentingly. By this he means not their 'physical eye', not, therefore, a type of actual visual deficiency, but rather an inner disposition that does not allow them to see his true person. (p. 111)

Honneth metaphorically draws on the perception of the protagonist in this novel to illustrate a deeper socio-psychological aspect of social relations through which recognition of the Other(s) comes to be expressed, in order to draw attention to how the suppression of recognition of the Others(s) might come about as a consequence 'of a *deformation* of the human capacity for perception with which recognition is connected'. Honneth captures this well: '[As the] author put it, [it is] "a matter of the construction of their inner eyes, those eyes with which they look through their physical eyes upon reality"'(p. 126). Overcoming such a deformation allows for the possibility of engaging with the complexity of human social relations. To some extent, such an approach resonates with de Sousa Santos's epistemological move to recover the 'sociology of the absences' (2001; see also Da Costa and McMichael, 2007; Rojas, 2007; M. Weber, 2007), which necessarily implies moving beyond the conceptions of human beings as atomistic individuals acting merely in terms of rational self-interest which remain at the core of mainstream development theory, and towards comprehensively relational analysis.

While a core aspect of my argument is that world historical development has been a relational process in which, historically and to the present, local (spatial) domains have had a global dimension in the sense that local social relations have been constituted of—and constituted by—encounters and inter-relations with distant others (cf. Hall, 1992, pp. 275–332; Halperin, 1997; Hobson, 2007; McMichael, 2004a, 2004b; Rosenberg, 2006), the degree, intensity and scope of such relations cannot be generalized without an appreciation of their specific situatedness within particular conjunctural and temporal dynamics and contexts (Cooper, 2005; McMichael, 1990). However, mainstream development theory and analysis has been constrained by the political imagination engendered by formal rather than substantive social and political relations. The consequences entail state-centred (and in many cases state-centric) analyses of development and inequality, within which the national imagination and the project of national development appear synonymous. Instead, they are contingently co-extensive, but clearly not synonymous. The formal comparative method is, as McMichael has argued, methodologically flawed, with the consequence of a severely distorted representation of social and political relations. My aim has been to reconstruct the implications of the omission of social relations from development, and suggest that this abstraction which this omission involves is a crucial enabling condition for the apparent coherence of neo-liberal approaches to development.

In the contemporary context, the activities around the World Social Forum (as an active site of counter-movements to neo-liberal politics in particular and capitalism more generally), for example, are not irrelevant to understanding the dynamics that underpin current attempts to consolidate versions of neo-liberal constitutions 'in the name of the poor' (Gill, 2002; Teivainen, 2002; Weber, 2004b). The analytical significance of social relations to political analyses of development is that they make visible social struggles as relationally constitutive of formations of a hegemonic development discourse otherwise ostensibly rendered in de-contextualized terms (cf. Balakrishnan, 2003).

Concluding Insights: Re-thinking Development

While early encounters between settlers and local peoples have had implications for identity and identity formation, they also established the substantive relations out of which the formation of the global political economy emerged. The substantive dynamics of these inter-relationships, whether we interpret them in terms of dependency or dependent development, always had a relational dynamic. While a combination of both the diachronic and the synchronic can better reveal the relationship between historical and contemporary contexts, it would nevertheless be inadequate if it were grounded ideologically with reference to formal political boundaries. For instance, diachronic and synchronic approaches may still proceed in ways that give primacy to the macro-subject of nation-states, where the nation-state is taken as ontologically given, thus replicating the fallacies and distortions associated with state-centred or state-centric analysis. What often appear as ostensibly macro-political problems or legal codes of conduct are not without a corresponding social basis.

> What Africans got was sovereignty. That was not the only demand that emerged from the political mobilization of the 1940s and 1950s. . . . But the issues of wages, labor conditions, poverty and opportunity never quite disappeared into the confines of national sovereignty—into questions for African and Asian governments for which outsiders had no responsibility—and they never quite disappeared into the anonymity of a world market that was supposed to allocate global resources in an optimizing manner. Those questions are still the focus of debates and of political mobilization. (Cooper, 2005, p. 230)

This contradictory dynamic reflected in social relations is constitutive of contradictions in the project of modernity, a project which has to be understood as encompassing the interactions of the colonial encounter (cf. Chakrabarty, 2000, esp. pp. 27–46; Cooper, 2005, esp. pp. 231–242). Social struggles over development are constitutive of the modern development project, and keeping this in sight is important in attempts to understand what moved history and why (cf. Balakrishnan, 2003; Cooper, 2005). These questions enrich our understanding of paths that were not taken or were suppressed in development struggles, and can potentially shed light on how to keep open the 'spaces of hope' of the present. As Cooper reminds us (2005):

> Scholarship on colonialism has, in its own way, emphasized that such issues cannot be separated from the history that defined them, and it has made clear how much is at stake in the way these issues are framed. Studying colonial history reminds us that in the most oppressive of political systems, people found not just niches in which to hide and fend for themselves, but handles by which the system itself could be moved. (pp. 241–242)

Notes

1   The argument I develop has been inspired by, and draws considerably on, the work of Philip McMichael, Julian Saurin, Sandra Halperin, and Justin Rosenberg.
2   For excellent critiques of these premises, see McMichael (2001) and Dalby (2005).
3   I do not suggest that new dynamics are not at play in this historical phase, but only that social relations and encounters have not been confined to the formal political boundary as often assumed by some globalization theorists.
4   One only has to recall the various struggles for self-determination in global politics: for example, Palestine, Sri-Lanka, or East Timor. However, we also know that this broad representation does not necessarily involve emancipation for all people within these communities. It did not and does not necessarily overcome other forms of domination, such as gender, class, and race relations.
5   Robert H. Jackson's (1990) *Quasi States* offers a similar account of the fate of the new states—an account that is relational—but nevertheless fails to theorize such relations in terms beyond the imagination of the hierarchy of states.
6   My sympathetic critique of Rosenberg's *Empire of Civil Society* (1994) resonates with his own, more recent, critique of this work, and that of others working from broadly similar perspectives (see Rosenberg, 2006, p. 337).
7   More recently, McMichael has incorporated social movement struggles for alternatives into the method of incorporated comparison (see McMichael, 2005).
8   I have provided a detailed account of the PRSP initiative and its relation to social struggles (Weber, 2002, 2004a, 2006; see also Jayasuriya, 2006).

References

Bair, J. (2007) From the politics of development to the challenges of globalization, *Globalizations*, 4(4), pp. 486–499.
Balakrishnan, R. (2003) *International Law from Below: Development, Social Movements and Third World Resistance* (Cambridge: Cambridge University Press).
Berger, M. T. (2007) Keeping the world safe for primary colours: area studies, development studies, international studies, and the vicissitudes of nation-building, *Globalizations*, 4(4), pp. 429–444.
Berger, M. T. & Borer, D. A. (2007) The Long War: insurgency, counterinsurgency and collapsing states, *Third World Quarterly*, 28(2), pp. 197–216.
Bleiker, R. (2001) The aesthetic turn in international political theory, *Millennium: Journal of International Relations*, 30(3), pp. 509–533.
Brenner, N. (1999) Beyond state-centrism? Space, territoriality, and geographical scale in globalization studies, *Theory and Society*, 28(1), pp. 39–78.
Brohman, J. (1995) Economism and critical silences in development studies: a theoretical critique of neoliberalism, *Third World Quarterly*, 16(2), pp. 297–318.
Chakrabarty, D. (2000) *Provincializing Europe: Postcolonial Thought and Historical Difference* (Princeton, NJ: Princeton University Press).
Cooper, F. (2005) *Colonialism in Question: Theory, Knowledge, History* (Berkeley: University of California Press).
Da Costa, D. & McMichael, P. (2007) The poverty of the global order, *Globalizations*, 4(4), pp. 588–602.
Dalby, S. (2005) Political space: autonomy, liberalism, and empire, *Alternatives*, 30, pp. 415–441.
De Sousa Santos, B. (2001) Nuestra America: reinventing a subaltern paradigm of recognition and redistribution, *Theory, Culture and Society*, 18(2–3), pp. 185–217.
Fine, B. (2001) Neither the Washington Consensus nor the post-Washington Consensus: an introduction, in B. Fine, C. Lapavitsas, & J. Pincus (eds) *Development Policy in the 21st Century: Beyond the post-Washington Consensus* (London: Routledge).
Fraser, N. & Honneth, A. (2003) *Redistribution or Recognition: A Political–Philosophical Exchange* (London: Verso).

Gill, S. (2002) Constitutionalizing inequality and the clash of globalizations, *International Studies Review*, 4(2), pp. 47–66.

Hall, S. (1992) The West and the rest: discourse and power, in S. Hall & B. Gieben (eds) *Formations of Modernity* (Cambridge: Polity Press).

Halperin, S. (1997) *In the Mirror of the Third World: Capitalist Development in Modern Europe* (Ithaca, NY: Cornell University).

Halperin, S. (2004) Dynamics of conflict and system change: the great transformation revisited, *European Journal of International Relations*, 10(2), pp. 263–306.

Halperin, S. (2007) Re-envisioning global development: conceptual and methodological issues, *Globalizations*, 4(4), pp. 543–558.

Higgott, R. & Weber, H. (2005) GATS in context: development, an evolving *lex mercatoria* and the Doha Agenda, *Review of International Political Economy*, 12(3), pp. 434–455.

Hindess, B. (2006) Terrortory, *Alternatives*, 31, pp. 243–257.

Hobson, M. J. (2007) Is critical theory always for the white West and for Western imperialism? Beyond Westphilian towards a post-racist critical IR, *Review of International Studies*, 33, pp. 91–116.

Honneth, A. (2003) The point of recognition: a rejoinder to the rejoinder, in A. Honneth & N. Fraser, *Redistribution or Recognition: A Political–Philosophical Exchange* (London: Verso).

Honneth, A. & Margalit, A. (2001) Invisibility: on the epistemology of 'recognition', *Supplements to the Proceedings of the Aristotelian Society*, 71(1), pp. 111–126.

Jackson, R. H. (1990) *Quasi-States: Sovereignty, International Relations and the Third World* (Cambridge: Cambridge University Press).

Jayasuriya, K. (2006) *Statecraft, Welfare and the Politics of Inclusion* (London: Palgrave).

McMichael, P. (1990) Incorporating comparison within a world-historical perspective: an alternative comparative method, *American Sociological Review*, 55(3), pp. 385–397.

McMichael, P. (2001) Revisiting the question of the transnational state, *Theory and Society*, 30(2), pp. 201–210.

McMichael, P. (2004a) *Development and Social Change: A Global Perspective*, 3rd ed. (London: Pine Forge Press).

McMichael, P. (2004b [1984]) *Settlers and the Agrarian Question: Capitalism in Colonial Australia*, 2nd edn. (Cambridge: Cambridge University Press).

Mc Michael, P. (2005) Globalization, in T. Janoski, R. Alford, A.M. Hicks & M.A. Schwartz (eds) *The Handbook of Political Sociology: States, Civil Societies and Globalization* (New York: Cambridge University Press).

McMichael, P. (2006) Peasant prospects in the neoliberal age, *New Political Economy*, 11(33), pp. 407–418.

Robinson, W. I. (2002) Remapping development in light of globalisation: from a territorial to a social cartography, *Third World Quarterly*, 23(6), pp 1047–1107.

Rojas, C. (2007) International political economy/development otherwise, *Globalizations*, 4(4), pp. 573–587.

Rosenberg, J. (1994) *The Empire of Civil Society: A Critique of the Realist Theory of International Relations* (London: Verso).

Rosenberg, J. (2006) Why is there no international historical sociology?, *European Journal of International Relations*, 12(3), pp. 307–340.

Rostow, W. W. (1960) *The Stages of Economic Growth: A Non-Communist Manifesto* (Cambridge: Cambridge University Press).

Sahlins, M. (1974) *Stone Age Economics* (London: Tavistock).

Said, E. (1978) *Orientalism, Western Conceptions of the Orient* (London: Penguin Books).

Saurin, J. (1995) The end of international relations? The state and international theory in the age of globalization, in J. Macmillan & A. Linklater (eds) *Boundaries in Question* (London: Pinter).

Soederberg, S. (2007) Taming corporations or buttressing market-led development? A critical assessment of the global compact, *Globalizations*, 4(4), pp. 500–513.

Taylor, M. (2007) Rethinking the global production of uneven development, *Globalizations*, 4(4), pp. 529–542.

Teivainen, T. (2002) The World Social Forum and global democratisation: learning from Porto Alegre, *Third World Quarterly*, 3(4), pp. 621–632.

Thomas, C. (1985) *New States, Sovereignty and Intervention* (Aldershot: Gower Publishing).

Thomas, C. (1986) *In Search of Security* (Brighton: Harvester Wheatsheaf).

Walker, R. B. J. (2002) International/inequality, *International Relations and the New Inequality*, 4(2), pp. 7–24.

Weber, H. (2001) The imposition of a global development architecture: the example of microcredit, *Review of International Studies*, 28(3), pp. 537–555.

Weber, H. (2002) Global governance and poverty reduction: the case of microcredit, in R. Wilkinson & S. Hughes (eds) *Global Governance: Critical Perspectives* (London: Routledge).

Weber, H. (2004a) The "new economy" and social risk: banking on the poor?, *Review of International Political Economy*, 11(2), pp. 356–386.

Weber, H. (2004b) Reconstituting the 'Third World'? Poverty reduction and territoriality in the global politics of development, *Third World Quarterly*, 25(1), pp. 187–206.

Weber, H. (2006) A political analysis of the PRSP initiative: social struggles and the organization of persistent relations of inequality, *Globalizations*, 3(2), pp. 187–206.

Weber, M. (2007) On the critique of the subject of development: beyond proprietary and methodological individualism, *Globalizations*, 4(4), pp. 460–474.

International Political Economy/Development Otherwise

CRISTINA ROJAS

Introduction

The opening to cultural differences in IPE/development is presented in academic circles as a disciplinary breakthrough. The cultural turn welcomes contributions from semiotics, ethnology, sociology, geography, and ethics. Surprisingly, despite the claim for this being a 'cultural approach', there have been few attempts to incorporate proposals from marginalized cultures. Absent from a cultural political economy are counter-discourses coming from critical development studies, including from subaltern, postcolonial, decolonial, and postdevelopment scholars. This paper argues for an international political economy/development otherwise which leads to a 'different place', a different 'beginning', and 'to spatial sites of struggles and building rather than to a new temporality within the same space' (Mignolo, forthcoming, p. 2). Thinking otherwise includes theorizing from economies and subjectivities that were never fully capitalist, the use of 'in-between' epistemologies, the incorporation of coloniality as the other side of modernity, and the envisioning of postcapitalist and postdevelopment possibilities.

The forgetting of colonialism and the suppression of noncapitalist alternatives has important consequences for the fields of development and political economy: the critique of capitalism is incomplete; different forms of resistance are overlooked, and alternative sources of innovation and creativity are ignored. Thinking otherwise avoids capitalocentrism and the colonization of knowledge. According to Gibson and Graham (1996, 2006) capitalocentric perspectives understand alternative forms of economy primarily in relation to capitalism, which is assigned the highest place, while alternative political economies are depicted as inferior and in the process of transition to capitalism. A colonial IPE/development shares with capitalocentric perspectives the hierarchical treatment of noncapitalist economies. In addition, colonial political economy: (1) historicizes capitalism by referring to alternative political economies as belonging to another time and by positing historical time as a measure of cultural distance (Chakrabarty, 2000); (2) understands capitalism as a process that emerges from within modernity, and ignores coloniality as the other side of modernity (Dussel, 2002; Quijano, 2000, 2001); and

(3) subalternizes alternative knowledges by discarding the idea of a rationality other than the one envisioned by modern epistemology (Castro-Gómez, 2002; Escobar, 2003; Mignolo, 2000). This paper analyses cultural, ethnological, oppositional, postcapitalist, and decolonial political economies/development, and consider the extent to which these alternatives allow for decolonization and disidentification from capitalism.

Cultural Political Economy

The proposal for a cultural political economy (CPE) originates in the body of literature known as the regulation school (Jessop, 2004; Jessop & Sum, 2001; Sayer, 2001). A CPE keeps the focus on the regulatory mechanisms within capitalism, while decentring the role of the state and re-instating the role that semiotics plays in the reproduction and transformation of capitalism. The economy is 'imaginatively narrated', socially constructed, and embedded in social and cultural relations (Jessop, 2004, p. 162).

As Sayer (2001) points out, CPE is not a new discipline; its roots remit to philosophers like Aristotle and classical political economists such as Smith, Ferguson, and Hume. For Aristotle, economic activity directed towards moneymaking was pathological, and Adam Smith criticized the tendency to value individuals for what they own rather than for what they are or do. In Sayer's view, a CPE should incorporate classical political economy as well as the embedding and disembedding effects of capital accumulation.

In a CPE the capitalist system is the main focus of analysis, and its meanings are called upon to explain both reproduction and variation within the system. Meanings secure economic repro-duction by selecting and retaining discourses that are supportive of the system; at the same time, meanings introduce new discourses that become a source of indeterminacy and change (Jessop, 2004, p. 164). Theoretically, CPE is closer to Gramsci's view of crisis as moments of uncertainty and struggle and, therefore, as moments of semiotic innovation. Discourses are selected based on their capacity to mobilize different narratives and their resonance with narratives of other strata of the population and with international audiences. To illustrate this, Jessop uses the example of the transition to the knowledge-based economy (KBE) which followed the crisis of the mass production-mass consumption regimes of Atlantic Fordism (p. 166). The success of the KBE is explained by its capacity to address different scales (regional, national, supranational) and different institutional, public, and private narratives in different fields (science, education, health, law, politics), and its ability to translate its field into different visions and strategies (smart machines, intellectual property, cybercommunities) into different political regimes (neo-liberal, neo-corporatist, neo-statist).

Without a doubt, a CPE opens the economy to cultural variation and uncertainty; however, because of its focus on the reproduction of the capitalist system, it underscores forms of resist-ance to capitalism. In this approach the forms of the state, ideology, and culture are all specified in relation to capitalism and its problems (Gibson and Graham, 1996). The capitalist system and transformations within capitalism are self-generating processes than can mask colonialism and other forms of subordination within capitalism. Following Jacinda Swanson (2005, p. 103), the-ories that see only capitalism reinforce capitalist hegemony by portraying capitalism as unchal-lenged and dominant; they represent noncapitalist alternatives as exotic and unfeasible; and politically, by conceiving change as requiring a whole-scale structural transformation, they tend to render small and local changes useless.

Moreover, by focusing on those meanings that succeed in the regulation of capitalism, the approach ignores the way in which successful cultural constructions subordinate and devalue alternative arrangements. Feminist analyses have demonstrated how, in order to succeed, the sexual division of labour entailed a subordination of household economies. Thinkers such as Vandana Shiva (2004) document how Western intellectual property rights regimes, central to a KBE, give northern countries a monopoly over knowledge, including over those originating in indigenous cultures. The defence of scientific rationality as singular and universal subordinates alternative knowledges and rationalities. As Latin-American scholar Anibal Quijano (2000, p. 541) points out, a global configuration of culture is made possible through operations that expropriate cultural discoveries of the colonized to the profit of the centre, and repress subaltern forms of knowledge production and its models for the production of meanings. Furthermore, by centring the analysis on discourses with high resonance and those whose meanings are retained by the capitalist system, a CPE analysis contributes to marginalizing dissident voices further, particularly those outside the 'prevailing web of interlocution'.

Ethnological Political Economy

Karl Polanyi inspired one of the most culturally sensitive approaches to political economy, through recognition that the economy is embedded in culture. *The Great Transformation* (1957) is an indictment of the destructive effects of market expansion on the culture of colonial societies:

> The catastrophe of the native community is a direct result of the rapid and violent disruption of the basic institutions of the victim (whether force is used in the process or not does not seem altogether relevant). These institutions are disrupted by the very fact that a market economy is foisted upon an entirely differently organized community; labor and land are made into commodities, which, again, is only a short formula for the liquidation of every and any cultural institution in an organic society. (p. 159)

In his view the same destruction took place in European societies: '[T]he elemental force of culture contact, which is now revolutionizing the colonial world, is the same which, a century ago, created the dismal scenes of early capitalism' (p. 158).

Polanyi was equally innovative in his search for alternatives ways in which to organize the economy, as he recognized reciprocity, redistribution, and householding as alternative forms to market rationality. Polanyi's insights provide the foundation for Naeem Inayatullah and David Blaney's (2004) proposal for an ethnological political economy (EPE) and a dialogue among cultures. They reject the idea that human livelihood is governed solely by an economic logic (p. 172), and concur with Polanyi on the need for mechanisms of social protection to re-embed the market in society (p. 174).

Inayatullah and Blaney call for a 'new civilization' that would subordinate the market to the purposes of human community (p. 174). To accomplish this task, they call for a cultural dialogue between noncapitalist and contemporary political economies for the creation of this new civilization, whose inputs would be drawn from both historical noncapitalist societies and from contemporary efforts to resist the implementation of a free market. Following Tzventan Todorov and Ashis Nandy, they consider dialogue an ethical imperative whereby self and other enter on an equal footing into conversation; this encounter would lead to a cultural transformation (p. 168). To enhance this dialogue they call for a disciplinary encounter between modern political economy and critical or postdevelopment scholars, given their commitment to recover alternative and marginalized voices (p. 183).

Despite the attention to cultural difference and the call for a dialogue between political economies, an ethnological political economy does not completely supersede capitalocentrism and colonialism. At the base of capitalocentrism is Polanyi's evolutionary perspective, whereby reciprocity is viewed as proper to primitive societies, redistribution is viewed as proper to archaic ones, and the market as proper to the modern economy; householding has no place in this schema and is positioned outside the typology (Gudeman, 2001). In Polanyi's reading, development relations of interdependence and sociability are relegated to the past, ignoring the existence of forms of solidarity in capitalist countries, within subsistence economies, and in economies of care, generally carried out by women. As a result of this evolutionary perspective, capitalism is placed in the centre and other economies are evaluated according to capitalism. For example, Inayatullah and Blaney's proposed notion of hybridity is dominated by the logic of capitalism, since hybridity is 'produced by the responses and adaptations of local people to the successive waves of the global expansion and intensification of capitalism' (p. 184). Moreover, an EPE understands noncapitalist cultures as distant in time and inferior to capitalism, as reflected in the tendency to qualify as 'romanticism' the recourse to pre-, anti-, or noncapitalist economic forms (p. 170). The adoption of noncapitalist economies is considered a return to 'primitivism' as the creation of a new civilization is tied 'to an engagement with our own society and history' as a source of moral community (p. 177).

Although an EPE recognizes cultural diversity and postulates an ethical commitment to listen to the voice of the other, the terms of the dialogue are dictated by capitalist rules. An EPE values noncapitalist economies according to capitalist standards. As Chakrabarty (2002a, p. 34) points out, an open dialogue between the 'modern and the nonmodern' cannot happen as long as one of the parties is in a position to decide unilaterally the final outcomes of the conversation; this dialogue 'is already structured from the very beginning in favor of certain outcomes'.

Oppositional Political Economies

The search for oppositional political economies conducted by Boaventura de Sousa Santos offers an interesting contrast to both CPEs and EPEs. He shares with CPE a concentration on moments of crisis; unlike in CPE the crisis is of modernity, and the solution must be found outside of modernity, since 'there are no modern solutions' to the problems created by modernity. He calls for an 'oppositional postmodernism' that poses a disjuncture between the modernity of the problems and the postmodernity of possible solutions, asking for 'theories and practices capable of reinventing social emancipation out of the wrecked emancipatory promises of modernity' (Santos, 2002).

Unlike a CPE's search for 'knowledge as regulation', Santos calls for 'knowledge as emancipation' (Santos, 1998, 2002). The latter does not concentrate on knowledges that successfully reproduce capitalism, but on knowledges that capitalism has marginalized or not tried (p. xxii). Instead of searching for factors contributing to the stability of capitalism, the approach concentrates on forms of resistance to capitalism carried out by social movements and local communities. Moreover, knowledge as emancipation does not aim to discard alternatives with low resonance but, on the contrary, to strengthen their potential to resist capitalism (Santos, 2006, p. xxii). Santos proposes a 'hermeneutics of emergence' which analyses diverse tendencies and possibilities and acts upon these possibilities and their capacity to produce not 'one civilization' but to encourage a diversity of alternatives to modernity (Santos, 2002, p. 465). A hermeneutics of emergence does not aim to exert control over the production and reproduction of observed regularities and to assert the validity of these regularities; knowledge as emancipation is plural in assuming that there are different ways of knowing and different knowledges (Santos, 1998, p. 130; Santos, 2002, p. 41).

Unlike a concentration on the meanings that support that which exists, Santos proposes a sociology of absences focused on the initiatives that have been suppressed or not allowed to exist. Anti-hegemonic struggles are a privileged form of politics aimed at linking different struggles

(Santos, 2001, p. 191). Linking is not carried out by suppressing differences but through practices of 'translation' and 'Manifesto'. The former aim to create mutual intelligibility between diverse struggles and to encourage self-reflexivity among movements, campaigns, and networks (p. 192). Unlike knowledge as regulation, which makes possible the 'technical heroism of the scientist' (Santos, 1998, p. 132), translation incorporates the social experience of oppressed classes and groups (p. 191). Unlike a proposal for a 'new civilization', translation respects the autonomy and diversity of practices; it aims to search for 'mutual intelligibility without cancelling differences' (p. 192).

Manifesto practices are based on a principle of action that reveals the incompleteness and inadequacy of struggles if they remain particular and local (p. 192). These practices allow transnational alliances based on commonalities, while recognizing tensions such as those between identity and solidarity, autonomy and cooperation, and recognition and distribution. Manifesto practices are multiple and each one opens possible paths towards an alternative society (p. 209). Their source of inspiration is the World Social Forum (Porto Alegre, Mumbai, Nairobi) and its premise that 'another world is possible'.

Their specific contributions to political economy are published in an edited book entitled *Another Production is Possible* (Santos, 2006). Following the hermeneutics of emergence, the book is the product of a network of researchers working in peripheral countries. The volume includes analyses of the Brazilian Landless Peasant Movement (MST), the cooperatives of garbage pickers in Colombia and India, and experiences of labour internationalism, among other contributions. The alternatives studied share several characteristics (Santos, 2006, p. xxxv): (1) there is an inter-relation between production and cultural, social, affective, and political factors; (2) the authors of these alternatives are from marginalized communities generally working without the support of the state and elites; (3) the alternatives are generally local and collective, based on principles of solidarity and reciprocity; and (4) the alternatives favour the self-management of group-owned companies.

Santos's proposal opens space to decolonize political economy by searching out and valuing knowledges that have been suppressed or discredited by modern political economy. However, the economic analysis is limited in its capacity to decentre capitalism. The understanding of capitalism as a form of production limits the role that culture and subjectivity can play in the dislocation of capitalism. While the authors recognize that production alternatives are hybrid initiatives, they argue that

> economic activities provide the material incentive, while the feeling of belonging and the educational and social integration efforts they generate help to keep up the energy and enthusiasm required to ensure continuity and success, without losing sight of original principles and goals. (Santos and Rodríguez-Garavito, 2006, p. xlix)

The point that a focus on production limits the capacity of alternatives to disrupt capitalism is clear in the comments of Anibal Quijano (2006), who defines these initiatives as 'alternatives to unemployment and poverty, rather than to capitalism'. This problem is more effectively dealt with by Gibson and Graham, as discussed in the next section.

Collective Disidentification with Capitalism

Katherine Gibson and Julie Graham's (1996, 2006) call for a postcapitalist politics goes further than previous approaches in its proposal for superseding capitalocentrism. Unlike Polanyi's evolutionism, their proposal for political economy provides room for different types of exchange (reciprocity, redistribution, householding, and market exchange) to co-exist together. They do not see production as the defining characteristic of economics, but as surplus appropriation. This shift in focus allows for a more inclusive understanding of the different places where wealth is generated—in the household, neighbourhoods, government, private sector, or voluntary sector—and a broader understanding of how the resulting social wealth is used differently in family firms, private firms, nonprofit organizations, communal enterprises, and cooperatives.

Gibson and Graham share with CPE a view of the economy as constructed in discourse, while avoiding the structure/meaning dichotomy. Thinking of the economy as constituted through contingent relations allows for a less deterministic understanding of agency and a conception of the economy as a space of recognition and negotiation (p. xxx). This contingency opens the economy to new vocabularies and new practices, which are a source of innovation and key to superseding capitalocentrism. In their view, '[T]he rules of syntax and grammar of our language are loose to the point of nonexistence, allowing for empirical encounters and creative expressions of the new, the unthought, the unexpected' (p. 60). This language destabilizes the dominance of economics and opens room for creativity—that is, for a diverse economy (p. 60). As they illustrate, in the global south and also in the north, there is a plethora of economic activities that cannot be labelled as capitalism; informal economies are one example (p. 58). Using this language of diversity they identify a variety of nonmarket transactions (household flows, gift giving, poaching, co-op exchange, barter, informal market), different ways of compensating labour (housework, family care, volunteer, slave labour, self-paid, reciprocal), and multiple forms of enterprise (communal, family firm, nonprofit).

A postcapitalist politics sees knowledge as a source for dislocating capitalism. Gibson and Graham, like Boaventura Santos, are committed to a 'sociology of absences' as a way of revealing that which has been suppressed or excluded, and of questioning the marginalization of the nondominant (p. xxxii). A main difference is in their understanding of the loci of absences. Gibson and Graham locate this absence in the subject. In their view, what constructs a capitalist society 'is partly our own subjection—successful or failed, accommodating or oppositional' (p. xxxvi). Thus, what makes capitalism hegemonic is not a method of production but the type of subject that makes capitalism function. Combating capitalism means refusing a long-standing sense of self and mode of being the world, while simultaneously cultivating new forms of sociability, visions of happiness, and economic capacities (p. xxxv).

Gibson and Graham's theoretical inspiration is feminism. Following Lacan, they conceptualize woman as a 'subject of lack', signalling her unfixed or incomplete identity (p. xxxiii). 'Subject of lack' does not imply a devalued identity but a source of possibility for a politics of becoming, which makes a new economic politics possible to imagine and enact. Collectively, the generation of new subjectivities makes possible disidentification with capitalism in such a way that they are not seen as deviations and neither are they evaluated with respect to capitalism (p. 56).

The creation of economic 'positivities' (p. xxxiv) compels Gibson and Graham not only to read into diversity but also to be co-participants in the creation of economic possibilities where none formerly existed (p. xxix). In their analysis, economic choices are subordinate to ethical principles such as democratic organization, solidarity, and group cooperation (p. 104). Decisions about wages, technology, and distribution of surplus are connected to the construction of ethical communal subjects (p. 125).

The Mondragon cooperative in the Basque region of Spain, analysed by both Santos and Gibson and Graham, provides a good illustration of the difference when evaluating from a productivist vs. a subjectivity perspective. According to Santos and Rodríguez-Garavito (2006, pp. xxviii–xxx), the main reasons for Mondragon's success are the support networks and the efforts made to ensure each co-op's competitiveness in the global market, which helps them survive and grow. Its success is qualified as 'relative' because it is not a major alternative to the capitalist sector of national and worldwide economies. What Gibson and Graham found meaningful about the cooperative was its contribution to a place-based politics of subjectivation, whose central element is the enactment of an ethical vision of the economy. Some of the values incorporated are: the equality of all worker-owners and the control that they exert on the distribution of surplus, the value of people over capital, the principle of solidarity in the assignation of wages, and the promotion of the social and economic reconstruction of a more free and just Basque society (pp. 103–105).

In their attempt at a disidentification with capitalism, Gibson and Graham do not aim to decolonize political economy. The central questions are whether postcapitalist politics benefit from adopting decolonial thinking, and whether decolonial scholars gain from a disidentification with capitalism.

Decolonizing Capitalism

I contend that adopting a decolonial perspective broadens both the scale and the scope of the critique of capitalism/modernity/coloniality, and also increases the availability of economic/ development imaginaries. The decolonization of political economy originates from another place, mainly from intellectuals from marginalized economies. This section deals specifically with two groups, the subaltern studies groups from South Asia and the Modernity/Coloniality Research Program.[1] As dependency theory constitutes an important antecedent for both groups, this discussion starts with the way in which decolonial thinkers draw from and supersede the limits of dependency theory.

Dependency scholars, like decolonial thinkers, have expressed dismay about the lack of space for the diversity of forms for organizing the economy in peripheral forms of capitalism in liberal and Marxist political economies. The emphasis on the co-existence of capitalism and feudalism, development and underdevelopment, and uneven forms of development and modes of production illustrate the attempt to capture this diversity. Dependency theorists have found the ahistorical analysis of capitalism equally problematic, particularly its disregard for the specificity of the experience of colonialism and economic dependence as factors contributing to the incomplete transition to capitalism. At the core of dependency is an attempt to link the history of capitalism in the north and in the south through the use of spatial and temporal metaphors such as world-system, centre/periphery, core/satellite, early/late development, and development/ underdevelopment. Notwithstanding, in their account of historical specificity, dependency theorists have blended in a single history the fate of developed and developing countries, immortalized in Frank's statement that 'one and the same historical process of expansion and development of capitalism throughout the world has simultaneously generated – and continues to generate – both economic development and structural underdevelopment' (Frank, 1962, p.5). This reading of the political economy of the south through the lenses of European capitalism limited the capacity to recognize and value the diversity of political economies and to capture the resistance to capitalism by actors outside the economic categories of class, such as peasants, women, blacks, and indigenous populations.

Decolonial scholars build upon and extend the scale and scope of the discussion opened by dependency in several directions. Like dependency, the scope of coloniality/modernity is global in reach, extending beyond the nation-state, but coloniality/modernity supersedes dependency's narrow economicism. The concept of the 'coloniality of power' developed by Peruvian intellectual Anibal Quijano (2000) underscores the existence of a global hegemonic power that has been colonial since the inauguration of the Atlantic circuit in the fifteenth century with the colonization of the Americas, and whose coloniality continues to the present. In his view, Europe not only controlled the world market but also incorporated all regions of the world into a model of colonial power, controlling subjectivity, culture, and the production of knowledge (p. 540). The problem, as Enrique Dussel (1995, p. 35) denounced, was that colonialism was covered over (*encubrimiento*). This *encubrimiento* made possible the construction of Europe as the centre of capitalism and modernity; thus colonialism is not a by-product of modern Europe, but made modern Europe possible (Lander, 2000, p. 525).

Unlike dependency's main focus on external conditions, the modernity/colonial perspective does not abandon the local. The South Asian Subaltern Studies Group focuses analysis on local politics—specifically, on the lack of representation of peasants' insurgency in Indian colonial historiography. According to Ranajit Guha (1982, 1994), liberal and Marxist historiography, including dependency theory, deny the rebel a sense of recognition as a subject of history. A reading of history according to the logic of capital depicts peasant struggles as pre-capitalist and feudal in nature. Against this reading, Guha claimed that there was an 'autonomous' domain of the 'politics of the people'. By criticizing this categorizing of peasant struggles as 'prepolitical', Guha pluralizes the history of power in global modernity and separates it from any universalist narratives of capital (Chakrabarty, 2000, p. 14; Chakrabarty, 2002a). Guha's criticism of nationalistic elites allows him to link local politics with global (colonial, imperial) domination. His postulate of 'dominance without hegemony' (1997) makes it clear that subalternity is not a matter of local or class politics but of subordination of countries and histories by colonial powers (Mignolo, 2001, p. 426).

A decolonial perspective overcomes the reification of space into a dichotomous centre/periphery, or core/satellite, by placing emphasis on place over space. As Escobar (2003) contends, place is the site of the subaltern *par excellence*, the excluded dimension of modernity (p. 55). Place is an 'epistemic perspective' committed to take seriously the epistemic force of local histories and to think theory through from the political praxis of subaltern groups (p. 38). It is the specificity of place[2] that makes possible new economic imaginaries, as there are places that were never fully capitalist (p. 56).

In addition, decolonial thinking expands the horizon of critical theory. First, it reveals the darker side of modernity. A reading of modernity as a self-generating European phenomenon that began with the Enlightenment sees only its emancipatory dimension while concealing its irrational and genocidal face (Dussel, 1995). Marxist political economy also prolongs the myth of the autogenesis of capitalism, and continues denying that anything external to Europe could be one of Europe's key constituting moments (Alcoff, 2000, p. 256).

Second, decolonial thinking unveil the racial and epistemic violence of modernity. This violence refers to the dispossession of the colonized of their historical identity, involving 'the plundering of their place in the history of the cultural production of humanity' (Quijano, 2001, pp. 58–90, 552). By labelling alternative forms of capitalism pre-capitalist or not yet modern, other forms of economy are condemned to disappear because 'a full-blown capitalism would or should be logically incompatible with feudal-type relationships' (Chakrabarty, 2002a, p. 10). It is violent also towards peasants and subaltern subjects who are conceptualized under the figure of the past and, consequently, have to mutate into industrial workers to emerge eventually as full citizens (Chakrabarty, 2002a, p. 11). Defining hierarchies legitimates those that exercise authority and supports their dominance while silencing the dominated (Rojas, 2002).

Third, decolonial perspectives change the content of the debate on capitalist development. Instead of asking why capitalism did not succeed in colonized countries, the question becomes: What are the consequences of a history premised on the inevitability of capitalist expansion? Instead of seeing the history of colonial countries as one and the same as the history of the colonizer, decolonial theory problematizes historical narratives. As Dipesh Chakrabarty (2000, p. 7) argues, capitalist history is immersed in an historicist narrative where capitalism is depicted as something that became global over time, by originating in one place (Europe) and then spreading outside it (Chakrabarty, 2000, p. 7). Categorization of time and space play an important role in this domination. People living in the colonies are 'assigned a place "elsewhere" in the "first Europe and then elsewhere" structure of time' (Chakrabarty, 2000, p. 8). Temporal difference is then converted into cultural distance, legitimizing civilizing missions.

Fourth, the colonial difference is epistemological also. The 'coloniality of power' not only naturalizes hierarchies of races, gender, and cultures but also introduces a 'coloniality of knowledge' where indigenous, Afro-descendent, and colonized peoples are considered incapable of serious thinking (Walsh, 2007, p. 229). This exclusion makes a dialogue or an argumentation community impossible (Dussel, 1995, p. 55).

The decolonization of knowledge is central to a decolonial IPE/development. Not all scholars agree where the epistemic renovation would come from. For Enrique Dussel (2001, p. 240), decolonial theorizing comes from the 'exteriority', defined as 'the place of the *reality* of the other'. It is from this standpoint that it is possible to critique all 'possible political economy (and even all possible economic systems)' (p. 189). Within capitalism this place is occupied by the proletariat, the unemployed, the marginal, the pauper, and the 'living labour' 'not *yet* subsumed by capital' (pp. 240–241). In his view, political economy does not recognize the reality of the other. On this point he quotes Marx:

> Political economy, therefore, does not recognize the unemployed worker, the working man, insofar as he happens to be outside this labour relationship. The rascal, swindler, beggar, the unemployed, the starving, wretched and criminal working man—these are figures who do not exist *for political economy* but only for other eyes, those of the doctor, the judge, the grave-digger and bum-bailiff, etc.; such figures are specters outside its domain. (quoted in Dussel, 2001, pp. 241–242)

In his view it is this position of exteriority that makes it possible to see the totality as an entity or object that can be analysed. Critical thought originates in the negativity (*negatividad*) of the victim (the worker, Indian, African slave . . .) (Dussel, 1998, p. 309).

Dussel (2002, p. 224) recognizes the existence of other cultures within modernity. A 'cultural plurality' develops on a 'trans-modern horizon', something beyond the internal possibility of simple modernity. Trans-modernity demands a whole new interpretation of modernity in order to include moments that were never incorporated into the European vision (p. 223). Trans-modernity affirms from without the essential components of modernity's own excluded cultures in order to develop a new civilization for the twenty-first century (p. 224). It is from these cultures that capitalism can learn, since they are a source of innovation:

> Like the tropical jungles with their immense quantity of plants and animals genetically essential for the future of humanity, the majority of humanity's culture excluded by modernity (which are not, and will not be, postmodern) and by globalization (because misery is 'necessity without money,' without solvency, and therefore is not of the market) retains an immense capacity for and reserve of cultural invention essential for humanity's survival. This creativity will also be needed if humanity is to redefine its relationship with nature based on ecology and inter-human solidarity, instead of reductively defining it on the solipsistic and schizoid criterion of increasing rate of profit. (p. 235)

As Santiago Castro-Gómez (1996, p. 169) points out, Dussel's great accomplishment was to discover a hidden place of observation which allows a different gaze than the one from the centre. However, it is problematic in making the exteriority of the other the other side of modernity or capitalism. The poor are made to be a transcendental subject and from this exteriority would give direction to Latin American history (p. 39). Furthermore, the thought of a popular culture, different from European, is problematic as well, as it is understood as excluded and alien to modernity, and therefore without its own consciousness. It is the role of the intellectual, in Dussel's case the liberation philosopher, to discover their alterity and bring voice to the excluded (p. 167).

Dipesh Chakrabarty (2000, p. 16) also believes that disciplinary renovation would come from the margins, which are multiple. Unlike Dussel, he is sceptical of narratives that read 'plenitude' and 'creativity' where 'lack' and 'inadequacy' were before (p. 35). He makes history a centrepiece to supersede coloniality; for him, history is 'the site where the struggle goes on to appropriate, on behalf of the modern ... these other collocations of memory' (p. 37). Notwithstanding, he shares Spivack's (1988) conviction that the subaltern does not have a place from where to speak. Even if it is possible to document constructions of self and community, the subaltern 'will never enjoy the privilege of providing the metanarratives or teleologies ... of our histories' (p. 37). Thus subaltern narratives are not outside capitalism. He warns that subaltern histories cannot be defined without reference to the category of 'capital'. Moreover, it is not possible to go 'beyond capital', especially at a moment when everything comes under the sway of capital (2000, p. 95). His proposal is to negotiate historical difference within capital (Chakrabarty, 2002b). Capital, he maintains, is a philosophical-historical category and 'historical difference is not external to it but is constitutive of it' (p. 106). In its reproduction capital encounters relationships that could be central to its own reproduction and relationships that do not contribute to such reproduction (p. 99). The subaltern is located between the two narratives, as he/she is located within the history of capital and at the same time 'remind[s] us of other ways of being human than as bearers of the capacity to labor' (Chakrabarty, 2000, p. 94). The subaltern can resist the penetration of capital but is not exterior to capital. Chakrabarty defines this position as a 'border zone of temporality'. There is no need to give up either Marx or 'difference', since resistance happens 'only *within* the time horizon of capital, and yet it has to be thought of as something that disrupts the unity of that time' (p. 95).

For Chakrabarty, the way out of this dilemma is a politics of translation and interruption. The former translates the archives of thought and practices into Marxist categories and at the same time modifies these thoughts with the help of Marxist categories (Chakrabarty, 2002b). Interruption of modern historical narratives is accomplished by pluralizing time, which allows different concepts of time to coexist (p. 109). This narrative asks for unlearning history as a development process that Chakrabarty equals to:

> ... learn to think the present—the 'now' that we inhabit so to speak—as irreducible not-one.... At the core of this exercise is a concern about how one might think about the past and the future in a nontotalizing manner. (Chakrabarty, 2000, p. 249)

Chakrabarty's project falls short as regards the proposal to decolonize capitalism, as he does not contemplate the possibility that knowledges from noncapitalist and nonmodern places could articulate from the colonial difference other knowledges, including Marxism, hidden from modern rationality. This change in perspective is crucial for understanding the struggles fought by indigenous and Afro-descendent peoples in Latin America, and concrete in Bolivia. As Walter Mignolo contends, to read the latter case as a turn towards the left continues hiding that what is at stake is a decolonial thinking which is changing the terms of the debate; in Evo Morales' Bolivia the left is translated into indigenous rationality, and not the other way around (Mignolo, 2006).

The Latin American Modernity/Coloniality Research Program (MC) advances a proposal which allows formulation of a political economy otherwise. For the MC, the border is epistemological, more than a zone of temporality (as for Chakrabarty). 'Border thinking' is a locus of enunciation from where those that are living in and thinking from colonial and postcolonial legacies reason (Mignolo, 2000, p. 5). The MC proposal is for an epistemic change of perspective, rather than a change in the content of the conversation (Escobar, 2003, p. 41). 'Border gnosis' is the subaltern reason striving to bring to the foreground the force and creativity of subaltern knowledges (Mignolo, 2000, p. 13). The narratives emerging from this border move towards a different logic, displacing the abstract universalism of modern epistemology and world history while leaning towards a network of local histories and multiple local hegemonies (p. 22).

This epistemological change requires a 'double translation' in a cross-epistemological conversation (Mignolo, 2000, p. 85). One translation is 'delinking' or epistemic disobedience (Mignolo, forthcoming, p. 2). Unlike CPE, whose concept of beginning directs one to Adam Smith or as far as Aristotle, Mignolo proposes a conversation with intellectuals writing from the experience of colonialism, such as the indigenous Waman Puma de Ayala in Peru in the seventeenth century, Ottabah Cugoano the emancipated slave in the eighteenth century, Mahatma Gandhi, W. E. B. Dubois, Juan Carlos Mariategui, Amilcar Cabral, Aimé Césaire, or Frantz Fanon. Waman Puma de Ayala, for example, wrote the *New Chronicle and Good Government* (1616) from the experience of colonialism in Peru, and Ottabah Cugoano published *Thoughts and Sentiments on the Evil of Slavery* (1787) from the experience and memory of African slavery in the eighteenth century. Catherine Walsh (2007) points to the recovery of 'other' thoughts from indigenous intellectuals in the Andes such as Nasa intellectual Manuel Quintin Lame (1883–1967), or Quechua-Aymara intellectual Fausto Reinaga in Bolivia; *pensamiento propio* (a thought of one's own) is an important component of both indigenous and Afro groups in the region (p. 230).

Another translation happens across struggles and experiences marked by subalternization, including gender, colonialism, and racialization. This translation sees as interwoven languages of biodiversity, sustainability, cultural rights, and ethnic identities and links identity, territory, and culture at local, national, and transnational levels (Escobar, 2001, p. 163).

This double translation is analysed by Arturo Escobar in the case of the Colombian Pacific region (Escobar, forthcoming). In the Pacific, Afro-Colombian and indigenous knowledges give origin not only to 'alternative worlds' but also to 'world and knowledges otherwise' about nature, the economy, and the world (p. 30). Activists' knowledges are crucial for this emergence. It is the activist engagement with place that is relevant in the production of alternative knowledge and an otherwise political economy. Escobar's study unveils the existence of 'alternative productive rationalities' combining ecology, culture, and politics (p. 167). In these economies 'the valuation of natural resources depends on qualitative process which lie outside the market, such as cultural perceptions, community rights, and social interests' (p. 168).

This translation is already underway among those groups that have been marginalized since conquest. For instance, there are contemporary indigenous movements worldwide, and specifically in Bolivia where discussions on the Constitutional Assembly are carried out under the leadership of Evo Morales, who is of Aymara descent, with a group of indigenous intellectuals aiming to incorporate decolonial thinking into several aspects of the country's social and economic organization

(Mignolo, forthcoming, p. 11). The double translation is evidenced in the writing of Aymara intellectual Felix Patzi (2004); in his view the transformation should start from the indigenous people's own philosophy and their own economic and political practices (p. 187).

The *Declaration of Nyéléni on Food Security* (2007) is a global example of a political economy whose rationality decolonizes and decentres the capitalist logic of food production and exchange. Central to the declaration is the concept of food sovereignty as a 'right of peoples' produced 'through ecologically sound and sustainable methods'. It involves recognition of the 'interests and inclusion of the next generation' and of 'women's roles and rights in food production, and representation of women in all decision making bodies'. Even further, food sovereignty 'implies new social relations free of oppression and inequality between men and women, peoples, racial groups, social classes and generations.'

Conclusion: IPE/Development Otherwise

The proposals analysed in this paper highlight the limits and possibilities of different cultural readings of IPE/development. Self-referential cultural construction of political economy has detrimental consequences. Monoculturally-defined IPE/development dispenses with others' visions; peasants, subsistence economies, and indigenous forms of economy are devalued and condemned to disappear in the name of a transition to a better capitalism. Self-referential IPE/development devalues colonial knowledges and deprives the world of alternative solutions.

This paper advocates an IPE/development otherwise which: (1) increases variation and negotiation within capitalism and creates room for otherwise political economies; (2) acknowledges the co-existence of diverse rationalities, allowing for a more democratic dialogue between political economies; and (3) creates room for a political economy imaginatively narrated in a noncapitalist and decolonial manner.

An IPE/development otherwise requires a change in perspectives that allows the recovery of other knowledges and rationalities generally marginalized or hidden by capitalism. A sociology of absences and a hermeneutics of emergence act upon marginalized alternatives and strengthen their potential resistance to capitalism. An IPE/development otherwise asks for narratives that pluralize time and history, where neither the past nor the future are reduced to one.

Epistemologically, practices of translation create mutual intelligibility between diverse political economies, abandoning teleological narratives such as transition where the future is one and the present is a continuous 'not yet'. A political economy otherwise brings different narratives into contact with each other, allows the marginalized to reveal their own interpretation, and opens space for accommodation, contradiction, and resistance.

An IPE/development otherwise is an ethic-political project asking for subjectivities able to disidentify from capitalism and to desire and create diverse economies. These subjectivities are enhanced through collective projects of solidarity, new forms of sociability, and alternative visions of happiness.

Furthermore, the analyses presented in this paper demonstrate not only that a political economy otherwise is possible, but that it does exist.

Acknowledgements

A preliminary version of this paper was prepared by the workshop 'Rethinking Development' in San Diego, 2006, and was presented at the 'Studies in Political Economy' conference in Toronto, 2006, and at the research workshop 'Modernity/Coloniality/Decoloniality' with the University of North Carolina and Duke University Consortium in Latin American Studies. I am grateful for the encouragement of Heloise Weber and the 'Rethinking Development' group. The group gave me the opportunity to establish conversations with Arturo Escobar and Walter Mignolo, leading scholars in the Modernity/Coloniality Research Program, and with their graduate students. I thank Barry Hindess, Naeem Inayatullah, Bob Jessop, and Judy Meltzer for their comments and suggestions. My research was possible thanks to a grant from the Social Sciences Research Council of Canada.

Notes

1 There is a Latin American Subaltern Studies Group (Beverly and Oviedo, 1993; Rodríguez, 2001) comprising postcolonial scholars in Africa, Asia, and First World countries. The Modernity/Coloniality Research Program is a network of scholars linked to North American and Latin American universities; the group includes, among others, Walter Mignolo (Duke University), Arturo Escobar (University of North Carolina), Santiago Castro-Gómez (Universidad Javeriana), and Catherine Walsh (Universidad Intercultural de los Pueblos Indígenas, Ecuador). For a description of the group see Escobar (2003) and Mignolo (2000, 2001).
2 Escobar defines place as the experience of a specific location with some measure of groundness (however unstable), sense of boundaries (however, permeable), and connection to everyday life, even it its identity is constructed, traversed by power, and never fixed (Escobar, 2001, pp. 139–174).

References

Alcoff, L. M. (2000) Power, knowledges in the colonial unconscious: a dialogue between Dussel and Foucault, in L. M. Alcoff (ed.) *Thinking from the Underside of History: Enrique Dussel's Philosophy of Liberation* (Lanham, Rowman & Littlefield Publishers).
Beverly, J. & Oviedo, J. (1993) *The Postmodern Debate in Latin America* (Durham, NC: Duke University Press).
Castro-Gómez, S. (1996) *Crítica de la Razón Latinoamericana* (Barcelona: Puvill Libros S.A.).
Castro-Gómez, S. (2002) The social sciences, epistemic violence, and the problem of "invention of the other", *Nepantla: Views from the South*, 3(2), pp. 269–285.
Chakrabarty, D. (2000) *Provincializing Europe: Postcolonial Thought and Historical Difference* (Princeton, NJ: Princeton University Press).
Chakrabarty, D. (2002a) *Habitations of Modernity: Essays in the Wake of Subaltern Studies* (Chicago: University of Chicago Press).
Chakrabarty, D. (2002b) Universalism and belonging in the logic of capital, in C. A. Breckenridge, S. Pollock, H. K. Bhabha, & D. Chakrabarty (eds) *Cosmopolitanism* (Durham, NC: Duke University Press).
Declaration of Nyéléni (Selingue, Mali) on Food Sovereignty (2007) http://www.nyeleni2007.org/spip.php?article290.
Dussel, E. (1995) *The Invention of the Americas: Eclipse of the 'Other' and the Myth of Modernity* (New York: Continuum).
Dussel, E. (1998) *Etica de la Liberación en la Edad de la Globalización y de la Exclusión* (Madrid: Editorial Trotta).
Dussel, E. (2001) *Towards an Unknown Marx: A Commentary on the Manuscripts of 1861–63*, Edited by F. Moseley (London and New York: Routledge.)
Dussel, E. (2002) World-system and 'trans'-modernity, *Nepantla: Views from the South*, 3(2), pp. 221–244.
Escobar, A. (2001) Culture sits in places: reflections on globalism and subaltern strategies of localization, *Political Geography*, 20(2), pp. 139–174.
Escobar, A. (2003) *Worlds and Knowledges Otherwise: The Latin American Modernity/Coloniality Research Program*, in G. O'Donnell, A. Hewitt, & A. Escobar (eds) (Amsterdam: Centre for Latin American Research and Documentation).
Escobar, A. (forthcoming) *Places and Regions in the Global Age: Social Movements and Biodiversity Conservation in the Colombian Pacific* (Durham, NC: Duke University Press).
Frank, A. G. (1967) Capitalism and Under development in Latin America (New York: Monthly Review Press).
Gibson, K. & Graham, J. (1996) *The End of Capitalism (As We Knew It)* (Oxford: Blackwell Publishers).
Gibson, K. & Graham, J. (2006) *A Postcapitalist Politics* (Minneapolis: University of Minnesota Press).
Gudeman, S. (2001) Postmodern gifts, in S. Cullenberg, J. Amariglio, & D. Ruccio (eds) *Postmodernism, Economics and Knowledge* (New York, London: Routledge).
Guha, R. (1982) On some aspects of the historiography of colonial India, in G. Ranajit (ed.) *Subaltern Studies* (Delhi: Oxford University Press).

Guha, R. (1997) *Dominance without Hegemony: History and Power in Colonial India* (Cambridge, MA: Harvard University Press).

Inayatullah, N. & Blaney, D. L. (2004) *International Relations and the Problem of Difference* (New York, London: Routledge).

Jessop, B. (2004) Critical semiotic analysis and cultural political economy, *Critical Discourse Studies*, 1(2), pp. 159–174.

Jessop, B. & Sum, N.-L. (2001) Pre-disciplinary and post-disciplinary perspectives, *New Political Economy*, 6(1), pp. 89–101.

Lander, E. (2000) Eurocentrism and colonialism in Latin American thought, *Nepantla: Views from the South*, 1(3), pp. 519–532.

Mignolo, W. (2000) *Local Histories/Global Designs: Coloniality, Subaltern Knowledges, and Border Thinking* (Princeton, NJ: Pinceton University Presss).

Mignolo, W. (2001) Coloniality of power and subalternity, in I. Rodríguez (ed.) *The Latin American Subaltern Studies Reader* (Durham, NC: Duke University Press).

Mignolo, W. (2006) ¿Giro a la Izquierda o Giro Descolonial? Evo Morales en Bolivia. *Revista del Sur*, 164(March–April).

Mignolo, W. (forthcoming) *Epistemic Disobedience and the DeColonial Option: A Manifesto*, unpublished paper.

Nandy, A. (1983) *The Intimate Enemy: Loss and Recovery of Self under Colonialism* (Delhi: Oxford University Press).

Patzi, P. F. (2004) *Sistema Comunal: Una Propuesta Alternativa al Sistema Liberal: Una Discusión Teórica para Salir de la Colonialidad y del Liberalismo* (La Paz, Bolivia: Comunidad de Estudios Alternativos.)

Polanyi, K. (1957) *The Great Transformation: The Political and Economic Origins of our Time* (Boston, MA: Beacon Press).

Quijano, A. (2000) Coloniality of power, Eurocentrism, and Latin America, *Nepantla: Views from South*, 1(3), pp. 533–580.

Quijano, A. (2001) Coloniality of power, globalization and democracy, *Trayectorias*, 4(7–8), pp. 58–90.

Quijano, A. (2006) Alternative production systems?, in B. de Sousa Santos (ed.) *Another Production is Possible* (London, New York: Verso).

Rodríguez, I. (ed.) (2001) *The Latin American Subaltern Studies Reader* (Durham, NC: Duke University Press).

Rojas, C. (2002) *Civilization and Violence: Regimes of Representation in Nineteenth Century Colombia* (Minneapolis: University of Minnesota Press).

Santos, B. de Sousa (1998) Oppositional postmodernism and globalizations, *Law and Society Inquiry*, 23(128), pp. 121–139.

Santos, B. de Sousa (2001) *Nuestra America*: reinventing a subaltern paradigm of recognition and distribution, *Theory, Culture and Society*, 18(2–3), pp. 185–217.

Santos, B. de Sousa (2002) *Toward a New Legal Common Sense: Law, Globalization, and Emancipation*, 2nd ed. (London: Butterworths).

Santos, B. de Sousa (ed.) (2006) *Another Production is Possible: Beyond the Capitalism Canon*, vol. 2 (London, New York: Verso).

Santos, B. de Sousa & Rodríguez-Garavito, C. A. (2006) Introduction: expanding the economic canon and searching for alternatives to neoliberal globalization, in B. de Sousa Santos (ed.) *Another Production is Possible: Beyond the Capitalist Canon* (London, New York: Verso).

Sayer, A. (2001) For a critical cultural political economy, *Antipode*, 33(4), pp. 687–708.

Shiva, V. (2004) The future of food: countering globalisation and recolonisation of Indian agriculture, *Futures*, 36(6–7), pp. 715–732.

Spivack, G.C. (1988) Can the subaltern speak?, in C. Nelson and L. Grossberg (eds) *Marxism and the Interpretation of Culture* (Urbana, IL: University of Illinois Press), pp.271–313.

Swanson, J. (2005) Recognition and distribution: rethinking culture and the economic, *Theory, Culture and Society*, 22(4), pp. 87–118.

Todorov, T. (1984) *The Conquest of America: The Question of the Other* (New York: Harper and Row).

Walsh, C. (2007) Shifting the Geopolitics of Critical Knowledge: Decolonial Thought and Cultural Studies 'Others' in the Andes, *Cultural Studies*, 21(2–3), pp. 224–239.

The Poverty of the Global Order

DIA DA COSTA & PHILIP McMICHAEL

Introduction

The 'poverty of the global order' refers to the institutional reproduction of a naturalized understanding of poverty, and its legitimation of the development industry. As required by the UN System of National Accounts, states and multilateral development agencies define development as accumulation, in positive measures of output and/or income. Other measures of well-being or the regeneration of social and ecological values remain unregistered and de-legitimized. In eliding or reducing multiple meanings of development to a monetary standard, poverty is naturalized as a measure of material scarcity, simultaneously impoverishing development. This process licenses the development industry to renew its reductionist view of inequality, everywhere, through the appropriation of alternative values and visions of development.

This impoverished vision of the global order also informs responses to post-modern approaches to development. Such approaches contest the legitimacy of development discourse as a misrepresentation of non-European cultures and a discourse of control (Crush, 1995; Escobar, 1995; Sachs, 1992; Said, 1978). Saul characterizes this tendency as the 'discursive world of "development stinks"', arguing that despite the shortcomings of development in externalizing cultural and environmental relations, 'this need not dictate the abandonment of any vision of "development"'(Saul, 2004, p. 229). Similarly, Sutcliffe surmises that 'criticism of the standard development model seems at times too total,' and that a nostalgic postdevelopmentalism runs the risk of 'losing the baby when we throw out the old bath water' (quoted in ibid.). And Schuurman adds:

> The very essence of development studies is a normative preoccupation with the poor, marginalized and exploited people in the South. In this sense *inequality* rather than *diversity* or *difference* should be the main focus of development studies: inequality of access to power, to resources, to a human existence – in short, inequality of emancipation. (quoted in Saul, 2004, p. 230)

As we wonder aloud why development studies has such a 'normative preoccupation' with the poor, we problematize the distinction between 'inequality' and 'difference.' Schuurman sees that inequality has diverse forms shaping the 'inequality of emancipation' (quoted in Saul, 2004, p. 230), but nevertheless affirms a binary between inequality and difference. We argue, however, that reinforcing this binary affirms the development establishment's economism as the core value. Alternatively, we propose that inequality and difference are relational, rather than oppositional or mutually exclusive constructs and experiences. Our phrase 'poverty of the global order' suggests that capital (and its fetishized representations) impoverishes not just (classes of) people, but the material relations that enable the imagining and realizing of new social futures. The relationship between inequality and difference becomes particularly evident when we consider that development is anchored not just in institutions and structures, but also in the lives of its subjects (Pieterse, 1998). Understanding how subjects of development receive, legitimize, and/or contest institutional and historical constructions of development is indispensable to understanding how development is accomplished (Baviskar, 2005; Gupta, 1998; Klenk, 2004; Li, 1999; Mosse, 2004), as well as to reformulating its possibilities.[1]

The poverty of the global order, then, concerns the production and representation of poverty (and development) in fetishized terms, and how this in turn legitimizes market rule,[2] as institutionalized in the development industry. Recent claims by development agencies to have given development a participatory 'human face' reproduce an impoverished global order dedicated to making capital accumulation work for the poor. However, micro-finance schemes make the poor work for capital, reinforcing the legitimacy of the development industry (Weber, 2004) but dispossessing extant cultures (Elyachar, 2005). The participatory reflex is a product of the very crisis of development, with the World Bank's recent 'poverty reduction' project illustrating the method of appropriation central to the development enterprise (Cammack, 2004; Cook and Kothari, 2001; Weber, 2006).

Current evidence of global economic inequality deepening via corporate globalization is experienced as a development crisis (cf. Sachs, 2005). It is generating questions about global development practices from the World Economic Forum to the development agencies, with World Bank President James Wolfensohn (2000) speaking of rethinking development 'because we have yet to solve old problems – above all that of the yawning gulf between the haves and the have-nots of the world'. While economic polarization is all too real, it is more than a material crisis. The crisis is institutional and epistemological, in the sense that development in its succession of forms across the last half-century has steadily reproduced inequalities and steadily sought to renew its legitimacy via organizational and definitional reformulations. Because this renewal depends fundamentally on appropriating alternatives, the crisis can only deepen as renewal reinforces economic reductionism (cf. Plehwe, 2004).

In our view, the need for new approaches ('poverty reduction') enables the development industry, but not its subjects. As we argue here, new forms of poverty alleviation in the neoliberal era renew the legitimacy of private forms of accumulation as the engine, and episteme, of development. A market episteme has two distinct but related repercussions for addressing the crisis of development. First, the crisis prompts the development establishment to obscure the roots of its legitimacy crisis by re-formulating poverty-alleviation methods with which to renew its original legitimacy (cf. Escobar, 1995). In addition to naturalizing poverty as a phenomenal, rather than a structural, feature of the global order, the development establishment mandates new institutional devices such as WTO protocols and 'governance initiatives'[3] that embed states and citizens further in the system of market rule. Second, the crisis *appears* to stem from the persistence of inequality, obscuring the deeper epistemological crisis of market rationality.

Distinguishing market rationality (formal economy) from substantive economy (Polanyi, 1968), we critique the poverty of economism and its scarcity paradigm, which fetishizes monetary relations and discounts substantive, socio-ecological conceptions of economy. We illustrate what it would mean to transcend the scarcity paradigm by examining two examples of substantive economy, in which questions of development and alternative values are addressed and realized through the device of representational power at the collective and the individual levels, respectively.

Naturalizing a Conceptual Poverty

To reiterate, the poverty of the global order is that its legitimacy depends not simply on progress in phenomenal terms (one-sided measures), but also on the progressive naturalization of its epistemological foundations. A key to this process is the construction of 'poverty' as an original, rather than a social, condition.[4] While we do not minimize the fact that most of the world's people's material needs are grossly unmet, the conceptual problem is that solutions to end deprivation proceed from an unproblematic empirical, or phenomenal, understanding of scarcity (of material means). There is little investigation of the relationships producing scarcity, and there is scant recognition that representing scarcity in market terms ignores other means of livelihood. Conventional solutions to poverty resort to market rule, and renew the development industry— they do not disturb conditions of inequality, becoming rather methods of controlling and re-producing dominant visions of what count as viable futures (cf. Fraser and Honneth, 2003). New ways of labeling old wine is a critical strategy for naturalizing the epistemological foundations upon which an unequal world is remade.

Shiva articulates one way of naturalizing poverty (and development):

> The paradox and crisis of development arises from the mistaken identification of the culturally perceived poverty of earth-centred economies with the real material deprivation that occurs in market-centred economies, and the mistaken identification of the growth of commodity production with providing human sustenance for all. (1991, p. 215)

To represent 'earth-centred economies' as poor, via comparative measures of wealth, identifies them as frontiers for capital accumulation, discounting alternative value systems, which is Shiva's point. Analogously, Kothari (1997) argues that alternatives exist in micro-initiatives by the poor, and that their survival strategies constitute the basis for imagining the future. However, 'earth-centred economies' and informal networks are not necessarily virtuous alternatives, and their diversity may be repackaged as commercial opportunity, and advertised as responsible corporate practice (Da Costa, 2007). Such romanticizations risk repeating development studies' normative preoccupation with the poor. Our point is that we cannot treat alternatives as inherent signs of resistance to the poverty of the global order, for they are frequently viewed as resources ripe for appropriation as new frontiers for capital accumulation—as we have seen, for example, with micro-financing initiatives and fair trade.

The Human Face of Development

The recent effort to humanize development in light of critiques of its top-down projects and singular visions has certain trademark characteristics. The discursive focus on individuals, humanity, and participation takes attention away from the wealth of resources diverted towards realizing the poverty of the global order, institutionally and epistemologically.[5]

While the participation of the poor in designing poverty alleviation programs may be important, rarely do these projects allow alternative constructions of what resources, interpretations, and rights are valuable to people concerned.

In this vein, Sen's contributions to humanizing development are exemplary. The journal *Studies in Comparative International Development* (2002) organized a debate concerning Sen's treatise *Development as Freedom*. Sen's reasoning about development pivots on a quality intrinsic to all individuals, prior to accumulation: '[T]the appropriate "space" is neither that of utilities (as claimed by welfarists), nor that of primary goods (as demanded by Rawls), but that of substantive freedoms – the capabilities – to choose a life one has reason to value' (Sen, 2002, p.74).

For Sen, substantive freedoms enable people to participate in the determination of what they should value and/or enable people in effect to construct their opportunities. The problem of development, then, seems to be absence of freedom, absence of adequate participation in democratic processes, and absence of adequate information about available opportunities. Critics argue that this model presumes the very thing that it claims to deliver, as a consequence of democratic participation and choice, namely a measurable equality, valuing individuality instrumentally as 'capital', and implying an ahistorical construction of individual agency (Stewart and Deneulin, 2002, p. 66). Sen's view is analogous to Wolfensohn's effort to give the Bank a human face. In viewing development as 'globalization with a human face. Globalization that is inclusive. Globalization that promotes social equity and works for the poor'(2000), Wolfensohn identifies global market access as the epistemological and practical point of departure.

We introduce Sen and World Bank reasoning to illustrate the impoverished economism common to liberal (and radical) conceptions of the global order. Such reasoning shares a particular view of the world, expressed in Wolfensohn's universalized claim that globalization 'is here to stay'. Our argument is that this homogeneous view of the world fetishizes a contradictory and politically-created process, depicting it as natural devoid of alternatives , even as it appropriates such alternatives. Wolfensohn deliberately seeks to incorporate many of the criticisms of the development project:

> This vision is firmly and genuinely country-owned. It rejects top-down development devised behind closed doors in Washington (or even in national capitals in member countries). It is holistic and comprehensive, taking account of the interrelationships among the different elements of development strategies. It is based on inclusion and participation, bringing together civil society, local competition, NGOs, the private sector and the poor themselves. Bringing them together in order to foster trust and sustainability . . . (Wolfensohn, 2000)

The World Bank's appropriation of participation—its opposition's discursive tool—is instructive because participation and the new 'country-owned' vision have been a key strategy in creating one world of shared interests. This vision gives rise to partnerships to produce Poverty Reduction Strategy Papers (PRSPs) compiled as 'performances:' '[T]o meet the charge that imposing conditions is undemocratic, the IFIs now insist that other stakeholders, such as NGOs, churches, unions and business, rather than just government, are involved in writing the plans' (Fraser and Honneth, 2003, p. 317). The view that the Bank does not and cannot project, for fear of losing its own legitimacy, is that the shared interest between these diverse groups can only be material accumulation—not social equality.

Under neo-liberal reform, participatory methods are presented as a new commitment to hear the voices of the poor (Narayan et al., 2000). Institutions such as the World Bank formally commit to using participatory methods to contain the potential of their critics' ideas to reformulate development. As it happened, the poor expressed dissatisfaction with government corruption while celebrating the Bank. During the 'Voices of the Poor' project, participating researchers conducted participant observation within the terms of the Bank's research project, describing the procedures by which the voices of the poor were sought, transferred into institutional logic, and used to build institutional and state legitimacy (Rademacher and Patel, 2002). Participation can indeed bite back, revealing the source of Bank institutional legitimacy as internally generated, but accomplished through the reduction of the social worlds of its subjects.

The State and Market Rule

Just as we argue that the development establishment bases its legitimacy on monopolizing development knowledge (appropriating alternatives), so governments implement official development knowledge to accumulate power and enrich their cadres. Thus Bose remarked of the post-independence Indian state: 'Instead of the state being used as an instrument of development, development became an instrument of the state's legitimacy' (Bose, 1997, p. 153). In other words, the national accounting system, in emphasizing paid employment, trade, and foreign investment, and discounting subsistence production and unpaid forms of work, structured accumulation at all costs into the public rationale of the development state. In the recent neo-liberal world ordering, accumulation is now filtered through disciplinary technologies mandated by the development establishment (IMF, World Bank, WTO) and instrumentalized through the privatization of states (Cammack, 2004).

Under the neo-liberal project, political elites seek legitimacy and creditworthiness by internalizing the rationality of global currency and capital markets. This transition reveals a complex legitimacy crisis of the state, indicative of the poverty of the global order. In a critique of international relations theory, Rosenberg terms this crisis the 'paradox of sovereignty'. The active construction and internalization of market rule within the operation of the state system suggests that sovereignty is 'both more absolute in its "purely political" prerogatives than other historical forms of rule, and yet highly ambiguous as a measure of actual power' (Rosenberg, 2001, p. 131). The subjection of politics to the market episteme is a fundamental part of the crisis, insofar as modern solutions to modern problems (e.g., 'planet of slums') are evaporating (cf. de Sousa Santos, 2002).

Market rule is increasingly implemented through IMF, World Bank, and WTO-ordained procedures, represented euphemistically as new forms of 'governance'. Under these institutional circumstances, market rule does not eliminate so much as transform states, which incorporate multilateral protocols and recalibrate policies away from public and toward private goals, often repackaged as empowerment. An additional, intensive dimension involves the subjection of producer, consumer, and social relations to the price form—where social protections (access to an environmental commons, public goods, subsidies, minimum wages, price controls on staple consumer items, trade tariffs, etc.) are regarded as (unnatural) frictions that distort market processes. In this sense, states reproduce, and are reproduced by, the market. Ironically, the market episteme is responsible for the demise of the (economistic) social contract at the same time as it intensifies the displacement of non-economic social and cultural forms and meanings—deepening inequalities supposedly resolved by market rule.

Where states do implement the new 'governance' requirements of participation, entrepreneurialism, and empowerment, they do so under conditions of (reproducing) inequality. For example, Baviskar's (2005) study of a watershed project in central India asks how the state, usually an object of harsh critique in this region and notorious for large, ecologically destructive projects, comes to be celebrated as having galvanized a massive people's movement. She traces the various methods, discursive and epistemological manipulations, exclusions, and corrupt practices through which 'participation' was adjusted to mean contained involvement by already endowed and protected individuals within villages in the government-administered watershed project. These powerful individuals were willing participants who collaborated with corrupt state officials while excluding 'ideal' participants, who were conveniently labeled unruly subjects—that is, those who had the capacity and knowledge to make the watershed project truly redistributive and socially just.

Baviskar's work brings the ethnographic eye to monolithic representations of the violence of development (Escobar, 1995). In showing how people participate in, legitimize, and contest development projects, she shows that individual agency and participation is tied to historical relations of unequal access to resources, rights, and power. As our critique of Sen and the Bank claimed, institutionalized participation has no meaning outside the contexts of inequality, hierarchy, and violence into which it is introduced through development projects. Baviskar's complex view of agency, which is neither outside the realm of, nor endlessly stifled by, structural power, motivates us to ask what exactly it means to argue, as Sen has, that freedom and participation bring equality.

Studying claims about creating equality and participation in ethnographic contexts of the accomplishment of rule is useful to understand how (not whether) success of development projects is produced (Li, 1999). In an analysis of a British-funded project of low-cost inputs to improve the livelihoods of poor farming families, Mosse argues that the formation of the semblance of policy coherence is accomplished through the enrollment of different interests to participate in a given project (2004, p. 649). Participation accomplishes rule because donor control enrolls diverse local interests 'effectively turn[ing] participation into a commodity' (Ibid., p. 650). In practice, participation was accomplished because participation meant jobs or contacts with powerful locals. Participation thus came to have institutional legitimacy because people strenuously fed back to 'headquarters' a coherent representation of the success of the participatory model regardless of project effects in transforming 'social relationships and ecologies' (Ibid., p. 662). Thus, affirming the success of the development project was not required by the development establishment as much as it was produced in conditions of social inequality within which people found themselves hoping for, establishing, and securing patronage relations with the project as their employer.

As in Baviskar's study, the people whose participation demanded something the development project could not deliver became inconvenient participants. '[S]taff who tried to be too participatory – spending too long investigating needs or women's perspectives ... would be seen as underperforming by both project and community' (Mosse, 2004, p. 655). In the end, the poorest are not the best subjects for participatory projects for they lack 'time or labour to realize new entitlements to water or forest resources, or employment; or as migrants were non-members of the new organizations through which these entitlements were realized' (Ibid., p. 652). These processes raise questions about who 'the poor' are, and what counts as poverty, considering the poorest are often not the most active and present participants. Ethnographic study of such processes shows that we know 'the poor' when we see them because they emerge through these multiple relations in particular contexts. While such complex particularity is routinely evident, 'the poor' are rarely recognized as a construction.

Reconceptualizing Equality

Development as an abstract vision of progress only becomes meaningful within particular contexts of rule and inequality when broader visions are realized through multiple rationales and projected desires. As the development industry apprehends these proliferating meanings, repackaging them into 'marketable' ideas and institutionally useful tools, it turns a substantive relation into a formal one, where participation in a project is for the sake of participation, whether the project is useful or meaningful or not. The reinterpretation and recycling of these proliferating meanings in universal packages is how the development industry renews its legitimacy.

The poverty of the global order lies in the constant imperative to reformulate people's multiple desires into a universal propensity to recognize, act on, and reinforce their economic self-interest. Rather than discounting multiple desires, development visions, and alternative equalities, they can be revealed, ethnographically, in subjective expressions of individuals and groups as they resist particular (unequal) relations of production and/or representation. Subjective expressions that seek to realize social visions irreducible to market relations are not so much idiosyncratic as historically situated.

When conceptualizing historically-grounded understandings of equality, the point is not that all subjectivities are equal but rather that subjectivity gives equality itself different meanings grounded in particular historical experiences of, and relations to, production and representation. Equality embodies a unity in diversity, insofar as subjects emerge through the negotiation of relations of production and representation. Accordingly, as implied in the UN Declaration of Rights (1948), the commitment to equalities in the social contract would be realizable if state legitimacy was grounded not in the formal (monological) concerns of capital, but in the substantive (historically diverse) concerns of citizenship.

A substantive notion of citizenship depends on transcending the reductionism of a market-based episteme. Economic reductionism stems from the market fetishism of formal economic theory, founded in the price form, and expressed through 'a situation of choice that arises out of an insufficiency of means … the so-called scarcity postulate' (Polanyi, 1968, p. 143). Distinguishing formal and substantive economy, Polanyi claims that the:

> two root meanings of economic, the substantive and the formal, have nothing in common. The latter derives from logic, the former from fact…. The substantive meaning implies neither choice nor insufficiency or means; man's livelihood may or may not involve the necessity of choice and, if choice there be, it need not be induced by the limiting effect of a 'scarcity' of the means; indeed, some of the most important physical and social conditions of livelihood such as the availability of air and water or a loving mother's devotion to her infant are not, as a rule, so limiting…. The laws of the one are those of the mind; the laws of the other are those of nature. (Idem.)

Notwithstanding that, since Polanyi wrote this, air, water, and love have been progressively commodified as international goods and services (cf. Barlow, 1999; Clarke, 2001; Hochschild, 2003), the point remains that formal market logic is a discursive imposition on the world. It represents the deepening power of capital to reconstruct the world in its image through a state system whose operation and legitimacy depends on the market institution. Polanyi's alternative, substantive economy, represents an 'ecological' view of 'the interchange with (man's) natural and social environment, insofar as this results in supplying him with the means of material want-satisfaction' (1968, p. 139). In our view, this alternative view of economy offers the possibility of a different, enriching global order, informed by a rejection of the fetishism of scarcity economics. We illustrate this through a discussion of 'food sovereignty' as a substantive challenge to the formal vision of 'food security'.

Food security concerns the question of material want satisfaction. Its essential goal is to provide populations with sufficient and predictable food supplies. Historically, it has been central to governing legitimacy, whether in communities, empires, or states (Spitz, 1985). In the latter half of the twentieth century, food security was redefined as 'best provided through a smooth-functioning world market' (Ritchie, 1993, fn 25), corresponding to the organization of transnational food flows by agribusinesses. Under the WTO's Agreement on Agriculture (1995), states no longer have the right to food self-sufficiency as a national strategy, despite the identification of human rights with sovereignty over natural resources in the 1948 UN Declaration. In converting food security to a(n unequal) market relation, thereby displacing peasant agri-culture *en masse*, the WTO regime subjects food, despite its global abundance, to the scarcity paradigm. Having been rendered scarce in market terms for impoverished ex-peasants, food becomes just another market value whose greater commercial production (e.g., Africa's impending 'second green revolution') for those with cash renews the legitimacy of the global developers.

Nonetheless, food sovereignty movements are building a counter-hegemonic, substantive understanding of food security in which material want-satisfaction is not subordinated to the market, but (re-)embedded in ecological principles of community and environmental sustainability. The Vía Campesina, which includes 143 farm organizations representing millions of farming families from 56 countries (Desmarais, 2007, p. 21), is an exemplar. The Vía Campesina vision is for 'the right of peoples, communities and countries to define their own agricultural, labour, fishing, food and land policies which are ecologically, socially, economically and culturally appropriate to their unique circumstances' (quoted in Ainger, 2003, p. 11).

We note that such a formulation demands that such rights be guaranteed, while the substantive content of rights remains open and to be determined by the communities and countries themselves (cf. Patel and McMichael, 2004, p. 249). From our perspective, the elaboration of this principle of self-organization subverts the reduction of agriculture, food, and development to market relations, and government complicity in such reductionism. Desmarais reports that this 'peasant' model

> does not entail a rejection of modernity, technology and trade accompanied by a romanticized return to an archaic past steeped in rustic traditions [but is based on] ethics and values [where] culture and social justice count for something and concrete mechanisms are put in place to ensure a future without hunger. (2007, pp. 56–57)

In asserting substantive ecology over formal economy, food sovereignty recombines production and representation (see, e.g., McMichael, 2006; Patel, 2006) in such a way as to restore democratic initiative to producers. How they choose to realize this initiative is neither pre-ordained nor prescribed by one-dimensional notions of equality that would suppress cultural practices in the name of poverty-alleviating development.

Substantive Economies

Demonstrating that food security and food sovereignty can be organized to reinforce each other mutually, Vía Campesina shifts the focus on scarcity as the only relevant inequality to the asymmetries of representation that reproduce inequality.[6] Vía Campesina changes the historically institutionalized subject of development by embodying and recognizing constructions of economy attentive to historical particularities and ecological limits. We believe that the formation of substantive economy must be understood as a struggle to make particular meanings and lived experiences of inequality and equality count institutionally, and members of Vía Campesina (whatever its limitations) are engaged in just such an endeavor (cf. Desmarais, 2007).

Holland and Lave (2001) understand history as a social practice that is made in person, because people make particular choices within contexts of enduring struggles. Some social actions in these struggles, more than others, come to be historically institutionalized (Holland and Lave, 2001, pp. 5–7). As such, studying the formation of 'history in person' captures how people come to make institutionally recognized struggles (such as development) mean something in their lives.

We animate such struggles via this conception of history in person. When people negotiate enduring institutional interventions in their lives, they shape social formations relevant to their life-historical contexts. From the perspective of examining history in person, the World Bank's claim to produce developed societies and subjects generates an enduring institutionalized struggle to bring equality. In practice, however, people make the Bank's institutional struggle count in their lives in their own, particular terms. Studying how people make World Bank intervention meaningful in their normative context and daily lives gives us insight into the making of history, the making of particular people, and what it means to a particular people to be in pursuit of equality in a given historically grounded context.

We view this relation between 'micro' contexts of people's lives and 'macro' historical/institutional relations as mutually conditioning, through process and struggle. Such a view is basic to our reformulation of inequality and substantive economies. In our understanding of substantive economies, the organization and distribution of scarce resources according to prioritized needs is inseparable from access to and control over means of representation. As we have noted already, inequality and difference are inter-twined.

Inadequacy, indifference, and asymmetry of representation are formative of the poverty of the global order—apparent in the words and actions of landless men in India.[7] After years of commitment against the central Indian government's pursuit of privatization and profit, the Communist government, the CPI (M), explicitly began to invite foreign investment and liberal reform for the agri-business sector in the late 1990s. Despite historical governmental efforts towards equality, today, agricultural and wage laborers continue to face high levels of seasonal unemployment, landlessness, and poor wages. In this climate, any available work produces huge competition in unskilled labor markets and consequent divisiveness within communities. This competition for work can be understood as an inequality produced out of scarcity (of jobs).

CPI (M) efforts to encourage the food processing industry are aimed at creating jobs and rejuvenating the 'sick' industrial sector. While the CPI (M) conceives of its legitimacy in terms of encouraging investment-creating jobs, agricultural laborers migrating to work in the food processing industry experience dilemmas beyond competing for scarce jobs. Ordinarily, and even in the face of appalling conditions of work, people represent their choices as not simply governed by cash and employment needs, but in terms of what kind of person to be and how much work, what kind of work, and what location of work matches their sense of being. For migrant laborers, the commercialization of rural life introduces a complicated set of dilemmas which are simultaneously economic, familial, physiological, political, and emotional. When asked how many days in a year he would be unemployed if he were to remain in Tarinipur, Ranjan Maity responded:

I spend one month on agricultural labor elsewhere. I spend about 25 days out of three months at the potato store. A total of three months in a year is spent outside the village. Work in the potato store is so tiring that sometimes I feel even if someone offers me 500 rupees and says 'Here do this!' I would want to say 'Forget it.' It is so tiring that I can hardly sleep. I feel that I should do a lot of work in a short time and just go home. When I come home I can't concentrate on work here because I am so happy to be back home. And yet, even as I have come back home sometimes I think of the money to be made there. (6 June, 2001)

The fine balance of his calculations is swayed by migrant labor from a neighboring village pushing down local wages. For people like Ranjan, migrating enables him to keep his rural home viable, and his family life stable and happy. However, seeking employment in potato stores also means weighing an horrific work-load against money. While Ranjan longs to be at home when he is working outside Tarinipur, he needs the lucrative potato store work that could make life in Tarinipur easier, and perhaps even enable him to spend more time at home.

Amulya Kaniara's experience also describes the dilemma of work in potato stores.[8] This is the kind of work likely to become generalized as a result of CPI (M) propositions for agribusiness schemes and export processing units. Amulya explained later that this was one of the most de-humanizing experiences of his life, one which he has sworn never to return to even if it means that he and his family would have to starve. Amulya is a landless, low-caste, wage laborer. His experience of and resolve to never return to that kind of work embodies Lukacs' insight about the soul of a worker: '[W]hile the process by which the worker is reified and becomes a commodity dehumanizes him and cripples and atrophies his "soul" . . . it remains true that precisely his humanity and his soul are not changed into commodities' (Lukacs, 1968, p. 172). Amulya does not allow his desperate need for jobs to determine what a man on the lowest rung of society can be expected to put up with. He refuses the logic that scarcity determines action.

While the institutionalized struggle towards equality views people as units with (or without) access to jobs, we examine how people's sense of self and life constitutes and is constituted by their lived experience of particular jobs. Amulya's decision not to work in such conditions may have negative economic consequences for his household, but it is nonetheless a rational decision which powerfully counters the 'poverty reduction' presumption that the lowest on the rungs have few options, nothing much to lose, and are therefore compelled to put up with the worst conditions, the lowest wages, and the deepest humiliations. Indeed, they are expected to be grateful because 'at least it is a job'.

Ranjan and Amulya's words are not idiosyncratic expressions of soul and subjectivity. Their words enable us to situate difference and alienation in its historically constructed connection with inequality. Ranjan and Amulya live in a context where the government has made enduring efforts towards economic redistribution through land reform, political decentralization, and other pro-poor policies. Despite this, Ranjan and Amulya must weigh life against jobs. We are not romanticizing Amulya's decisions as difference, higher on the hierarchy of human values compared to Ranjan's decision to keep working in potato storage units. Their words and actions lie 'between transgression and reproduction' and show the multiple ways in which people negotiate their historical context in person (Willis, 2001, p. 171).

Jan Breman's study of laborers in India offers another example of people's negotiation of institutional meaning-making. A father responding to institutional accusations that 'these citizens' care too little about education responds:

We force them [children] to work and live on their earnings, they say. It is a cruel joke they are heaping on us. We also have fatherly sentiments and we also know the value of education. But when I am refused work in the field and my old mother comes back saying she too has no work on that day, we momentarily cease to be fathers and against our wish ask our children to go out to work. (Punalekar, quoted in Breman, 1996, p. 113)

This father transgresses institutional mandates and his own aspirations to school his child because he cannot compete for a job as well as his child can—yet he finds himself institutionally judged to be reproducing his own inequality.

His dilemma points to alienation from institutional mandates. It exemplifies the poverty of the global order and its inability to represent justice for citizens whose choices amplify deep contradictions between poverty alleviation and market logics. Like feminist international relations theory, we recognize that cheap labor is a 'necessary' reification of the unequal state system and the poverty of the global order. There is no such thing as cheap labor unless it is labor made cheap (Enloe, 2004) through the political construction of comparative social inequalities in particular places. However, the market can inflict disciplinary force on this father's life precisely because transactions loom much larger in his life and because what he values has no representation in institutional visions.

While post-development critics might recognize Amulya's actions as difference and this father's actions as inequality, we recognize both as relational expressions of representational inequality and alienation from institutional notions of economy. Amulya and Ranjan's words do not easily lend themselves to incorporation into World Bank logic, because in their decision to choose work (Ranjan) or not (Amulya) they weigh affection against money. Competition between these values cannot become visible within the World Bank's model of rationality, since its foundational legitimacy relies on projecting money as preordained winner. Thus, despite the current organized commodification of love, Amulya and Ranjan's words are likely to be alienated rather than incorporated for they reveal too much of the soul in this competition. Along with material inequality, then, Amulya and Ranjan are simultaneously marginalized from the means of representation. What we mean by this is that they have no audience that listens to and acts on what (kind of work or relation to home) matters to them.

We maintain that it is important to take account not only of the many cultural registers through which people understand and experience 'development', 'scarcity', or 'need', but also the representational inequality which disciplines people into legitimizing their low value in the economic order (cf. Mohan, 2004). This is why we propose additionally viewing inequality as people's (in)ability to realize meanings and motivations that matter to them. Our argument is that inability to realize meanings in institutional form is a materially-grounded expression of a historical lack of access to and control over means of representation. Struggles to speak and to be heard must be conceptually recognized as kernels of the 'social dramas of development and citizenship', revealing people's constructions of legitimate state–society relations (Caron and Da Costa, forthcoming). Amulya's expression of an inequality that transcends a phenomenal form of poverty is historical in that it is both product and critique of his times. Indeed, our difficulty in seeing Amulya's evaluation of the state of the world as more than idiosyncratic expression is a product of the very historical relations that marginalize Amulya in the first place.

The poverty of the global order lies in inability to see beyond the scarcity principle, and recognize the diversity of values that could inform different conceptions of development and equality, based on a combination of economic and representational justice. Until the means of representation are actively redistributed to result in substantive reform of institutional and disciplinary orders, poverty and inequality cannot be addressed adequately.

Conclusion

This paper has three related themes designed to identify and transcend the poverty of the global order. The first theme highlights the binarism expressed in the distinction between material inequality and difference/diversity that animates the current debate between modernist and post-modernist approaches to the development paradigm. This sets up artificial distinctions between development as economic justice and development as an undefined political emancipation. We argue that binarism falsely divides the two ways in which inequality is expressed via relations of production and representation, respectively. Indeed, our argument is that inequality and difference are mutually conditioning, because difference is materially grounded, and because material inequality, being relational, brings different meanings to those material relations. An enriching conception of development would value such meanings instead of abstracting them into a formalistic equation of equality with access to money.

The second theme is that to the extent that the binary remains, development critics are doomed to reproduce the naturalizing reflex of the development industry itself, in reducing development questions and choices to the scarcity postulate. Viewing development as being about economic justice alone discounts alternative conceptions of equality that value other choices concerning the organization of material life, not just the attempt to transcend material constraints.

Our third theme addresses the ways in which the development industry, and states, co-opt resistance and renew the legitimacy of development by reducing alternatives to the common denominator of economic gains in the marketplace. This trend, represented and implemented via the discourse of governance, merges the international relations and development paradigms, requiring states to author their own internalization of market rule. These neo-liberal procedures, in holding states accountable for poverty reduction, embed public priorities in private relationships. Arguably, the structure and episteme of the World Trade Organization, as flawed as it is, represents the highest stage of mutual infection of developmentalism and the state system. Governance, on behalf of globalization, reduces all inequalities to questions of market rationality. Governance is prosecuted by states through the surveillance and protocols of the WTO on behalf of development visions that ultimately reduce the social world to a de-politicized checkerboard of competitive and expendable units of efficiency.

We view this formalistic appropriation of alternatives as servicing the legitimacy of the development establishment's market episteme and its ontological representation in the machinations of the WTO. It is this reductionism that compounds the barriers to a critical reformulation of development—to rethinking equality as a complex combination of access to means of production, reproduction, and representation rather than access to economic opportunity across a homogeneous world. In confirmation of our argument, the poverty of this reductionism is calling forth substantive economies via counter-movements across the world, premised on principles of strategic diversity rather than standardized materialism.

Acknowledgement

The authors acknowledge helpful feedback from Rajeev Patel on a previous version of this paper.

Notes

1 Thus in the crisis in Argentina (2001), the coordinator of a worker-run factory claimed, 'We're demonstrating that success is not profit but the creation of work and social inclusion. . . . We are not just workers taking back our jobs. What we want is an entirely different model for our country' (quoted in Garrigues, 2004, p. 8).
2 'Market rule' comes from Arrighi (1982).

3   An example is President Bush's proposal to establish the Millennium Challenge Account, via which his administration would substitute grants for existing loans to Southern states complying with neo-liberal forms of governance (Soederberg, 2004).

4   Jeffrey Sachs, for example, claims: 'Two hundred years ago the idea that we could potentially achieve the end of extreme poverty would have been unimaginable. Just about everybody was poor, with the exception of a very small minority of rulers and large landowners' (2005, p. 26; see also Escobar, 1995).

5   For systematic analyses of the World Bank's project of development knowledge monopolization, see Cammack (2004) and Goldman (2005).

6   The idea of asymmetry of representation and meaning derives from Reddy's conceptualization of the disciplinary force in the asymmetry of monetary exchange between rich and poor, where an 'equal' transaction generally has more consequence for the poor than the rich (Reddy, 1987, p. 65).

7   Some of the ethnographic detail here is based on research in West Bengal, India (August 2000–August 2001).

8   Asked how many bags a worker had to carry to earn Rs. 120 ($ 1 = Rs. 43 in 2000 at time of interview), Amulya replied:

There is no fixed rate. The rule with the potato cold storage is that you have to fill up one store in 10–15 days. So one has to work from eight in the morning till 10 at night. So you have to carry these potato bags, each weighing about 60 kg. And climb up these makeshift ladders up to 50 feet high. If any one person falls or slips, all the others also fall. Sometimes while falling, if a leg gets stuck in the ladder, it can even break. I have seen it happen. What happened to me is that I hurt my knee very badly. Even then I continued to work for about four to five days. After that I just could not work. So I stayed back. But there was no-one to look after me, not even to ask me how I am, no-one to help me walk. They all went off to work. I just lay there in pain, crying. Then I decided to come back home. No, they didn't pay me because I had not completed my quota. They gave me my bus fare.

References

Ainger, K. (2003) The new peasants' revolt, *New Internationalist*, 353 (Jan/Feb), pp. 9–13.

Arrighi, G. (1982) A crisis of hegemony, in A. Amin, G. Arrighi, A. G. Frank, & I. Wallerstein (eds) *Dynamics of Global Crisis* (New York: Monthly Review).

Barlow, M. (1999) *Blue Gold* (San Francisco, CA: International Forum on Globalization).

Baviskar, A. (2005) The dream machine: the model development project and the remaking of the state, in A. Baviskar (ed.) *Waterscapes: The Cultural Politics of a Natural Resource* (New Delhi: Orient Longman).

Bose, S. (1997) Instruments and idioms of colonial and national development: India's historical experience in comparative perspective, in F. Cooper & R. Packard (eds) *International Development and the Social Sciences* (Berkeley: University of California Press).

Breman, J. (1996) *Footloose Labour: Working in India's Informal Economy* (Cambridge: Cambridge University Press).

Cammack, P. (2004) What the World Bank means by poverty reduction, and why it matters, *New Political Economy*, 9(2) pp. 189–211.

Caron, C. & Da Costa, D. (forthcoming) There's a devil on Wayamba Beach: social dramas of development and citizenship in north-west Sri Lanka, *Journal of African and Asian Studies*, 42(5).

Clarke, T. (2001) Serving up the commons, *Multinational Monitor*, 22(4), http://www.essential.org/monitor/mm2001/01april/corp2.html.

Cook, B. & Kothari, U. (eds) (2001) *Participation, The New Tyranny?* (London: Zed).

Crush, J. (ed.) (1995) *Power of Development* (London: Routledge).

Da Costa, D. (2007) Mirrors of value? Advertising and political theatre in the hegemonic constructions of women in India, in S. Deshpande (ed.) *Theatre of the Streets: The Jana Natya Manch Experience* (New Delhi: Janam).

Desmarais, A. A. (2007) *La Vía Campesina: Globalization and the Power of Peasants* (Point Black, NS: Fernwood Books).

de Sousa Santos, B. (2002) *Towards a New Legal Common Sense* (London: Butterworth).

Elyachar, J. (2005) *Markets of Dispossession. NGOs, Economic Development, and the State in Cairo* (Durham, NC: Duke University Press).

Enloe, C. (2004) Margins, silences and bottom rungs: how to overcome the underestimation of power in the study of international relations, in C. Enloe, *The Curious Feminist: Searching for Women in a New Age of Empire* (Berkeley, University of California Press).

Escobar, A. (1995) *Encountering Development* (Princeton, NJ: Princeton University Press).

Fraser, N. & Honneth, A. (2003) *Redistribution or Recognition: A Political-Philosophical Exchange* (New York: Verso).

Garrigues, L. (2004) Argentine workers build new economy, *Yes* (Spring), pp. 7–8, http://www.yesmagazine.org/article.asp?ID = 717.

Goldman, M. (2005) *Imperial Nature: The World Bank and Struggles for Social Justice in the Age of Globalization* (New Haven, CT: Yale University Press).

Gupta, A. (1998) *Postcolonial Developments: Agriculture in the Making of Modern India* (Durham, NC: Duke University Press).

Hochschild, A. (2003) Love and gold, in B. Ehrenreich & A. Hochschild (eds) *Global Woman: Nannies, Maids, and Sex Workers in the New Economy* (New York: Metropolitan Books).

Holland, D. & Lave, J. (2001) History in person: an introduction, in D. Holland & J. Lave (eds) *History in Person: Enduring Struggles, Contentious Practice and Intimate Identities* (Santa Fe, NM: School of American Research Press).

Klenk, R. (2004) Who is the developed woman? Women as a category of development discourse, Kumaon, India, *Development and Change*, 35(1), pp. 57–78.

Kothari, R. (1997) *Poverty: Human Consciousness and the Amnesia of Development* (London: Zed Books).

Li, T. (1999) Compromising power: development, culture, and rule in Indonesia, *Cultural Anthropology*, 14(3), pp. 295–322.

Lukacs, G. (1968) *History and Class Consciousness: Studies in Marxist Dialectics* (New Delhi: Rupa & Co.)

McMichael, P. (2006) Reframing development: global peasant movements and the new agrarian question, *Canadian Journal of Development Studies*, XXVII(4), pp. 471–483.

Mohan, D. (2004) Reimagining community: scripting power and changing the subject through Jana Sanskriti's political theatre in rural North India, *Journal of Contemporary Ethnography*, 33(2), pp. 178–217.

Mosse, D. (2004) Is good policy unimplementable? Reflections on the ethnography of aid policy and practice, *Development and Change*, 35(4), pp. 639–671.

Narayan, D., Patel, R., Schafft, K., Rademacher, A. & Kah-Schulte, S. (2000) *Can Anybody Hear Us? Voices of the Poor* (New York: Oxford University Press).

Patel, R. (2006) International agrarian restructuring and the practical ethics of peasant movement solidarity, *Journal of Asian and African Studies*, 41(1–2), pp. 71–93.

Patel, R. & McMichael, P. (2004) Third Worldism and lineages of global fascism: neo-liberalism and the regrouping of the global South, *Third World Quarterly*, 25(1), pp. 231–254.

Pieterse, J. N. (1998) My paradigm or yours: alternative development, post-development or reflexive development, *Development and Change*, 29(2), pp. 343–373.

Plehwe, D. (2004) The World ('Knowledge') Bank's Global Development Network (GDN) and transnational/global civil society: reclaiming development theory/policy or decentralizing neoliberal policy advice? Presentation to International Studies Association meeting, Montreal, March.

Polanyi, K. (1968) The economy as instituted process, in G. Dalton (ed.) *Primitive, Archaic and Modern Economies: Essays of Karl Polanyi* (Boston, MA: Beacon).

Rademacher, A. & Patel, R. (2002) Retelling worlds of poverty: reflections on transforming participatory research for a global narrative, in K. Brock & R. McGee (eds) *Knowing Poverty: Critical Reflections on Participatory Research and Policy* (London: Earthscan Publications).

Reddy, W. (1987) *Money or Liberty* (Cambridge: Cambridge University Press).

Ritchie, M. (1993) *Breaking the Deadlock: The United States and Agricultural Policy in the Uruguay Round* (Minneapolis, MN: Institute for Agriculture and Trade Policy).

Rosenberg, J. (2001) *The Empire of Civil Society* (London: Verso).

Sachs, W. (1992) *The Development Dictionary* (London: Zed Press).

Sachs, J. (2005). *The End of Poverty: Economic Possibilities for Our Time* (New York: Penguin).

Said, E. (1978) *Orientalism* (New York: Pantheon).

Saul, J. S. (2004) Globalization, imperialism, development: false binaries and radical resolutions, in L. Panitch & C. Leys (eds) *Socialist Register* (London: Merlin).

Sen, A. (2002) Response to commentaries, *Studies in Comparative International Development*, 37(2), pp. 78–86.

Shiva, V. (1991) *The Violence of the Green Revolution* (London: Zed).

Soederberg, S. (2004) *The Politics of New International Financial Architecture: Reimposing Neoliberal Dominance in the Global South* (London: Zed Books/New York: Palgrave).

Spitz, P. (1985) The right to food in historical perspective, *Food Policy*, 10(4), pp. 306–316.

Stewart, F. & Deneulin, S. (2002) Amartya Sen's contribution to development thinking, *Studies in Comparative International Development*, 37(2), pp. 61–70.

Weber, H. (2004) The 'new economy' and social risk: banking on the poor? *Review of International Political Economy*, 11(2), pp. 356–86.

Weber, H. (2006) A political analysis of the PRSP initiative: social struggles and the organization of persistent relations of inequality, *Globalizations*, 3(2), pp. 187–206.

Wolfensohn, J. (2000) Rethinking development – challenges and opportunities. Paper presented at the UNCTAD meeting, Bangkok, 16 February, http://www.irvl.net/thetenth_ministerial.htm.

Willis, P. (2001) Tekin' the piss, in D. Holland & J. Lave (eds) *History in Person: Enduring Struggles, Contentious Practice and Intimate Identities* (Santa Fe, NM: School of American Research Press).

Conclusion: Towards Recognition and Redistribution in Global Politics

HELOISE WEBER & MARK T. BERGER

As mapped out at the beginning, and outlined in detail in the various contributions, this volume has sought to broaden and deepen the critique of 'international development'. This has been grounded in an explicit effort to integrate questions of recognition and redistribution into the theory and practice of global development. Our assumption has been that efforts to rethink development will involve a need to re-conceptualise and re-theorise the dominant narrative of international development (often framed with reference to the formal comparative method) through a critical re-interpretation of the history of the organisation of the politics of development in *relational* terms.

A comprehensive approach requires an evaluation of the way in which the identity of the developmental subject has been conceived mainly in economistic and technocratic terms. We have sought to consider the social and political effects of the technocratic framing of human beings (and societies) in the wider context of spatial and temporal dynamics. For example, we have explored how the orthodox framing of the 'question of development' has been deployed to justify and legitimate social relations as being primarily mediated through property relations. This has led us to question the epistemological premises of mainstream development theory and the practices it has engendered, as evidenced in the various contributions which have identified and critically analysed practices of domination and exploitation in the context of the articulation of struggles for alternatives.

At the same time, the way alternative discourses have either been appropriated or suppressed has also been illustrated. Our position recognises that alternatives are not necessarily progressive or emancipatory. While we do not aspire to offer an 'ideal type' theory of development, we are, through our collective critique of the dominant approach, creating a conceptual space with practical implications for the various social and political struggles which challenge the institutional organisation of scarcity as the normative basis of development. By reflecting on identity issues in relation to the concept of recognition (of self and self-to-others), we consider how a theory of development based on the individual, competition, and commodity exchange could be displaced by dialogical approaches and more inclusive substantively grounded recognition approaches (Fraser and Honneth, 2003; Shapcott, 1994).

We have demonstrated the extent to which social and political struggles have been global in scope. We have also alluded to the fact that post-colonial critique—while of central importance—is not sufficient to render visible the way in which a contradictory international development project is organised and contested at various sites and through various agencies under current social and political conjunctures. Nor is it sufficient merely to challenge the intensification of global capitalism. To this end, our efforts at rethinking development have deployed counter-readings of the history of development, in order to try and render visible the social consequences of developmental determinism and the practices of domination they engender. Implicit (if not always explicit) here has been an emphasis on a dialectical approach to conceptualising alternative political spaces for those many struggles, and the ways in which they are relationally situated within the global. They directly challenge development as an attempt to constitute social relations primarily as property relations. Ultimately, we have sought to highlight how questions of identity are deeply inter-related not just with questions of redistribution, but more fundamentally with the contradictions of an international development project that organises and produces scarcity and dispossession (cf. Da Costa and McMichael, 2007). In this context, we have drawn attention to the dialectical relationship between structural power and the violence of the nation-state and the way in which identity has been utilised (intentionally or unintentionally) throughout history to manage the contradictions of capitalism.

Our primary objective has been to rethink development beyond hitherto dominant approaches which have foregrounded development as a spatial political and/or economic problem reflected in the categories of North and South, and First, Second, and Third Worlds. On the basis of such analyses, development has been conceived as a problem confined to the South, to underdeveloped, less developed, or developing nation-states, or to the Third World. We have argued that such an approach is limited on several levels. It fails to capture the politics of development in social and relational terms. Given that the current international development agenda is constitutively constructed in normative terms, and directed at explicitly redressing experiences of vulnerabilities, heteronomy, and deprivation, a concern with the contradictions it engenders is both timely and necessary.

This project has been concerned with taking seriously the social ontological (and political) implications of the critique of methodological territorialism and individualism. In turn, this has meant the exploration of alternative approaches through which the contradictions identified can be understood and a comprehensive political analysis of the relationships between development, inequality, and human (in)security can be achieved. Our aim has been to try and open up an alternative analytical lens, premised upon a relational approach in order to arrive at a more appropriate picture of contradictory developments of global politics. Such a relational approach can render social and political power relations visible and aid in overcoming practices of exclusion and dispossession. To this end, we remain motivated by a shared interest in the emancipatory potential of development. However, we recognise that this emancipatory potential is not visible, or tenable, without a rethinking of the foundational assumptions that have privileged evolutionary narratives of development, and downgraded or made invisible social struggles for political alternatives.

References

Da Costa, D. & McMichael, P. (2007) The poverty of the global order, *Globalizations*, 4(4), pp. 588–602.
Fraser, N. & Honneth, A. (2003) *Redistribution or Recognition: A Political–Philosophical Exchange* (London: Verso).
Shapcott, R. (1994) Conversation and coexistence: Gadamer and the interpretation of international society, *Millennium, Journal of International Studies*, 23(1), pp. 57–84.

Index